THE 100

BEST TRENDS

2005

Emerging Developments
You Can't Afford to Ignore!

GEORGE OCHOA AND MELINDA COREY

Adams Media

Avon, Massachusetts

To Martha, the next generation

Published by Adams Media, an F+W Publications Company
57 Littlefield Street, Avon, MA 02322 U.S.A.
www.adamsmedia.com

ISBN: 1-59337-098-9
Printed in Canada.

J I H G F E D C B A

Library of Congress Cataloging-in-Publication Data
Ochoa, George.
The 100 best trends, 2005/by George Ochoa and Melinda Corey.
p.   cm.
ISBN 1-59337-098-9
1. Business forecasting. 2. Economic forecasting. 3. Globalization.
I. Title: One hundred best trends, 2005. II. Corey, Melinda. III. Title.

HD30.27.O27 2004
303.49'09'0511–dc22

2004009502

This publication is designed to provide accurate and authoritative information with regard
to the subject matter covered. It is sold with the understanding that the publisher is not
engaged in rendering legal, accounting, or other professional advice. If legal advice or
other expert assistance is required, the services of a competent professional person
should be sought.
—From a *Declaration of Principles* jointly adopted by a Committee of the American Bar
Association and a Committee of Publishers and Associations

Many of the designations used by manufacturers and sellers to distinguish their products
are claimed as trademarks. Where those designations appear in this book and Adams
Media was aware of a trademark claim, the designations have been printed with initial
capital letters.

This book is available at quantity discounts for bulk purchases.
For information, call 1-800-872-5627.

Acknowledgments

It took three agents to bring this book into being: the late Jane Jordan Browne, Scott Mendel, and Danielle Egan-Miller. We thank them all. We also thank our editor Jill Alexander, along with Kirsten Amann and Larry Shea.

Contents

Introduction

If there's one thing we know about the future, it's this: it has already begun. The changes that will shape our lives in the next ten to twenty years are already in motion—from demographic changes to technological marvels; from social trends to novel ways of doing business. The pace of transformation can be bewildering, but if we scrutinize the present, we can see the footprints of change even now. *The 100 Best Trends* is a snapshot of 100 of those footprints: the 100 most important trends now shaping the near future.

Trends are more than just fads or fashions, things that are hot now but may not survive the winter. Trends are patterns of change that have been in formation for several years and are expected to endure for at least several more years. The macarena was a fad; a multicultural population (greater cultural diversity among Americans) is a trend. *The 100 Best Trends* presents each trend in an essay that says what the trend is, gives historical background on the trend, describes the evidence for it, and sketches its major aspects and implications. This book is intended for business readers who need to know about the most important trends affecting their operating environment and customer base. It is also intended for general readers who want a better understanding of the directions in which their world is heading.

Trends arise in every category of human activity, from the most leisurely to the most purposeful. To cover this broad range, *The 100 Best Trends* is divided into ten chapters, each focusing on one area: business and industry; demographics; entertainment and the arts; health and medicine; lifestyles; marketing; politics; religion and spirituality; science and technology; and the sexes. Within each chapter, the trends are presented in alphabetical order by title. Some of the titles are self-explanatory; others will make sense once you delve into the essay. "Digital Broadcasting" is exactly what it says; "Seventy Million Navel Geezers" has to do with the aging of the baby boomers, well known for their penchant for navel gazing.

The scope of the essays varies as the trends do, from broad concepts ("Omni-Connectedness," the desire to be electronically linked all the time) to narrow social or political phenomena ("Hipublicans," young, hip Republicans). Most essays focus on the United States, but some cover international trends, among them "Globalization Returns," "China Rising," and "Remembering the Forgotten Continent" (Africa). Whether the topic is scientific ("The Incredible Shrinking Science," on nanotechnology), spiritual ("The Religion Shopping Mall"), commercial ("Conglomer-media"), or sexual ("More Free Milk: Cohabitation Abounding"), the aim throughout is to present the trends concisely in a plain, lively style with a minimum of jargon. An increase in spare time is not one of the trends discovered in our research, so the reader's time is respected here.

In a time of rapid change, it helps to understand the underlying patterns of change—not only because those patterns are interesting, but also because knowing about them confers an advantage in the pursuit of prosperity and happiness. It is our hope that *The 100 Best Trends* will help give you that advantage.

1

Business and Industry

Clicks and Bricks

1 At the end of the 20th century, retailing visionaries pondered the eventual demise of actual brick-and-mortar stores at the hands of their online competitors. Some thought that physical stores couldn't provide the variety and ease of use that a Web site could. In 2000, ClickZ.com columnist Jeffrey Graham wrote, "Without an integrated online approach that allows them [physical stores] to offer the type of value that customers will increasingly demand, they will be dead in the water." A few years into the new century and the verdict is in: store and site are still standing, together. Says Hamed Shahbazi, chairman and CEO of Info Touch Technologies, the age of brick-and-mortar and online integration has arrived: "The 'Clicks and Mortar' paradigm sets an end to this conflict by creating a balance between online and offline operations, which is well suited for both traditional and dot com retailers. . . . It is important to emphasize that 'Clicks and Mortar' is not just a trend or craze; it is here to stay."

Department stores, clothing outlets, and specialty shops are now integrated; together the sites accounted for more than $149 billion in sales between 2000 and 2003. In addition, many online or catalog merchants have adopted brick-and-mortar components, such as the Apple Store, Bliss Spas, and American Girl. In fact, the Gartner Group, a consulting firm, projected that 98 percent of dot-com sites would fail if they did not have a brick-and-mortar component. Now, even service industries are integrating an interactive—not just an informational—online presence with their brick-and-mortar agency storefronts.

Among the basic ways brick-and-mortar stores have integrated an online presence in their stores are Internet kiosks, at which customers can order from a complete inventory and browse in-store advertisements and promotions on the online site.

These changes in shopping venues have created a new kind of buyer, the multichannel consumer. He or she is a buyer who uses multiple shopping outlets for the same store, such as the brick-and-mortar store, Web site, and catalog. Research showed that store shoppers who buy online from the same retailer spend about $600 more annually. Trichannel buyers (store, Web site, catalog) buy from a store 70 percent more frequently than average store customers.

But brick-and-mortar stores are not standing still. Many of them are retooling themselves as destination stops that recall the entertainment and fantasy that they provided a century ago, when department stores were new. At Chicago's Marshall Field's flagship store, plebeian late-century design has been gutted to reveal stately wood moldings and other architectural glories. The aim is to make the brick-and-mortar department store what its online version cannot be: a source of wonder for all five senses, a visual, auditory, olfactory, tactile, and even gustatory experience. If done right, these stores will be a reason to leave the computer screen.

Come Fly with Me

2   In early 2003, airline traffic was stymied. The war in Iraq and the threat of global transmission of SARS (severe acute respiratory syndrome) were largely responsible for two-digit declines in domestic and

international travel, according to the Air Transport Association, as reported in the *New York Times*. Yet, by early 2004, some discount carriers posted profits in the fourth quarter of 2003, with some of them marking their success by increasing earnings and traffic or instituting cost-cutting measures.

In various ways, airplane flight is being transformed. As a business, it is reshaping itself to fit a more fragmented, consumer-savvy market. New varieties of airlines and destinations target regions not served by major carriers; competition overall has increased, leading to lower or stabilized prices across the board. What's more, the entertainment factor of airline travel is increasing, making flight a source of amusement, if not fun. The jet-set status of the 1960s may be gone, but the Kate Spade uniforms, personal TVs, and especially increased on-time arrivals don't hurt.

In general, the move toward discount airlines is invigorating the industry, with three airlines—Southwest Airlines, America West, and AirTran posting profits in the last quarter of 2003 and touting more customers. Some discount airlines are like JetBlue Airways, which serve many major destinations but cut costs by not serving traditional full-meal selections, among other practices. JetBlue also prizes itself on its stylishness, advertising its uniforms as "Pradaesque." One of the ways Southwest is trying to save costs is by eliminating travel agent commissions. The plan, implemented in December 2003, is expected to eliminate $40 million in annual expenses, according to the *New York Times*.

Other discount airlines are spinoffs of established airlines. Among them is Song, the discount arm of Delta Air Lines, which began service in 2003. In part, Song (and some other airlines) distinguishes itself through positive attitude and style. At its inception, Song marketed itself as being "[f]ounded by optimists and built by believers" and offering to "give style, service, and choice back to people who fly." Indicators of the company's sunniness are the friendly Song "talent" (or flight attendants) and roomy, brightly colored seats of blue, purple, green, and orange. Ultimately, Song plans to serve organic meals and equip planes with leather seats and individual screens for watching movies and accessing the Internet. In all, what with the gray-and-green Spade designer outfits, Song aims to be more hip than its competitor, JetBlue.

Still other discount airlines moderate prices by establishing their hub in smaller cities that have lower operating costs, such as lower enplaning charges. Examples include AirTran, which is based in Orlando, Florida, and Allegiant Air, which is consolidating its operations in Las Vegas. Many discount airlines establish themselves by serving more medium-sized and niche locations. For example, among Allegiant Air's destinations are Las Vegas and Des Moines, Iowa. Other discounters specialize in such medium-sized locations as Lansing, Michigan, and Fort Collins/Loveland, Colorado.

At least in part, the added competition appears to have spurred major airlines to improve service. According to the national Airline Quality Rating (AQR) study for 2002, several of the big airlines improved their ratings from the previous year. AQR areas of study included baggage handling, customer complaints, denied boardings, and on-time arrivals. Of the airlines that made the top ten ranking for overall performance, those improving their ranking included Alaska, America West, American, Continental, Delta, Southwest, United, and US Airways.

The airline industry's plans for the future include research and development programs to promote good health while traveling. In one initiative, companies including Goodrich will develop an airline seat cushion that encourages proper seating posture and decreases pressure on the veins of the lower extremities that can result in deep vein thrombosis (DVT).

To attend to less glamorous needs, airlines have pledged to adopt their own and government-mandated procedures to fight infectious diseases such as SARS. Some airlines, like Northwest, have integrated SARS training into their infectious disease education program, though most airlines do not plan to implement other training until advised to do so by the World Health Organization (WHO) or Center for Disease Control (CDC). Speaking in general to Newsday.com, Marty Cetron, deputy director of the CDC's division of global migrations and quarantines, said, "[I]t's prudent to prepare for the worst and hope for the best."

Conglomermedia

3 Over the past half-century, many parts of the media industry have undergone great consolidation, reports the *Progressive*. Between the 1960s and 1980s, huge numbers of newspapers ceased publishing, and those that remained became owned by a handful of major chains. Similarly, the book publishing industry shrank in its number of publishers and owners. The major cable TV and music industries also became owned primarily by a few conglomerates.

Consolidation increased markedly during the past decade. Previous laws that had prevented television stations from producing their own shows, kept movie companies from owning their own theaters, and limited ownership of TV and radio stations within a market and within a family of owners were relaxed. As a result, television and radio stations are now owned by a handful of corporations and private individuals. As of 2004, the largest media players and their properties include:

- **Time Warner**—CNN, Warner Bros., Time, AOL, WB, TNT, HBO
- **Disney**—ABC, Walt Disney Studios
- **General Electric**—NBC
- **News Corporation**—Fox movie and television, Fox News on cable
- **Viacom**—CBS, UPN, MTV, Paramount, Simon & Schuster

Some proponents of media consolidation pointed to the Internet as an answer to the concerns that the media would become a monopoly. These proconglomeration businesses said that as the Internet grew as an information medium, it opened up the media market. Individuals could establish new media strongholds, which eroded the need to impose strict ownership rules on traditional media outlets.

Media owners also pointed to the increased threat of terrorism as a call to broaden media units. The media power used to cover terrorist events like the 9/11 attack was raised as evidence of a need for more conglomermedia. Consolidated media coverage was presented as a way of ensuring public service.

In reality, the Internet is pervasive, and it is a force in decentralizing the arts. But it does not yet have the media power of the major television and film outlets, so it is not equivalent competition with them. Further, the typical media conglomerate is less focused on providing public service with its media than it is with using all of its parts to generate revenue, say by producing a movie, promoting it on its TV and radio stations, broadcasting the movie after its release, and making recordings related to the movie on its own label. This is what the Viacom/CBS matrix—which includes Paramount, CBS, Showtime, multiple TV stations, over 150 Infinity Radio stations, and Blockbuster Video—can do.

For years, various media critics have decried the increasing concentration of media ownership in the hands of a few corporations. In his 1989 book, *Culture Inc.: The Corporate Takeover of Public Expression*, Herbert Schiller called for active political involvement that would "aim at reducing private monopoly" over the media and discourage it from being a "salable commodity." He also hoped to see "public support and encouragement of noncommercial expression and creativity" to counter the commercial media. In recent years, these movements have not occurred and show few signs of developing.

Rather, over the past two decades, the U.S. government has hastened the trend of concentrated ownership of media outlets. Among its acts have been the passage of the business-friendly Telecommunications Act of 1996, and the 2003 FCC decision relaxing rules for corporate media ownership.

These June 2003 changes are sweeping. They include increasing the proportion of television stations that companies can own, from stations reaching a total of 35 percent of the U.S. population to stations reaching 45 percent. Companies can own more local TV stations; a company can own two in a five-station market and three in an eighteen-plus market. Companies can own newspapers or radio stations as well as TV stations in markets with nine or more TV stations. Companies can own up to eight radio stations in a forty-five-plus station market. In all, the FCC changes mean that in the largest cities, a company may own up to three television stations, eight radio stations, a daily newspaper, and a cable operator. The decision also allows the television networks to buy more stations. These acts toward relaxation of corporate control sit in contrast to the 1934 Communications Act, which aimed to prevent corporate concentration.

Whether the American public cares about the control of the media by a few players is questionable. PBS reported on a study by the Project for Excellence in Journalism that showed that people aren't bothered by the prospect of most media outlets being held by a few hands. Unless the American public gets weary of overly similar programming and credits it to the shrinking circle of media owners, that circle will grow ever tighter. Imagine the nation's media outlets owned by a single conglomerate, such as AOLGeneral ElectricNewsCorporationTimeWarnerVivendiUniversalViacom—or AGENTVV.

Creative: Not a Dirty Word

4 Everyone praises creativity, but creative people have always had something vaguely disreputable about them. If someone who is not famous says he is an actor, artist, or writer, the implication is that this person is poor: the actor waiting on tables, the artist starving, the writer living in a garret. But the stock of creative people is rising as cities and businesses realize that money can be made from them. And the spectrum

of people who are considered creative is getting broader—not just artists and writers but also scientists, academics, lawyers whose craft is designing tax shelters, and even managers who think "outside the box."

A greater premium began to be placed on creativity in the 1980s, when scientists, software engineers, and other knowledge workers began to be valued for driving fields such as biotech and information technology. At that time, the business world showered its appreciation on science, but not necessarily on the arts and humanities. Increasingly, however, the trend has been to value artists and humanists as drivers of economic growth.

Richard Florida, in his 2002 book *The Rise of the Creative Class*, theorizes that creative people are crucial to the modern economy because they produce new forms and designs that can be marketed and used widely, and because they think on their own, drawing on far-flung knowledge to solve new problems. They include a "super-creative core" of people who invent new forms, such as artists, writers, musicians, academics, scientists, engineers, actors, designers, architects, editors, analysts, and general opinion-makers. And they include "creative professionals" who solve problems creatively, such as financiers, managers, lawyers, and physicians. With the net thrown this wide, Florida counts 38.3 million creatives in the country, about 30 percent of the U.S. work force—up from less than 20 percent in 1980. Another book, *The Cultural Creatives* (2000) by Sherry Ruth Anderson and Paul H. Ray, puts the number of "Cultural Creatives" even higher, at 50 million. Anderson and Ray's criterion is somewhat different from Florida's: they view Cultural Creatives as a distinct subculture interested in things such as spirituality and personal growth.

How to count creatives, and whether their numbers are as big as these authors say, is open to debate. But it seems certain that creative people, however counted or grouped, are important to economic growth in today's fast-changing world. We live in an era of lowered trade barriers, globalized competition, and rapid technological development. In this setting, a country's economic standing rests not primarily on cheap labor or protection of old industries, but on new ideas and the ability to

thrive in changing circumstances. As this fact becomes more widely rec-
ognized, creativity will continue its shift from being viewed as the opposite of moneymaking to a condition of it.

As Florida documents, creative people tend to cluster in certain
kinds of cities: those with flourishing art and music scenes, interesting
history, active nightlife, ample outdoor recreation, young people, and
gays. The last may be surprising, until one considers that most creative
people grew up feeling like outsiders, so they value places that welcome
people of different persuasions, orientations, and lifestyles. Also, creativity
is fueled by contact with different perspectives, so creative people tend to
appreciate diversity and avoid conformity. With this in mind, Florida has
come up with a "Creativity Index" that ranks cities according to how
many creative people live there, how much high-tech industry and patent
innovation exists there, and how many gays live there (the "Gay Index").
The top large city for creatives turned out to be San Francisco, followed
by Austin, San Diego, Boston, and Seattle. (Despite its reputation as a
mecca for artists, New York came in ninth.) Albuquerque, Albany, and
Tucson were the top three medium-sized cities, and the top three small-
sized cities were Madison, Wisconsin; Des Moines, Iowa; and Santa Bar-
bara, California. Bottom-ranked cities included Memphis, Alabama;
Youngstown, Ohio; and Shreveport, Louisiana.

As demand for the services of creative people rises, so does their
price. Florida reports that the average salary for a member of the creative class in 1999 was nearly $50,000, considerably higher than for
working-class or service-class workers. David Brooks has wittily
described the culture of at least some creative class members in
Bobos in Paradise: The New Upper Class and How They Got There
(2000). Brooks's term *Bobos* stands for "bourgeois bohemians,"
people who combine an artistic-idealistic worldview with a taste for the
comforts of money.

As the clout of creatives rises, look for cities and businesses to step
up efforts to attract them, both with cultural/lifestyle amenities and hard
financial incentives. But don't be surprised if many artists remain
starving and many writers still live in garrets. The most genuinely

creative people tend to care more about what they create than whether they can make money with it—which means that a lot of their creations will bring in little or no money. And since everyone has a novel in their drawer or a doodle on their phone pad, there will always be fierce competition among creatives, keeping down their price. There will be more demand for creatives, but probably also an undiminished supply.

Digital Deflation

5 It is easy to see how digital technology has affected certain parts of our lives: just look at the PC, the CD player, the DVD player, and the Internet. What is harder to see is the big picture of how it affects our total economic condition. Investment analyst Graham Tanaka thinks there is something larger going on: digital deflation.

In Tanaka's book *Digital Deflation* (2003), he uses that term to mean better living, but not more expensive living, through digital technology (devices that use data converted into ones and zeroes). Thanks to ongoing advances from scientists and engineers, products and services are rising in their value to consumers without rising proportionately in price. The result, effectively, is that new consumer goodies cost less than they would have if prices had kept rising in proportion to value. This effect is digital deflation. This year's MP3 music player has double the storage capacity of last year's, with little or no price increase. Prices stay stable, but you get more value for your money, because advances in digital technology improve quality without raising price.

The benefits of digital deflation are also found in many products and services that are not obviously "digital." Tanaka gives the example of how pharmaceuticals may be improving in safety and efficacy because of the digital technologies (supercomputers, analytical software tools, etc.) that support their development.

Digital deflation has been going on at double-digit rates each year for decades, and Tanaka predicts that it will continue at this pace until advances in digital technology hit a physical wall that cannot be surmounted—something that will probably not happen for at least ten and possibly twenty years or more. In fact, digital deflation will grow as industries that are currently making little use of information technology (IT) start benefiting from it. This will make them part of the New Economy as Tanaka defines it: a New Economy company is one that used digital deflation to deliver more value to the consumer per dollar. As digital deflation grows, Tanaka predicts all kinds of good economic outcomes: higher output and productivity with lower inflation; higher standards of living without higher prices; steady and growing consumer demand as impressively new products are marketed; recessions that are less sharp than in the past; and an economy that can stand to hire more workers without increasing inflation.

The benefits of digital deflation can be maximized, Tanaka argues, if the governments of the United States and other nations would only count it more fully in the economic data they use to guide policy. If they did so, they would see that inflation is 1 or 2 percent lower than believed in just about every economy benefiting substantially from digital technology. By correcting the data, they would see, among other things, that they can print money more freely and lower interest rates without fear of producing inflation. The result, he says, would be greater, and sustained, global economic growth.

Is Tanaka right? No consensus has yet been reached. Productivity has clearly been growing steadily over the years: by one estimate, the average annual growth in productivity in the nonfarm sector in the United States was 2.6 percent a year from 1995 to 2002. But there is debate about how much of that growth was due to technology; many factors, such as corporate environment and attitudes to work, can have an impact on productivity. Further, there is a widespread suspicion that many of the vaunted "improvements" offered by digital technology amount to less than meets the eye. Do we really need a speakerphone with our cell phone, or a still-roomier MP3 player? Based on corporate performance data, Paul A. Strassmann argued in *Computerworld* in 1997, "It's a myth that computers have measurably increased the overall productivity of information management." In 2003, Richard Holway, director of the consulting firm Ovum Holway, voiced his suspicion that businesses often buy and use new IT not because of real advantages but "because it is there."

The extent of "better living through digital technology" and the proper way to measure it remains elusive and controversial. Yet, Tanaka's basic point seems on target: overall, digital technology is producing better products and services without raising prices; and governments should, and probably will, measure this and factor it into their policy decisions. In the meantime, individual investors who buy his argument can take digital deflation into account in their investment decisions. For example, they might look for areas that are nontech but that are likely to benefit in coming years from digital deflation (such as health care), or rate a company with what Tanaka calls "the Digital Deflation test": seeing if the company is improving its products and services by using advancing technologies. The rest of us should look forward to fancier but still attractively priced DVD players—until some post-DVD technology comes along to replace that.

Globalization Returns

6 Long an unstoppable juggernaut in world economics, globalization has recently seemed more like a 97-pound weakling. Terrorism, war, slow growth, and international disputes have hindered the continued integration of the world's economies into one big free-trade

zone. Nevertheless, don't count out globalization yet. Further global economic unification is inevitable, and there are signs that the pace of it is already picking up.

Globalization has been growing since the post–World War II era, when many countries realized that they could find mutual advantage in trading freely across national borders, with a minimum of tariffs, subsidies, and other government regulations aimed at protecting native industries. The European Economic Community, now the European Union, was formed to work for economic integration of Europe. The major world economic powers formulated the General Agreement on Tariffs and Trade (GATT) to encourage free trade; GATT ultimately gave rise to the World Trade Organization (WTO), in 1995. In the decades since World War II, technology made the world smaller, with jet airplanes, satellite communications, and the Internet facilitating the spread of ideas, people, and capital around the world. In the 1990s, with the Cold War ended and free trade driving economic growth in many countries, it seemed that nothing would stop the onward march of globalization.

Then 9/11 happened. The September 2001 terror attacks prompted the United States and other countries to place new restrictions on international travel and shipping. Security and war dominated summits of world leaders that once would have focused on trade issues. The world economy, already sluggish, sank further into the doldrums, and world trade and global capital flows went into decline. Politicians looked to protect jobs in their nation's own industries rather than shoot for a distant abstraction like globalization. And the United States, once the admired leader in globalization, became an object of global scolding because of various unilateral actions. In September 2003, WTO talks in Cancún, Mexico, collapsed. The breakdown put in jeopardy the WTO's self-imposed deadline of January 2005 for reaching a new global free-trade agreement.

Still, despite all the bad news and controversy, globalization is unlikely to stop growing. For one thing, it is already here, in spades. Further, globalization does not depend only on the trade agreements of governments, but more fundamentally on basic economic principles.

As Bill Mann of Fool.com puts it, "people naturally gravitate toward buying the same goods at the lowest price available." It also depends on what Thomas Friedman, in his book *The Lexus and the Olive Tree: Understanding Globalization* (2000), calls the Electronic Herd—the faceless masses of investors, traders, and multinational corporations that every day shift funds, factories, and jobs to whichever country seems best equipped to produce goods efficiently at low cost. Since the Electronic Herd and the consumer preference for buying cheap are unlikely to go away, globalization is all but certain to continue growing, despite the best efforts of trade negotiators. Antiglobalization protestors who vocally oppose every round of free-trade talks because of the allegedly toxic effect of free trade on poor nations are also unlikely to stop it. At least some antipoverty groups will find it more productive to try to influence free-trade accords in ways that benefit the poor.

The sluggish economy has hurt globalization, but according to the 2003 A.T. Kearney/*Foreign Policy* magazine Globalization Index, globalization is not just a matter of economic ebb and flow. In 2003, the Index reports, "other aspects of globalization sustained their forward momentum. Political engagement has deepened, and levels of global personal contact and technological integration have continued to grow." Globalization should also be measured by the regional ties that countries form. In October 2003, for example, Singapore and Thailand urged their partners in ASEAN, the regional association of Southeast Asian countries, to work together for a common market—and announced that the two of them would move ahead in tandem if no one else cared to follow their lead.

A significant new power bloc is the Group of 20-plus or the Group of 21, conceived by India and Brazil and consisting of resource-rich, economically ambitious developing nations around the world. This coalition, which is committed to free trade and has a sophisticated sense of its own interests, exerted considerable influence at the Cancún meeting before the talks fell apart. Charlene Barshefsky, former U.S. trade representative, told the *New York Times* that the coalition was "much better organized and more savvy" than previous coalitions of developing countries. Despite stumbles along the way, more countries around the world are getting savvy enough to want to increase globalization.

Networked Businesses

The traditional model for a business is a top-down hierarchy: a chairman, under whom is a president, under whom are senior vice presidents, under whom are more vice presidents, and so on all the way down to the guy who sweeps the factory floor. When such a company wants to expand, it adds more factories, departments, and subsidiaries, all ultimately reporting to one big boss. This hierarchical business model is as old as the Egyptian pharaohs and will probably never go away completely. But in our wired, globalized era, it is now competing with the networked business model—and that model is increasingly beating it.

A networked business is one that makes its money through linkages with partners more than through in-house, top-down operations. A networked business keeps its overhead low; outsources tasks to specialists who can do them at low cost; acts as a hub of productive exchange (for example, between customers and vendors); takes advantage of modern technology to keep its network flowing; and ignores regional and national boundaries, cheerfully hiring contractors in Singapore while soliciting customers in Denmark from its base in Hoboken.

A prime example of a networked business is the online auction house eBay, which has become a huge success by facilitating exchanges between buyers and sellers of everything from paintings to computers. Unlike a brick-and-mortar auction house, it has no warehouse of dusty goods to maintain, no fast-talking auctioneers to pay; rather, it functions as a business-web or b-web, a networked business that links suppliers, distributors, customers, and commerce service providers via the Internet and other electronic media. Prices are set by moment-to-moment negotiations among buyers and sellers, rather than by a central agency. In *Digital Capital: Harnessing the Power of Business Webs* (2000), by Don Tapscott, David Ticoll, and Alex Lowy, the authors argue that participation in b-webs is a necessity for surviving and thriving in the digital economy.

Networked businesses have been most visible in e-commerce, and for good reason. The essential fact about the Internet is that it is a network, a global linkage of computer networks sharing information electronically. As such, it is of interest to the burgeoning scientific field of network theory—and it is a huge opportunity to businesses that can take advantage of its radically decentralized structure. The best way to do so is for a company itself to become networklike, connecting to customers in this direction, to suppliers or service providers in that direction, leaving itself free to concentrate on whatever its core competencies might be.

But even companies whose main business is not Internet-related are increasingly discovering the benefits of a networked business model. In a 2002 report called *Networked Pharma*, the business information company Datamonitor predicted that, by 2015, networking would be the preferred competitive strategy for the pharmaceutical industry. This is a big claim, given that pharmaceutical companies are traditionally extremely hierarchical behemoths with huge capital investments in R&D and manufacturing. But Datamonitor argues that they will improve their productivity and profitability by networking instead. Ideally, the result would be a limber, responsive, and unbureaucratic company that is neither burdened with excess production capacity in times of slowdown nor limited by tight production constraints in times when business is booming.

No major pharmaceutical company is yet fully networked, but many have taken steps in that direction, for example, through partnerships with biotech companies and contract research organizations. In 1999, the drug giant Roche launched a "virtual" organization spinoff called Fulcrum Pharma Development that conducts trials of new medicines and takes the products to market by outsourcing all facets of the drug development process. It is at heart a project management team, coordinating up to twenty contractors per project while acting as the point of contact for its clients. According to Datamonitor, Fulcrum has achieved time savings of up to 28 percent and cost savings of up to 49 percent.

Networked business models vary greatly, from ones that are thoroughly or mostly decentralized to ones in which one company functions as the central leader but forms partnerships as needed. In years to come, successful new businesses will increasingly be fully networked ones, taking full advantage of globalized connections and a telecommuting work force. Meanwhile, older businesses will increasingly become networked, in whole or in part, just to stay competitive with the upstart business-webs around them.

Scandal, Inc.

8 Scandals are not new to the business world, but in recent years the number of them, from Enron to Martha Stewart, has been growing. Public outrage has led to calls for increased regulation. As always in such periods, the people trying to reform business practices are locked in a struggle with people who have deep pockets and a big stake in the status quo. Yet, the struggle has already resulted in new legislation and a movement toward increased corporate governance—that is, stronger control by boards of directors over how CEOs run publicly owned companies. We are still in the age of Scandal, Inc., but it may already be giving way to the age of Scrutiny, Inc.

The underlying theme of all the scandals is the same: greed. But the individual issues have been legion. There have been companies that crashed and burned, taking unsuspecting investors with them, after using deceptive bookkeeping to inflate the value of their stocks—notably the energy-trading company Enron and the telecommunications giant WorldCom. A dose of celebrity entered Scandal, Inc., in June 2003, when home-decorating queen Martha Stewart was indicted for offenses related to her sale of stock in the biotech company ImClone.

The mutual fund industry, which manages funds for 95 million people, also has become a poster child for Scandal, Inc. A mutual fund operates by having many individual investors pool their money in one professionally managed portfolio of assets—but it turned out that not all those investors were created equal. Top executives were charged with providing confidential information to big investors; failing to give appropriate discounts to customers; and, through practices known by such arcane names as late trading and market timing, rapidly trading money in and out of their own mutual funds to make huge profits at the expense of ordinary investors. Executives charged with wrongdoing included Gary L. Pilgrim and Harold J. Baxter, founders of PBHG Funds, and Richard Strong, head of Strong Capital.

All this corruption has lowered public confidence in the nation's captains of industry. A Harris poll in December 2002 showed that nearly 30 percent of Americans have "hardly any" confidence in the people running major companies, a large jump from the fewer than 15 percent who responded that way back in 2000. On the other hand, public confidence has been even lower at other times, notably 1973, when the proportion of people with hardly any confidence was more than 30 percent. Still, whenever corruption becomes outrageous enough, there are inevitably efforts at reform, and some of those are already in process. The question is, how deep will they go this time, and how long will their effects last?

Congress, the SEC, and state regulators have all tried their hand at reform, and all have had limited success. In 2002, Congress responded to the cluster of scandals that included Enron and WorldCom by passing the Sarbanes-Oxley Act, which put in place antifraud provisions and corporate governance reforms. But under the influence of the well-heeled mutual fund lobby, the act granted exemptions to the mutual fund industry that left the door open for the scandals that rocked the industry the following year.

In the wake of the mutual fund scandal, the House of Representatives approved legislation to deter trading abuses and increase the independence of fund boards. But some lawmakers complained that the legislation had been watered down from earlier versions under the influence of industry lobbyists. Meanwhile, the current SEC chairman, William H. Donaldson, drafted plans for a new system of risk management assessments to improve the commission's surveillance of market wrongdoing. But this was closing the barn door after the horse had escaped; in previous years, periodic SEC examinations of the mutual fund industry had failed to uncover the major trading abuses that have now surfaced. It had taken investigation by state governments to do that. One such state official, New York attorney general Eliot Spitzer, complained in November 2003 that the SEC was still being too lax with the mutual fund industry.

Some state regulators have been dogged in pursuing corporate wrongdoing. But leaving regulation to the states keeps open the possibility that companies will relocate in states with more laissez-faire environments—and that possibility in turn discourages some states from launching investigations that might alienate companies.

Perhaps the best hope for preventing future waves of scandals lies in a movement toward corporate governance. Corporate boards of directors, which are supposed to represent shareholders, have traditionally rubber-stamped the decisions of CEOs and rewarded incompetence with big salaries and bonuses. No surprise, given that many of these boards have been stocked with friends of the CEOs in a culture that assumed the CEO could do no wrong. But according to Roger Lowenstein, in a December 2003 *New York Times Magazine* article called "A Boss for the Boss," that culture is changing: "[R]egulators, investors, academics and even corporate directors are coming round to the idea that . . . a better way must be found to govern the corporation from within." Directors shaken by scandal are growing more likely to challenge or question the decisions of CEOs, even as legislation and regulation (such as the Sarbanes-Oxley Act) take incremental steps to strengthen standards for directors.

Even with Scrutiny, Inc., struggling to be born, never underestimate the power of greed. Scandal, Inc., still has life left in it.

Specialized Consultants

9 According to consultants themselves, the golden age of consulting is over. In the 1990s, businesses had the money to hire consultants to help them make strategy and business decisions about their new technological and Internet business ideas. It was the culmination of the growth of consulting over the past half-century, when the once-quiet business became a high-profile profession with celebrity status.

But the downturn in the economy made businesses turn away from high-cost consultants who provided general coverage for their company. In fact, in a change from years of increasing earnings, revenues in 2001 were flat. In response, since the beginning of the 21st century, the companies who hire consultants have been looking for targeted results. Companies have also cooled on consulting due to recent scandals in the accounting industry, such as the scandal that brought down one of the Big Five, Arthur Andersen. The backlash from scandals, along with an uneven economy and legislation (the Sarbanes-Oxley Act) that limits the role of accountants in consulting, has reshaped the consulting business. Consultants now have to assure clients that they follow stronger watchdog laws and provide results to the client.

With cash-strapped and wary companies wanting consultants who offer more for less, some consulting firms of the future may cut operating costs and become more efficient by becoming more specialized. While traditional consulting firms will continue, others will be limited in size and offer specialty or boutique consulting.

Currently 45 percent of consultants are independent contractors. As freelancers, they are hired on a project-by-project basis. The single-project hire benefits the employer, who limits financial commitment and eliminates the need to pay company benefits. In so doing, the company follows the larger economic trend toward networked businesses that acquire much of their staff through outsourcing.

Of course, some areas of consulting will be in high demand over the next decades. They include highly scientific fields, such as biotechnology, and emerging fields, such as mobile commerce. There will also be continued interest in human resource and health care consulting. In addition, there will always be room for unexpected areas of specialization, such as psychic consulting. One established psychic consultant is Cynthia Hess, known as "New Mexico's Most Listened to Psychic." A radio and television personality, she predicts upcoming public events such as political futures and celebrity deaths. She also offers consulting to individual clients, presumably advising them on their personal future, their competitors', and, if they want, the future of consulting.

Telecommuting Grows

10 For a variety of reasons, the number of telecommuters is expected to increase by several million in the 21st century. Currently, over 24 million Americans work from their home; by 2010, the number is likely to reach 40 million. According to futurist David Pearce Snyder, one-third of all gainful employment will take place in the home by 2015, and futurist Joyce Gioia says that the number of people telecommuting from home will increase by about 60 percent in the early 21st century.

Workers cite a desire to eliminate the stress of commuting and the need to take care of family as prime reasons for working from home. This includes elder care: the Families and Work Institute estimates that 42 percent of workers currently provide some care for their elderly parents and demand is expected to continue. Affirming the need for flexible work environments, U.S. Secretary of Labor Elaine Chao said, "Companies must be more flexible, adaptable, decentralized, worker-friendly and family-friendly than ever."

Employees champion telecommuting by noting the various ways they have increased their productivity by telecommuting. By not commuting, workers gain an average eight additional working weeks per year, which translates into about fifty-three extra minutes per day. According to the International Telework Association and Council, most teleworkers are 25 percent more productive than office workers.

For their part, employers have found that telecommuting results in lower costs for workplace real estate (with average savings of $8,000 annually), reduced travel and gasoline expenses, and decreased absenteeism.

The continued use of telecommuting is helping to fuel the growth of networked businesses—companies constructed more like spread-out networks than top-down pyramids. It is also likely to result in long-lasting changes in management styles. Managers used to on-site staff being evaluated through observation and interaction have had to adapt to results-oriented performance.

Changes in technology and the natural environment are also likely to occur as telecommuting grows. A simple but broad technological change is teleconferencing, which has become even more popular in light of terrorism fears. For telecommuters, teleconferencing allows several independent contractors from across the world to be united face-to-face.

The natural environment will be affected if the increase in virtual employment results in reduced pollution levels. According to Department of Transportation studies, telecommuting may reduce the number of automobiles owned and the amount of gasoline consumed. The lower consumption of gasoline may reduce dependence on foreign sources of oil.

Telecommuting is also likely to be useful for retirees, who will increase in number as the century continues. As baby boomers reach traditional retirement age, they may be unable to retire on their savings and pension, and will look to part-time employment. They may be able to supplement their income with part-time or consulting work done by telecommuting. This move toward hiring older telecommuters fits with a general trend toward hiring interim workers.

Although there are many advantages to telecommuting, there are, inevitably, drawbacks. Among them, some experts cite the dangers of an excess of success. When self-motivated telecommuters accomplish their work goals more quickly than they could on-site, they may feel guilty. Says one telecommuting adviser, fast-working telecommuters should abandon the guilt and just "enjoy the spare time and go to the gym." There is also the problem for the telecommuter of always being available on the job. The Internet makes the workplace omnipresent. Says venture capitalist and partner at Sequoia Capital Michael Moritz, "[T]here will be fewer places to escape from work, to escape from advertisers, and to escape from school."

In many ways, the desire to work at home is natural, and historic. In 1895, 50 percent of work was located in the home. Although the professions then and now differ, the result may be the same—work and home combined, naturally. The rise of telecommuting also fits with increasing interest in and demand for flexibility in the workplace. Given a young work force that will be dwindling over the next decades, companies will have to exercise flexibility in working conditions, such as telecommuting. Says Alan Halcrow, editor of *Workforce* magazine, flexibility will become commonplace. Work will, he says, "kind of move around in the day—people working four hours and then taking four hours to take care of their children, and then going back to work." In this type of world, telecommuting earns its keep.

2

Demographics

The Fattening of America

11 The United States is growing larger. It is not establishing a new state; its citizens are picking up excess pounds. In fact, the nation's people have increased their weight so much that the head of the U.S. federal health agency called it the country's top health threat. According to Dr. Julie Gerberding, the director for the Centers for Disease Control and Prevention, 65 percent of U.S. adults are either overweight or obese. Poor diet and lack of exercise are far more likely to kill Americans than any biological threat, imported menace like anthrax or smallpox, or disease like SARS.

Yet, over the past few years, Americans have tried in some ways to eat more healthfully. They have reduced the overall fat in the national diet and have eaten less meat. Despite these changes, Americans have gained weight. Even supposedly active young adult Americans, who decreased their intake of dietary saturated fats and cholesterol over the past seven years, increased their average weight by ten pounds.

This weight gain is reflected in a rising obesity rate. According to statistics cited by Dr. Gerberding, 38.8 million American adults as of 2000 have been classified as obese. What's more, the rise in obesity in the United States has been going on for decades. In a 1999 national survey, 35 percent of the 1,615 people over age twenty who were tested were overweight and 26 percent were obese. In 1994, 33 percent were overweight and 23 percent were obese. Even back in 1991, one-third of the population was considered obese, which then marked a 32 percent increase over the previous decade.

Now for the truly bad news. Obesity is associated with an increased risk of heart disease, hypertension, some cancers, type 2 diabetes, and reduced life expectancy, among other health problems. The major health problems are even affecting children. Registered dietician Nadine Pazner says, "We're seeing heart disease in young people, high blood pressure in children, and what we used to call maturity-onset (type 2) diabetes showing up in people in their twenties and thirties. Even kids in high school are showing up with it."

To make things worse, obesity is increasing the national health budget, which the American public ends up paying for in increased taxes. Treating obesity-related health conditions costs individuals and the health care system about $39 billion annually.

Obesity has not just increased in the United States. According to Kelly D. Brownell, Ph.D., professor of psychology, epidemiology, and public health at Yale University, "[O]besity is on the rise in country after country, as each becomes more like America." In 1997, the World Health Organization declared a global obesity epidemic.

Causes for this increased weight are varied. Americans have unprecedented access to a poor diet—to high-calorie foods that are widely available, low in cost, heavily promoted, and good tasting. There is also the unending psychological allure of food. Says Dr. Margo Denke, associate professor of internal medicine at the University of Texas Southwestern Medical Center and researcher at the Center for Human Nutrition, "Food . . . fills a growing dissatisfaction with the depersonalization of America— food is a fabulous reward that never fails." Nutritionists point to another culprit in the rise in weight gain: the supposedly helpful spate of foods that are labeled "low-fat" or "fat-free" but are high in calories.

Another problem has to do with American thriftiness. Americans don't like to waste food, especially when it is served in restaurants. Add to that condition the fact that restaurants today are serving larger portions and that processed foods are getting bigger. For example, a chain-bakery blueberry muffin is 430 calories and 18 grams of fat. Its size is about 6 ounces, while the USDA lists the typical medium-sized muffin as 2 ounces. Further, a recent study showed that people do not notice the changing size of their portions. They eat more of a larger portion, particularly when it is a junk food. This practice was verified in a study organized by the Food and Brand Research Lab at the University of Illinois at Champaign-Urbana.

Not only are Americans eating more, they are eating more quickly, and this increases the possibility for sustained weight gain. Instead of moderating the dinner experience by eating at home or a restaurant in front of a place setting, it is now acceptable to eat anywhere. This can mean eating in a car, on the job, in a store, at the movies, or anywhere imaginable.

It can be frustrating for those who want to adopt a proper diet to even figure out what a healthy diet is. While most nutritionists advocate fewer processed foods, many debate the correct proportions of food types, primarily proteins, carbohydrates, and fats.

Exercise and restraint are necessary to maintain normal weight levels, says Dr. Brownell, because evolution will not do it for us. The environment has changed greatly over the past 200 years, he says, but evolution has not: "[I]t takes thousands or millions of years for evolution to catch up and change our ancient genes. The environment has changed way too quickly." People used to live in an environment where food was scarce. They managed by eating large quantities of high-calorie food when they found it. Now we live in a land of abundance and we have to learn to adapt to it. He also suggests that we can improve our health by reforming the food industry. He suggests subsidizing healthful foods and increasing the cost of unhealthful foods. Greg Critser, author of *Fat Land*, a study of the fattening of the United States, says that it might be useful to bring back gluttony as one of the deadly sins.

But such sanctions would subvert the nation's drive to create easy abundance. According to the Department of Agriculture, says Dr. Marion Nestle, Chair of the Department of Nutrition and Food Studies at New York University, "our food supply provides an average of 3,800 calories every single day for every man, woman and child in the country. . . . And it's roughly twice what the average person needs." According to physiologist James O. Hill, getting fat is less an aberration than "a normal response to the American environment."

Honey, I Shrunk the Middle Class

12 Under the tax cuts put into law in 2003, the already wealthy will prosper. The 1 percent of Americans living on investments or who have employment that pays more than $250,000 per year will receive greater tax benefits than other Americans, and the 400 richest taxpayers, who in 2003 made an average $174 million each, will benefit even more. Not only has the income of the top 400 increased fourfold since 2000, they are likely to pay even less than the average 22.3 percent in federal income taxes that they paid in 2003. There will be yet more of a reduction in their taxes from the 90 percent level they paid in the Eisenhower administration and the 39 percent they were reduced to by the 1990s. To apply the old adage, the rich will get richer.

For a variety of reasons, the middle class in the early 21st century will be slimming down. In general, fewer people will have the components that made for 20th-century middle-class comfort, such as a job that pays the bills, a residence big enough for the family, the ability to pay medical bills, and leftover funds for a car or vacation.

This widening of the distance between the well-off and everyone else continues a pattern that has been going on for over a quarter of a century. One reason for the gap is education. A study by the nonprofit Economic Policy Institute, a think tank in Washington, D.C., reported that nationally from 1973 to 1977, wages of workers with advanced degrees rose 6 percent above the inflation rate. Incomes of those with college degrees only remained nearly steady and wages of those with only a high school diploma fell 14 percent against inflation.

Linked to the increasing erosion of wages for workers without advanced degrees is the decrease in well-paying blue-collar jobs. Traditional blue-collar jobs that require little educational training off the job, such as manufacturing and heavy and light industry, have declined over the past quarter-century and will continue to decline over the next decades. Service jobs at all levels will increase, but most bring low salaries: an average store cashier earns $15,000 per year, without health benefits.

Not having health benefits can immediately increase costs for the uninsured. Not only do the uninsured have to pay for doctors' services, they have to pay higher rates than insurance companies. Particularly in hospitals, uninsured patients pay "gross charges," or list prices for medical services. Insured people get a discount from the negotiations of their insurance companies or government health programs (Medicaid, Medicare), which pay reduced rates to medical professionals, while hospitals charge uninsured people the full rate. With medical costs increasing much faster than pay raises, and with an aging population requiring more forms of medical treatment, it will be increasingly difficult for average Americans to fit medical costs into the middle-class budget.

Many other factors challenge the accepted middle-class way of life. For example, statistics show that college and advanced degrees usually result in higher salaries. But the cost of college and graduate school education, which many employers deem necessary, is increasing in cost by double-digit percentages each year. Because of increased state mandates and a highly expanding college-age population, usually less expensive state schools will increase tuition and yet be unable to serve all applicants in the traditional classroom educational experience. Private colleges may become prohibitively expensive for all but the well-to-do, as they had been in generations past.

Ballooning housing costs, shrinking pension plans, and the general rise in the cost of living also present threats to the newly modern middle class. From this point at the start of the 21st century, it seems the great shrinking game for the bottom 99 percent of Americans has just begun.

Multicultural People

13 What do Vin Diesel, Tiger Woods, and Hispanic census figures have in common? All testify to the transformation of America from a society that is assimilationist and racially divided to one that is multicultural but perhaps less racially divided.

For most of U.S. history, the population fell into two main categories: white and black. According to the U.S. Bureau of the Census, white people were the vast majority, peaking at 90 percent from 1920 to 1950, with blacks making up most of the remainder. Asians in those days constituted less than half a percent, and Hispanics weren't even counted. White people weren't all from one country, of course; many were recent immigrants. But most of them came from Europe, and were expected quickly to abandon their native cultures and adopt a more or less uniform American one. They were expected to learn English, like baseball, honor George Washington, and believe in the Constitution and the Judeo-Christian tradition. The universality of the American way was marred mainly by segregation, which in the days before the civil rights era kept the black population apart and below. America was a melting pot, with blacks in a separate pot.

But a funny thing happened on the way to the 21st century. In the last fifty years, immigration from Europe declined while immigration from the rest of the world soared. Latin America, in particular, contributed vast numbers: nearly half of the foreign-born people in the United States today are from Hispanic countries. The Asian-American population also mushroomed, increasing more than thirtyfold, while the U.S. population as a whole grew by less than twofold. The African-American population grew more quickly than the white population, but neither grew as quickly as either Asians or Latinos. The result is that Asian-Americans are now 4 percent of the population, and Hispanics, at 12.5 percent and rising, have begun to surpass blacks as the country's biggest minority group. Meanwhile, in the past fifty years, whites have fallen from being 90 percent of the population to being only 75 percent. In another fifty years, estimates are that whites will make up barely more than 50 percent of the population. Soon after that, the United States will no longer have a clear majority race, but only an assortment of minorities.

As this trend accelerates in the coming years, many people fear the Balkanization of America. As universities expand their "Asian Studies" and "Latino Studies" departments, there is concern that children will be less likely to grow up with positive views (or any views) about George Washington and the Constitution. Islam and Hinduism are spreading, and a growing number of Americans don't even speak an Indo-European language, much less English.

However, in his book *The Monochrome Society* (2001), sociologist Amitai Etzioni offers reason to think that any fears about America's growing multiculturalism are unnecessary. Numerous surveys show that despite the demographic changes of the past fifty years, Americans of all races and ethnicities share basic values and beliefs, including a commitment to the American way. As far as basic attitudes go, says Etzioni, "[w]e are much more a monochrome society than a rainbow society." For example, one poll asked Americans whether high school students should "be required to understand the common history and ideas that tie all Americans together." Not only did 85 percent of all parents say yes, but foreign-born parents (88 percent) and Hispanic parents (89 percent) were even *more* likely to say yes. Far from refusing to learn English, foreign-born parents are more likely than the population at large to want schools to teach English to their children as quickly as possible. In most surveys of opinion on current issues, there is more similarity than difference among Asians, Latinos, blacks, and whites.

Demographic change is not likely to make the country fly apart. What it is likely to do—and is already doing—is introduce Americans to previously little known cultures, and pique their interest in knowing more. (Globalization and the Internet are helping, as trade and communication with other countries proliferate.) In the last decade, music by Latino artists has gone from marginal to mainstream—with Jennifer

Lopez, Ricky Martin, and Christina Aguilera all becoming household names. After 9/11, sales of books about Islam shot up, as Americans took notice—more often curious than hostile—of the growing population of Muslims in their midst. In 2002, *Flower Drum Song* was revived on Broadway, with an entirely new script that erased the stereotypes of forty years ago and showed a new, richer understanding of Chinese-American history. That same fall, Deborah Treisman came on board as fiction editor at the staid *New Yorker* magazine, expressing her preference for voices from less well known cultures.

While no less loyal to their adopted country than previous generations of immigrants, the new immigrants are more likely to celebrate and want to preserve their ethnic heritage. The United States less resembles a melting pot than a salad bowl now, with numerous ingredients retaining their flavor while contributing to the mix. Numerous businesses are making money by selling to ethnic markets within the United States. Witness the enterprises that are thriving by serving just the Hispanic market—everything from Goya Foods to the Telemundo and Univision television networks to the periodicals *El Diario* and *Latina.*

With all these changes happening, the question of racial identity is likely to become more complicated, and perhaps less important. Is golf champion Tiger Woods Asian-American, African-American, or what? Essentially, he is whatever he wants to be. Hispanics are not a distinct race at all: the U.S. Census Bureau notes that they can be of any race, and many Hispanics are a biological mix of European and Native American genes, often with African ones thrown in. Fifty years ago, being black almost always entailed being poor, but now there is a growing black middle class that is statistically likely to share the views and buying habits of the rest of the middle class. Further, Americans of all races and ethnicities are more likely than ever to marry outside their group: since 1970, the proportion of such marriages has increased by 72 percent. More than 40 percent of third-generation Asian-American women, for example, marry non-Asians.

Expect more Americans in the coming years to identify themselves as multiracial or multicultural. Actor Vin Diesel gave himself the "multicultural" tag in publicity interviews in 2002, when he won box-office success as a new, rougher-edged, racially vague kind of movie spy in *XXX*. Greater diversity without greater division: that is the wave of the future for America's ethnic groups.

Seventy Million Navel Geezers

14 The end of the baby boomers is coming. Sixty years from now the kids born of post–World War II hope will be gone. But they will go out in high style. They'll live longer than any generation before them, work longer, and entertain and educate themselves more. They'll also generate higher health care costs and collect more private and federal pensions than ever before (and maybe reshape the way future generations think of these services). And they'll do it all in a big way. Even after early and midlife deaths, there will be 70 million of them. Famous for being "navel gazers," they will now be navel geezers.

The growth in the numbers of older people in the United States over the past 100 years is staggering. According to the Federal Interagency Forum on Aging Related Statistics, in 1900, the number of U.S. residents age 65 or higher was 3 million, or 4 percent of the total population. By 2000, there were 35 million people 65 or older, representing about 13 percent of the population. But by 2030, two decades after the first baby boomers turn 65, projections indicate that one in five U.S. residents will be 65 or older. Even by 2020, Americans over 65 will outnumber teenagers two to one. By 2030, there will be 70 million senior citizens in the United States. They'll live longer, too. By 2030, the number of the population over 85 is expected to increase from 4 to 19 million. Up to 381,000 of them are expected to reach age 100.

As the number of older people increases and that of young people decreases, more older people will be needed to work. For example, about 22 percent of men over age 65 and 12 percent of female seniors are expected to be working in 2020, reports the Association of Bay Area Governments, in California. Because of the influx of older workers, says deputy director of the Council of Aging of Santa Clara County, California, Paul Isaacs, "The pace [of work] will be altered to cater to a changing society. You won't be working 20 hours a day." Part time work schedules will be adjusted to the changing demographics.

A huge aging population less interested or able to drive but still desiring to be active will push for more public transportation. In addition, thousands of local and state public and private services now offer paratransit programs that take older Americans to medical, shopping, and entertainment destinations. Many communities are also improving sidewalks and resting areas to make public transportation safer and more appealing.

As for the general life span of the generation, it is about 30 to 40 years longer than it was for the generations that preceded it. In 1960, the average life expectancy was 70 years. In 1997, it was 79 for women and 74 years for men.

The health picture for future older Americans varies. Decreased fat intake and increased mobility have been positive influences on the generation as a whole. But some specific diseases, such as cancer, are expected to increase. According to Holly L. Howe, Ph.D., and executive director of North American Association of Central Cancer Registries, "The number of cancer patients age 85 and over is expected to increase four-fold" between 2000 and 2050.

One of the greatest strains on individual and government pocketbooks as the population ages is health care. According to projections done by researchers at the Institute of Business and Economic Research/Center for the Economics and Demography of the Aging, University of California, Berkeley, the cost of federal programs is set to rise substantially. According to their findings, they project that the costliness of federal programs as a share of the GDP will increase by 35 percent by the 2030s. Nearly all of that is expected to go for health care to the elderly, which will rise from 8 percent of the GDP in 1999 to 21 percent in 2075. Medicare is projected to have a median share of 11 percent of GDP in 2075. Increases in payroll taxes, cuts in benefits, or revamping of the entire government health care system are anticipated.

One reason for this projected restructuring of the health care system is that the aging of the United States is not expected to end with the baby boom generation. As the country ages, it will increase its old-age dependency ratio throughout the 21st century. This will necessitate further payout of government health care programs, which with Social Security, already account for one-third of the federal budget.

How America resolves the problems of getting older will be one of the major concerns of the late 21st century.

World Population: Slowing Growth

15 Over the past fifty years, the world's population rose at a hectic pace. According to the World Bank Group, global population soared from 2.5 billion people in 1950 to greater than 6 billion in 1999. In fact, throughout most of the 20th century, the world population increased each year by about 2 percent. At that rate, the population would reach 10.6 billion by 2025. By 2600, the 2 percent growth would mean a population of 6.3 trillion, an amount that would leave barely enough room on earth for any human to turn around. If the problem of space did not occur, a lack of food would. In the groundbreaking book *The Population Bomb*, author Paul Ehrlich posited that the population was increasing at such a high rate that there would not be enough food to feed everyone.

Studies now show that neither of these scenarios is likely to occur. The planet Earth is not likely in the foreseeable future to have the rapid population growth it had in the 20th century. Instead, it will have fewer people than previously expected. According to a 2003 report by the United Nations, the world population in 2050 is expected to be only 8.9 billion, down from the 9.3 billion it projected earlier.

Reasons for the decline in the rate of population growth are varied. A primary reason is the increase in HIV/AIDS. According to the recent U.N. report, the countries most affected by AIDS will have half a billion fewer people in 2050 than had been projected. Another reason for lower world population is decreased fertility. In the last two decades of the 20th century, fertility dropped by 1.5 births per woman. In most advanced countries, the birth rate is under the replacement rate of 2.1 births, the rate necessary to keep population stable. The birth rate in developing countries has also declined, from 6.3 to 2.9. Generally, the decline in non-AIDS related birth rates can be traced to the families' increased affluence and/or family planning.

The United States is one developed country expected to increase its population, due to immigration. Aside from the United States, all population growth sites over the next fifty years will be developing countries. They include Bangladesh, China, Congo, Ethiopia, India, Nigeria, and Pakistan.

Overall, the increase in world population over the next decades is to come largely from the world's poorest countries. According to the World Bank Group, the next billion of the world's population over the next fifteen years will include nearly 600 million from low-income countries. About 375 million will come from middle-income countries, and high-income countries will add 30 million, or 3 percent.

Geographically, they break down as follows, according to the World Bank Group:

- **South Asia**—310 million
- **Sub-Saharan Africa**—230 million
- **East Asia and the Pacific**—220 million
- **Middle East/North Africa/Latin America/Caribbean**—230 million
- **Europe and Central Asia**—9 million
- **High-Income Countries**—30 million

A 2001 study, published in *Nature*, forecasts a possible scenario of the world population rising to 9 billion in 2070, and dwindling afterward. The study "The End of World Population Growth," by Wolfgang Lutz, Warren Sanderson, and Sergei Scherbov, demonstrates that there is about an 85 percent probability that the world's population will stop growing before the end of the century. The study presents a model of aging populations and ultimately decreasing numbers for the most modernized societies (in accord with that model, the U.N. report predicts that Europe's population will dwindle from 728 million to 632 million in 2050). Meanwhile, population rates in the countries of the Southern Hemisphere are projected to increase, resulting in substantial population redistribution. Commenting on these projected changes, John Bongaarts of the New York–based Population Council says, "The world is becoming less European, less white, less North American."

As for the population of the United States, there is no need to worry. As it has for centuries, it will grow. By 2050, thanks to immigration and a healthy fertility rate, estimates show that the U.S. population will rise from 285 million to 409 million.

According to the World Bank, every minute 380 women become pregnant across the world. Most of these pregnancies and births will occur in developing countries, and births in developed countries will continue to decline. According to the United Nations Population Division, already 44 percent of the world's population lives in countries where the fertility rate has fallen below the replacement level. How these countries change and coexist will define the new world for the 22nd century.

3

Entertainment and the Arts

Decentralized Art

16 In the 20th century, New York was the center of publishing, theater, and the fine arts, and Los Angeles was the center of the film and pop music industries. But as the 21st century wears on and technology improves, both high and low arts are breaking away from traditional geographic centers. We have entered the age of decentralized art.

New technology has been the most important factor in driving this trend. Digital cameras, desktop publishing, the Internet, and other innovations are rapidly changing the two halves of any living art: production and distribution.

In most arts, production has traditionally been the cheaper of the two halves: writing, for example, requires nothing more than paper and pencil, whereas publishing requires printing presses, warehouses, and a sales force. But in some arts, even production costs can be high: the typical Hollywood film, for example, costs tens of millions of dollars to make. Enter new technology: digital video can drastically lower film-making costs, making it easier for movies to be made outside of Hollywood. Mike Figgis, who filmed *Time Code* on digital video in 2000, has said, "It's beyond imagination what this is going to do to film-making. What has been an exclusive medium of high finance, banking and financial exclusivity is now going to become something that is within reach of everyone."

Technology is also decentralizing the distribution half of the arts. The Internet has made it possible in principle for everyone to be a publisher, art gallery owner, record company, and movie exhibitor. By posting pictures on the Internet, a painter in Montana can exhibit her works to as large a potential art-buying audience as one in Manhattan. A writer can attract more readers on a popular online literary journal than in some print ones. Film distribution on the Internet is still in its infancy, because high-quality digital prints of feature-length films come in huge files, difficult to transmit electronically. But producers of short films are increasingly in demand on the Web, and several low-budget, non-Hollywood films have gone on to surprisingly big box-office returns on the strength of Web publicity (most memorably, *The Blair Witch Project* in 1999).

Technology has even affected the link between production and distribution in a way that promotes decentralization. A writer without a publisher is an unread writer, and a publisher without writers has no books to sell; different as they are economically, each side has always needed access to the other. In previous periods, because long-distance travel and communication were slow and expensive, the best way to achieve this access was by placing them in physical contact. Hence, the arts tended to cluster in one or a few locations—publishers in New York, and movie studios in Hollywood. But the widespread availability of e-mail, cell phones, and express shipping means that a writer in New Mexico and an illustrator in Florida can easily collaborate with a publisher in Dublin, who can outsource distribution to a global sales force. Hollywood itself is barely located in Hollywood anymore: many big-budget American movies today are filmed in Vancouver or eastern Europe, often with foreign financing and aimed heavily at foreign audiences.

Technology is not the only factor encouraging decentralized art. Cities throughout the world have realized the importance of the arts in promoting economic development. The arts attract creative people who drive economic growth, and they bring in tourism and recreational dollars. From Bilbao, Spain, where the Guggenheim Museum has spurred revitalization, to Detroit, now sporting a new symphony hall, city planners are looking to the arts for urban renewal. One effect of this trend is to increase the number of the world's artistic centers, further decentralizing art.

Is decentralization a good trend for the arts? With about 9 million Web sites in the world as of 2002, would it increase the world's total aesthetic merit if each Web site owner posted his own poems/films/yodeling for the world to enjoy? Maybe not—but then nobody is going to wade through all 9 million galleries in search of the rare gems. There will always be a need for critics, reputable publishers, hoary museums, and name-brand conglomerates to serve as filters directing audiences to artworks they are likely to enjoy. Corporations that are in the filtering business (such as movie studios) usually have deep pockets for marketing and distribution, and all that money will serve as a brake on decentralization, persuading even an upstart artist to sign with a big record label or movie studio. But even in the filtering side of the arts, decentralization is taking place. Movie fans are now as likely to look for guidance to someone like Harry Knowles—publisher of the independent movie-criticism Web site Ain't It Cool News—as to TV ads or reviews in major newspapers.

Despite the benefit decentralization brings—most notably, bringing art to more people in more geographic locations—something of value might be lost in the process of breaking up old geographic centers of art such as New York or Los Angeles. A side effect of centralization was the aesthetic cross-pollination that resulted from having artists living close together, debating over coffee and swiping ideas from each other's studios. But the Internet makes possible a digital version of this effect, as artists debate in chat rooms and swipe from each other's Web sites. Meanwhile, decentralization encourages the rise of brand-new regional centers of the arts, such as Austin, Texas. As artistic decentralization continues, many other places will soon join it.

Digital Broadcasting

17 Who wants a digital TV set? Hardly anyone—yet. About 25 million old-fashioned analog TV sets are sold each year, versus 150,000 digital television (DTV) sets. Unlike the analog TV sets in use since the days of *I Love Lucy*, which use video technology to display images, a DTV set works the way a computer does: by processing digital information, data that has been converted into ones and zeroes. Even when people become aware that this is what DTV does, most see no reason why they would want it. Digital radio is even more obscure: what's wrong with an old-fashioned transistor radio? Even so, the transition to digital TV and radio broadcasting is already underway, and it is likely to accelerate in coming years.

By the way, the much talked-about phenomena of digital satellite systems and digital cable systems are not the same thing as DTV. Those just refer to digital transmission; the signals being transmitted might originate as analog signals and be displayed on analog sets. In true DTV, filming, transmission, and display are all done digitally.

Here are reasons why a consumer might want to own a digital set:

• A sharper, wide-screen picture, with up to six channels of Dolby sound, through the miracle of high-definition television (HDTV). Among other benefits, the wide screen (16:9 aspect ratio) allows you to watch DVDs of movies in their original wide-screen format, turning your home into a mini-theater.

• Interactive TV, permitting viewers to download data, images, sounds, etc., as well as receive more traditional broadcasts. In other words, it's TV with some of the features of Web pages or interactive CDs/DVDs. One possibility that is already available in some models is a TV integrated with a PC to provide a "home infotainment center."

• Multicasting, in which a station uses its digital channel to broadcast several simultaneous shows from which the viewer can choose;

these shows would be standard-definition (fuzzier) rather than high-definition (sharper). One likely possibility is for a station to multicast several standard-definition shows during the day, and switch to a single high-definition show at night.

If you think that none of this sounds like enough reason to plunk down good money for a high-priced digital TV set, you're not alone. Millions of Americans feel the same way. Those who have digital sets don't have much digital programming to receive. Several years back, the FCC set deadlines for commercial and public stations to convert to digital formats, but some of those deadlines have come and gone without the stations meeting the mandated steps. In part, broadcasters are dragging their heels because not enough customers own digital sets. It's a chicken and egg problem: which will come first, the customers or the programming? Without broadcasts, audiences aren't interested; without audiences, broadcasters aren't interested. Then there is the problem of competing formats, as in the old 1980s wars over videocassette recorders. Customers don't want to buy one kind of DTV only to have it become the Betamax of its day.

Even so, digital TV is inevitable. One reason is that our computers are conditioning us to like and expect a high-definition image. Even the lowest-grade computer monitor displays a sharper resolution than an analog TV does. As we become accustomed to surfing the Web, watching DVDs, and working on a PC, the old-fashioned TV screen is going to start looking obsolete.

The omnipresence of computers makes a difference in another way. As we come to spend more of our time online, we will be reluctant to leave our easy chairs to switch machines. People will want to have their TV sets integrated with their PCs so they can get all their entertainment and information in one seamless center. Such a home infotainment center requires DTV.

To these consumer incentives, add incentives for business. A mass conversion to DTV would create a new consumer electronics industry as consumers bought DTV sets. Broadcasters would gain multiple new channels for selling advertising. Then there is strong appeal for the FCC, which gains revenue from licensing the use of the radio spectrum, including the channels used for analog signals. The FCC set a vigorous timetable that envisions the digital transition completed by 2006, with 85 percent of U.S. households having the capability to receive a DTV signal.

Even though most people still receive television signals the old-fashioned way, look for DTV to grow in prominence—especially if a "killer application" arises that makes DTV look like a necessity. In addition, digital radio, which is at an even younger stage than DTV, is likely to increase its presence. With digital radio, you may be able to store songs on a hard drive, fast-forward past commercials, and link to sites where you can buy albums or concert tickets as you listen.

When CBS and NBC began regular color broadcasts in 1954, only 1 in 100 U.S. households owned a color TV set. Ten years later, color TV sets were commonplace. Similarly, if you don't own a DTV set today, just wait a few years. You will.

Digital Hollywood

18 Hollywood may have a taste for novelty, but in its basic technology, it has long opted for something exceedingly old. Since the invention of the movies more than 100 years ago, the cinema has relied on the same equipment: chemical emulsion on celluloid film. But in the biggest cinematic revolution since the advent of talkies, that equipment is now being replaced by digital technology: technology based on the conversion of information into ones and zeroes.

This transition has been happening in every phase of the movie business, though not all at the same pace: the shooting of movies (production); the fine-tuning of movies with special effects and editing (postproduction); the dissemination of movies from studios to theaters (distribution); and the showing of movies to paying audiences (exhibition). Most movies are still shot on 35mm celluloid film, which has a depth and richness that until recently was difficult to attain with other formats.

In postproduction, the pace of change has been faster. Even movies that are made on 35mm film are now routinely digitized so they can be more easily edited and spruced up with special effects. Editors now rearrange digitized pieces of film on computers, rather than having to fuss with physical snipping and cementing of celluloid. Digital effects have transformed special effects in ways both obvious and invisible. Everyone knows that the Hulk is a computer-generated creature, but when a car is digitally erased from the background of a medieval epic, only the filmmakers know about it.

The slowest transition has been in distribution and exhibition. Even though movies are regularly digitized in postproduction, they are just as regularly converted back into old-fashioned celluloid prints for shipping to theaters and projection on movie screens. The studios would love to save money by releasing their movies to theaters as digital files sent via satellite or network lines; however, the vast majority of theaters are not yet equipped with digital projectors. At current prices, converting a screen to digital projection costs about $150,000. True, they may gain bigger audiences if digital projection turns out to be a draw. But that gain may not be enough to offset the cost of conversion. Since the studios are the ones that stand to save the most money (right now, they spend $1.36 billion a year to produce and distribute celluloid prints worldwide), exhibitors say the studios should pay for the conversion. Still, many experts think the transition to digital distribution and exhibition will be complete by 2010, if not sooner.

For the film industry, the shift to Digital Hollywood presents both risks and opportunities. When the day comes that movies are routinely shipped as digital files, piracy may become as big a problem for film studios as it now is for the music industry. Already the studios are working on encryption systems and other techniques to protect digital products from being stolen.

Theater owners will get a windfall by using their digital projectors not only to show movies but to present souped-up ads before the movies (goodbye, old-fashioned slide shows; hello, digital displays) and offer videoconferencing. The nation's biggest theater chain, Regal Entertainment Group, is already doing that with digital projectors in many of its theaters.

Film producers may benefit more than anyone from Digital Hollywood if they can eliminate their greatest source of tension on the set: actors. The 2002 film *SIMONE* imagined the rise of a computer-generated star who looked fully human, got rave reviews, but demanded no salary, limo, or air-conditioned trailer. At present, even fantastical computer-generated creatures, such as Gollum in the *Lord of the Rings* movies, require human actors to supply their voices and block out their movements. Still, filmmakers are taking small steps to supplement human performances with digital ones, and producers are increasingly replacing or supplementing real sets with digital ones. Coming attractions: Hollywood continues to go digital.

Pirates of the Internet

19   The word *pirates* conjures up images of 17th century sailors armed with cutlasses, boarding Caribbean ships and relieving them of treasure chests. But 21st-century pirates are likely to be armed not with cutlasses but computers. The treasure they steal is likely to be digitized information, and the pitching sea on which they find it is the Internet. Nor are these pirates adorned with savage-looking eye patches. They are likely to look like suburban teens, or perhaps the reader of this book.

So far, digital pirates have become best known for stealing music. Using file-sharing software such as KaZaA, LimeWire, Morpheus, and BearShare, about 60 million Americans have downloaded music free of charge on the Internet and traded it with other pirates. (The phenomenon is also called peer-to-peer, or P2P, networking.) File-sharers are unlikely to see what they are doing as wrong: Sonya Arndt, a fourteen-year-old pirate in California, told the *New York Times*, "It shouldn't be illegal. It's not like I'm selling it." Music companies and recording artists have another view: record labels are suffering from the loss of sales, performers from the loss of royalties. In September 2003, the empire struck back, as the Recording Industry Association of America (RIAA) sued 261 people for up to $150,000 per song for allegedly downloading music illegally. The strategy certainly intimidated the people who were sued, but it also gave a public relations black eye to the recording industry, which looked like a cyber-age bully, trying to shake millions of dollars out of middle school students. Nor was it clear that the strategy would clear the Internet seas of music pirates. The news that lawsuits were coming brought a dip in music down-loading activity, but file-sharing numbers soon sprang back up.

Digital piracy is already spreading to other areas. For piracy to exist, all that is needed is a valuable commodity regularly conveyed along a poorly protected route. In the 21st century, the poorly protected route is the Internet, and the valuable commodity is digital information: music, movies, TV shows, software, corporate secrets, bank accounts, war plans. As more types of data are routinely shuffled through electronic networks (or can be easily uploaded onto a network), and as the technology for getting to the data becomes more widely available, the opportunity for piracy increases.

Hollywood movies are a prime example. At present, a digital file containing a high-quality, feature-length film is too big and cumbersome for the ordinary home PC user to download. But as technology becomes cheaper and more convenient, consumers will probably start swapping free movies as easily as they now swap free songs.

Like the music industry, future victims of digital piracy are likely to crack down with detective work and legal action, but that will probably only fuel technological efforts to evade detection and legal vulnerability. In 2002, the music industry succeeded in shutting down the file-sharing system Napster, which used a central index server that made it vulnerable to a lawsuit. But another generation of file-sharing programs, such as LimeWire and BearShare, sprang up to take its place, and these did not use central servers. Some, such as Blubster, use encryption software, circuitous routes through proxy servers, and other technological tricks to make it harder for the music industry to find and identify pirates. Some pirates are resorting to darknets, private file-sharing networks that are difficult for outsiders to crack.

With digital pirates always improving their armaments, perhaps the best way to battle them is to join them, by helping anyone who wants digital commodities to get them in the cheap and easy online format that makes piracy attractive. Apple's iTunes Music Store is doing strong business by offering legally downloadable songs at low price. Low price is still more expensive than free, but many consumers will pay a small premium for legality, especially if the sellers throw in greater convenience and service.

Then there is the prospect of an entirely new business model: the recording industry could continuously offer all its songs to all comers, so that anyone with an Internet connection can hear any song, anytime, in streaming audio. The price would have to be right, and a system for collecting fees and distributing the proceeds would have to be developed, but if such a system evolved, music piracy might become as obsolete as Caribbean pirates stealing pieces of eight. To battle their own pirates, movie studios and other purveyors of digital goods will have to come up with their own solutions. In the meantime, the pirates of the Internet will probably continue to sail the digital seas.

Respectable Video Games

20 Time-wasters, cyber-crack, desensitizers to violence: these are some of the kinder things that have been said about video games. Yet, the status of video games, including the violent first-person shooter games that are most often denounced, is starting to change. At last, unlike Rodney Dangerfield, they are getting some respect.

The turning point was a University of Rochester study, published in *Nature* in May 2003, that showed that playing first-person action video games improves visual attention skills. In the study, college students who played such games were better than nonplayers at localizing objects in a cluttered environment, spreading visual attention over a wide area, perceiving and tracking numerous objects at once, and switching attention rapidly. Nonplayers who received ten days of training in a first-person shooter game also improved their visual attention skills, while those who trained in a nonviolent puzzle game did not.

Once blamed for everything from Johnny's poor grades to the Columbine massacre, shoot-'em-up video games suddenly appeared *good for you*. Media reports speculated that video games might be useful for improving everything from elderly people's peripheral vision to the attentiveness of airport security personnel. In September 2003, no less than *Reader's Digest* suggested that video games could help improve the driving skills of its Middle American readers.

Meanwhile, public advocacy campaigns to ban or restrict violent video games have come, so to speak, under fire. In June 2003 a federal appeals court overturned a St. Louis law that forbade minors from purchasing or renting violent games. Experts who claim to be able to prove a link between violent video games and real-life violent behavior are increasingly countered by other experts who find no strong evidence of such a link.

Even as action video games have gained new respectability, the video game market has been stretching to include a panoply of nonviolent games for audiences other than aggressive boys. As it has done so, it has built a broad-based constituency and growing sales. Girls are now being raised on games like Barbie Pet Rescue and Magic Wardrobe; primary schools use The Logical Journey of the Zoombinis to teach logic; grandmothers play casino games; sports fans enjoy video football and basketball; and adults live vicariously through the Sims. The arena for game-playing is ever-spreading, from GameCube and PlayStation 2 consoles to CD-ROMs to multiplayer online games in which players lose themselves in fantasy identities. The Entertainment Software Association recently estimated that the U.S. market for game software was $6.9 billion in 2002 and would climb to $8 billion in 2003. The average American household today is more likely to have a video game player than a computer, and almost as likely to have one as it is to have a VCR.

Video games are even becoming patriotic. The military is increasingly partnering with the game industry to produce video games to train soldiers and attract recruits. One such game, Full Spectrum Command, released for military use in February 2003, trains squad leaders in commanding soldiers in complex urban warfare scenarios. Another game, America's Army, released in 2002, is designed to get teens interested in enlisting by taking them through a virtual basic-training regimen.

As the video game industry rises in status, at least one company is doing what all social climbers do: it is moving to a more respectable address. In 2003, Electronic Arts, a video game giant worth $2.5 billion in annual sales, began building a spanking new studio in Los Angeles. Though the company (maker of games such as The Sims, Madden NFL Football, Harry Potter, and Medal of Honor) is still based in Silicon Valley in northern California, the L.A. facility was expected to put it on more of a par with nearby Hollywood movie studios. That might improve its ability to attract top animators, writers, set designers, and other movie-making talent and to make collaboration deals with the film industry. Once upon a time, the movie industry itself was vaguely disreputable, but it has long since become part of the establishment. Expect video games to do the same. As games become more ubiquitous and sophisticated, and as their good publicity increases, the day may soon come when polite dinner party conversation will be as likely to revolve around the latest video game as the latest movie.

Safe Thrill-Seeking

21 For decades, Americans have found thrills by testing their physical limits. While some people do this with crime, drugs, liquor, or sex, an increasing number try to satisfy their need to take risks in ways that they can control and are legal.

As passengers, they sit on scary rides that are faster, higher, and noisier than ever. As participants, they play sports whose extremes of heat, cold, heights, or speed could kill them. Among popular thrill-seeking sports activities are auto racing, bungee jumping, paragliding, skiing, surfing, and white-water rafting. In all these sports, most people take precautions that allow them to experience thrills but remain relatively safe.

According to some researchers, the need to seek thrills may be linked to one's physiological makeup. University of Delaware professor in clinical psychology Dr. Marvin Zuckerman says that thrill seekers may have a consistent low level of activity in the frontal lobes and may lack certain key neurotransmitters. To achieve mental balance, he says, thrill seekers must engage in extreme physical behavior. Through their actions, they stimulate a desired "dopamine response," which others achieve without risk-taking actions.

There may also be a difference among genders for risk taking. In an independent 2001 questionnaire study aimed at determining differences in risk taking among men and women, testers said, "As far as we could conclude, the stereotype towards men and risk taking is true." While the two sexes were roughly equivalent in their enjoyment of roller coaster riding, quitting jobs without having another job, riding on motorcycles, and shoplifting, men take more risks and participate in more dangerous activities than do women. These activities include driving while intoxicated, having unprotected sex, and driving more than 25 miles per hour above the speed limit. In all, men were found to be greater risk-takers than women.

But there are a couple of thrill-seeking sports that women like more than do men. They are white-water rafting and rock climbing. These preferences may jibe with the findings in a recent government report on why the sexes take risks. According to this 1997 report from the President's Council on Physical Fitness and Sports, females are differently motivated from men. Rather than being drawn by competition, women are moved to participate in risk-taking sports for self-improvement and to achieve team goals.

Athletes who engage in risk-taking sports may be drawn by the promise of danger, but must, out of necessity, protect themselves from its excesses. To do this, they take many precautions. For example, bungee jumpers, whose jumps range from under 200 to over 3,000 feet, curtail injuries and fatalities by properly connecting themselves to the cord and making sure the cord is properly connected to the jump platform. Statistically, the dangers of bungee jumping equal the danger level of driving a distance of 100 miles; there is about a 2 in 1 million chance of death.

The 11 million skiers and 4 million snowboarders in the United States make about 50 to 55 million ski visits every year. According to First Tracks!! Online Ski Magazine, skiers encounter about 2.5 medically significant injuries per 1,000 skier visits. Skiing- and snowboarding-related fatalities total about 35 per year. To promote continued attention to safety, the National Ski Association of America, the National Ski Patrol, and the Professional Ski Instructors have enacted a program called National Safety Initiative 2000. Among safety procedures that have lessened injury are helmets with proper venting and reduced hearing diminution; increased use of bilingual signage; and areas for tree and glade skiing.

Similarly, in 2003, the American Canoe Association presented a series of recommendations about how to prevent death and injury in paddle sports, the most dangerous of which is canoeing. It is responsible for more fatalities than any other paddle sport (75 percent), most caused by riders not using flotation devices. Other problems associated with fatalities included moving in the canoe, riding in an aluminum canoe, and use of alcoholic beverages.

There are many types of virtual thrill-seeking experiences for those who like their excitement supersonic. Of particular interest is space sports. They are recreational activities that occur in zero-G atmosphere, such as zero-G gymnastics, zero-G freefall, and zero-G travel. Web sites such as *www.spacetourist.com* allow viewers to devise their own spaceship and dream trips.

Finally, for those who seek a more immediate thrill, there is the tried-and-true roller coaster and other adventure-oriented rides. These types of controlled activities make up what Temple University psychologist Frank Farley calls technological wonders that represent "the new science of thrills." According to Farley, they offer "physiological thrills and sensations that you can't get anywhere else" and that sate what he calls the thrill-seeking "Type T" personality. In all, Farley says, the roller coasters and dangerous rides fit "the American pastiche. It's a Type T nation." He continues, saying, "We're creating human-made frontiers."

Web Lit

22 For some time, a popular topic at cocktail parties has been whether the computer would ever replace the book. No, goes one line of thought, people will always want to be able to crack spines and flip pages; yes, goes another line of thought, people will increasingly do everything on the computer. While this debate has gone on, it has quietly been made more complicated by the proliferation of a new kind of literature: writing that is created, distributed, and read on computers, without necessarily ever being committed to print. If you want to read this literature, you won't find it on the printed page—and in that sense, it has already replaced the book. Welcome to the world of Web Lit.

Web Lit is not one genre but many: the online journal, the e-zine or Webzine (an online magazine or newsletter), the e-text or e-book (an electronic book), the blog. It includes the personal stories and articles posted on innumerable subject-specific Web sites, such as those that specialize in, say, diabetes, and feature a place for readers to give their accounts of coping with the illness. It includes the online-only material offered by the Web sites of periodicals like *Newsweek*: the full-length interviews and columns that are available only on the Web. Some Web Lit venues are direct replacements of print venues. Some print journals, for example, have responded to rising costs and shrinking subscription lists by giving up print publication altogether and moving online. Other venues would probably not exist were it not for the World Wide Web. They include a few household names—such as *The Drudge Report, Salon*, and (in the humor market) *The Onion*—along with millions of lesser-known or wholly unknown sites.

Web Lit includes online fiction magazines, some of which have won awards once reserved for print journals. *McSweeney's*, for example, is associated with the respected writer Dave Eggers and has earned recognition in the O. Henry Awards and Pushcart Prize competitions. Some online magazines specialize in literary fiction, others in genre fiction, such as science fiction, fantasy, and horror. The benefit for writers is an increase in the number of markets to which they can submit; the downside for readers is the increase in the number of writers who probably should never have been published. Nevertheless, some online journals have built up a readership based on the good taste of the editors and the quality of the writers. Popular online journals include *The Blue Moon Review, Intertext, Monkeyplanet,* and *Zuzu's Petals Quarterly*. Most online fiction journals have had trouble turning a profit, though some have tried innovative approaches to getting paid. *Mind's Eye Fiction* came up with the idea of letting readers read the beginning of a story for free, then, if they liked it, having them pay to read the ending.

E-books are another growing form of electronic literature. Some e-books begin life as a print book. Project Gutenberg has made a specialty of converting books that are in the public domain into electronic form. Since many of these volumes, such as the novels of Mrs. Humphry Ward (circa 1900), are out of print, they would virtually go out of existence were it not for this conversion to e-text. Many other e-books begin life in electronic form and remain there, unless a reader wants to buy a Print-on-Demand (POD) copy of the book. The independent publisher iUniverse has made a business out of helping writers self-publish in this new digital age.

One form of Web Lit that has recently received a great deal of attention is the blog. Short for Web log, a blog is an online personal journal. In early 1999, there were 23 known Web logs; as of mid-2003, there were nearly 3 million and counting. A typical blog combines personal observations, commentary on current events, and links, but blogs can take unusual turns. One blog by writer Michael Dagley at *http://buddydon.com* morphed into an online, chapter-a-day novel. New software made it possible for anyone to build their own blogs without knowing programming code, while some Web sites specialized in letting people post their own blogs. One such site, Blogger.com, trumpeted the democratic nature of blogs with its slogan "Push-Button Publishing for the People."

Democracy is characteristic of Web Lit in general, making it part of the broader trend of decentralized art. In principle, anyone can post their fiction or commentary to the Web, though in practice it takes a combination of talent, grit, marketing savvy, and luck to build traffic to one's opus. Web Lit has also brought changes to the style and format of literature. These changes include the creation of new forms, notably hypertext fiction, which is characterized by multiple paths through the same text, multiple endings and beginnings, interactive features, maps that the reader can navigate, and audiovisual attachments. There are also more subtle changes, such as a taste for short sentences and paragraphs and bite-sized sections with subheadings; these changes have already been influencing the world of print lit. One online journal, *Story Bytes*, specializes in very short stories—as short as two words long.

As Web Lit grows and evolves, it will likely continue to spawn new forms and exert a growing influence on literature in general.

4

Health and Medicine

AIDS Across the Continents

23 In the coming decades, AIDS (acquired immune deficiency syndrome) is expected to expand its reach over six continents. Based on reports to the Centers for Disease Control (CDC), the cumulative number of AIDS cases in the United States was 816,149 through December 2001.

Over the next decades, HIV/AIDS will present itself in various ways geographically and demographically. Because the disease is contracted more often through heterosexual encounters, the number of women with the virus will grow. As of 2003, approximately 50 percent, or 19.2 million, of the 38.6 million adults living with HIV/AIDS across the world are women.

The next decades will see rising numbers of AIDS cases and increasing attempts to prevent and treat the condition. Sub-Saharan Africa, the site of the highest incidence of HIV/AIDS, is the region projected to have the greatest continuing growth. In 2001, it had 3.5 million new infections, bringing its overall total to 28.5 million afflicted. According to the UNAIDS (the Joint United Nations Programme on HIV/AIDS) report, there had been hopes in Africa that AIDS may have reached its "natural limit," but these hopes are unfounded. The report notes that if "a natural HIV prevalence limit does exist in these countries, it is considerably higher than previously thought." For example, in Botswana, the HIV prevalence rate among pregnant women in urban areas had not stabilized. It rose in just a few years from 38.5 percent in 1997 to 44.9 percent.

In answer to this growing incidence of HIV/AIDS, some countries, including South Africa, Uganda, and Senegal, have instituted health and public policy programs that have decreased the prevalence of HIV in pregnant women and others. Among their areas of attack are promoting condom use and strengthening rules for blood collection. In general, programs using these and other safeguards have been successful. In Cambodia and the Philippines, HIV prevalence rates have been reduced or have stayed at low levels.

Yet, in some cases, moves to reduce cases of infection have met cultural roadblocks. Across all affected continents, there is resistance to using condoms. Reasons include the condom's awkwardness, discomfort, and perceived unmanliness. In Uganda, where over the past several years the spread of AIDS has been cut by a nationwide public policy program of abstinence or delayed first sexual encounters, some young women are complaining on economic grounds. They indicate that forsaking sex or marriage with financially stable men deprives them of financial support for their families.

In recent years, pockets of other geographic regions have seen sharp growth in incidence of AIDS. For example, reports UNAIDS, aside from sub-Saharan Africa, the area with the greatest number of people living with HIV/AIDS is Asia and the Pacific. As of the end of 2001, there were an estimated 6.6 million in the region with HIV. In China alone, there were an estimated 850,000 people with HIV at the end of 2001, nearly double the 1997 number of 430,000. Increasing the spread of the disease in China are unsafe practices such as reusing drug-injection needles and lack of sanitation in blood donation.

Currently in India, the overall percentage of those afflicted by HIV is low, less than 1 percent of the population at the end of 2001. Yet, it still puts HIV numbers at 3.97 million. In Indonesia and Vietnam, HIV/AIDS rates are increasing, and it is the leading cause of death in Thailand.

The disease is also spreading rapidly throughout Eastern Europe and central Asia. UNAIDS refers to HIV/AIDS in the region as "the fastest-growing epidemic in the world." By the end of 2001, HIV/AIDS had been contracted by 1 million people there. As in many other countries, only a small fraction of HIV/AIDS patients are receiving antiretroviral medication. In some countries such as Ukraine and Tajikistan, spread of the virus is made worse by lack of information about the disease, particularly for young adults under twenty-one years of age.

In Latin America, an estimated 1.5 million people have the HIV virus. Among the hardest-hit countries are those in the Caribbean basin, notably Haiti and the Bahamas. Overall, the region's high HIV prevalence rates are second only to those in sub-Saharan Africa. But medical and public policy programs in the region are reducing hospitalization rates by providing drug therapies. Through several multinational coalitions throughout the region, countries are developing stronger HIV/AIDS programs and negotiating better prices for antiretroviral drugs.

An estimated half million people are living with HIV/AIDS in North Africa and the Middle East. As yet, treatment facilities reach only a small fraction of patients. Among countries with epidemics is the Sudan. High incidences of unsanitary injected drug use and unsafe practices in prisons account for some of the increase in HIV/AIDS cases.

In the United States, Europe, and other Western industrialized nations, HIV/AIDS incidence continues to grow and in many cases, can be linked to a return to unsafe sexual practices. Some experts believe that the wide availability of highly active antiretroviral therapy (HAAR) may be contributing to a less serious commitment to AIDS prevention.

Throughout these regions, another way AIDS treatment is compromised is by false medicine. For example, in recent years there have been rumors of cures or unorthodox treatments that turn out to be dangerous, such as nonworking vaccines in Nigeria that promoted the spread of HIV/AIDS.

For the future, the UNAIDS report stresses the importance of instituting "large-scale protection programs" for all citizens, from those with high-risk behavior to knowledgeable members of high-income nations to the population as a whole. These, along with facilities and medications for treating HIV/AIDS, are crucial to reducing the wider growth of the epidemic. It is one of the major economic and humanitarian issues of the 21st century.

Alternative Medicine

24 For medical and practical reasons, complementary and alternative medical treatments will rise throughout the 21st century. As defined by the National Center for Complementary and Alternative Medicine, a U.S. government agency, complementary and alternative medicine "is that group of diverse medical and health care systems, practices, and products that are not presently considered to be part of conventional medicine." Complementary medicine includes practices used in addition to traditional medicine. Alternative medicine includes practices used instead of traditional treatment, such as folk medicine, herbal medicine, diet fads, homeopathy, faith healing, New Age healing, chiropractic, acupuncture, and naturopathy.

According to a report by the Institute for Alternative Futures, complementary and alternative approaches to health and medicine are among the fastest-growing branches of health care. For example, over 150 million consumers used herbs, and other alternative health substances, with sales totaling $17 billion in 2000. The institute projects that by 2020, at least two-thirds of Americans will use some form of alternative approach to health care. To confirm growing U.S. interest in alternative medicine, an executive order in 2000 formed the White House Commission on Complementary and Alternative Medicine Policy. Further, a group of physicians and lay experts testified to the U.S. Congress that already proven mind-body therapies could substantially reduce the number of doctor visits and save over $50 billion annually. They might also reduce ever-increasing expenditures on prescription drugs.

Alternative therapies also appeal to people because they provide a source of control over one's health. According to a survey in the late 1990s published in the *Journal of the American Medical Association*, most of the over 80 million Americans who used some form of alternative medical treatment used the therapies to prevent rather than treat illness.

Increased use of the Internet will continue to fuel knowledge and use of alternative medical practices. Despite the White House Commission on Complementary and Alternative Medicine's caution that voluntary standards are needed to maintain the quality of Internet information on alternative medicine, tens of millions of Americans seek health and medical information online, often at alternative medicine sites.

Among the most popular of alternative substances is the herbal supplement, and its place in the Food and Drug Administration hierarchy suggests the flux in which the substances exist. Like other alternative products, herbal supplements are not regulated as drugs by the Food and Drug Association, but instead as foods. As such, if they are shown to be unsafe, the FDA can take them off the market, as it did with the herb found in some weight-loss and bodybuilding supplements. Further, in 2003, the FDA published new proposed guidelines for supplements that require manufacturers to label their products accurately and to package them without additives.

Over the next few years, the U.S. government will study some of the most popular supplements to increase scientific knowledge about them, such as analyzing their active ingredients and how they work in the body. They hope to determine whether the ingredients can be standardized for public use.

Among alternative approaches that have gained the interest of the medical community is the ancient practice of Tibetan medicine. Dating from the 4th century B.C., Tibetan medicine uses plants, minerals, and animal organs to treat acute and chronic conditions. The practice, built upon the Four Classics of Tibetan medicine, is being used in parts of China and is being studied by modern scholars and medical professionals. The Institute for Alternative Futures projects that by 2010, there will be 24,000 physicians and other health care professionals trained in Asian medicine.

In addition, other types of alternative medicine are expected to become more prominent. For example, estimates are that there will be 103,000 chiropractors in practice by 2010. Generally, says the institute's report, this will dovetail with a move toward health care that includes a large wellness component. It will have varieties of types of self-management for disease prevention. Says Pat De Leon of the American Psychological Association, "Health science has reached a point where it is no longer accurate to talk about psychology versus biology; the mind versus the body; or nature versus nurture. These processes are inextricably linked."

Do-It-Yourself Health Care

25 According to a 2001 study, the average cost of health care rose 11 percent over the course of the year. That makes the cost increase five times that of the rate of inflation. Health companies credit much of the rise to the development of new pharmaceuticals and technologies, which become popular and costly to the consumer. Fewer health care providers and lower payments to hospitals also increase costs to the consumer.

Whatever the reasons, analysts project that health insurance costs will continue to rise at double-digit rates well into the 21st century. In response, consumers and providers are seeking new ways to afford good health. Traditional health care constructs, such as indemnity or fee-for-service (or point of service) plans, HMOs (health maintenance organization), and PPOs (preferred provider organization), may be headed for a makeover to cut costs. As they change, others will attempt more unconventional solutions to health care. Some of the proposed solutions are conservative variations on belt tightening, while some reimagine the doctor-insurance-patient structure. Nearly all involve making health care more consumer oriented, or in plain terms, turning health care into a do-it-yourself endeavor.

Over the next years, alternative forms of health insurance will probably continue to involve self-selected partial service. In this way, health insurance of the future, unless nationalized health insurance is initiated, will involve limiting coverage to match one's needs or funds. This will bring health insurance more in line with home and automobile insurance. One employer-based health plan involves alternating between self-payment and traditional coverage. The pay-as-you-go plan is particularly appealing to healthy young people, who have relatively limited health care bills. Many plans are already adopting variations on this health care model of offering more choices but less reimbursement.

However, such self-directed health insurance comes with risks. One is the shortcuts people take to lessen health care costs. For example, rather than paying to see a doctor, some people go straight to a medical lab for testing. The process eliminates physician costs, but does not provide treatment advice, which one gets only from a medical doctor. Another problem is grossly inadequate coverage masquerading as full-fledged health care. The *Wall Street Journal* cited an employer-sponsored health insurance that charged only $10 to $20 per pay period but had a maximum payout of only $1,000. That amount is far less than the cost of any hospital stay or series of specialized medical tests.

One possible counter to the high cost and time spent on doctor visits is visiting a doctor virtually. These visits, which range up to $25 each, are online meetings with a doctor that let the doctor dispense medical advice without seeing the patient in person. Another way people reduce health costs is by using at-home testing. Instead of paying for preliminary testing, there are already a number of tests for conditions such as pregnancy, ovulation, cholesterol, hepatitis, and HIV. To the pharmaceutical companies that produce the tests, they're a bonanza, toting up over $1 billion in annual sales.

Another alternative to traditional health insurance is the discount health medical card. The sponsoring organization offering the card arranges for its members to receive discounts from 25 percent to 80 percent on medical, dental, vision, chiropractic, and pharmaceutical services with providers linked to the plan. Online nurse service is also available on some plans.

Given the government's high participation in the health care industry, many politicians have various plans for reform. Some politicians and tax reformers suggest that the health care system could be simplified through the introduction of medical savings accounts. Like IRAs, which encourage and provide tax benefits for saving for retirement, medical savings accounts will encourage people to save for medical needs. Instead of paying into a health care plan, people can contribute to a medical savings plan that they use only when needed. Unused monies carry over on a per-year basis.

For patients who have ample health care funds, tiered health care will ensure high-quality treatment. According to Robert J. Blendon and Catherine DesRoches in *Issues in Science and Technology Online*, "[T]he new approach to cost containment, which asks individuals to pay more for their own health care, is going to lead to tiering, in which those with higher incomes will be able to afford a wider range of health care services than much of the middle class and those with lower incomes." For example, according to Dr. Clark Howard at *www.clarkhoward.com*, hospitals are already courting well-heeled patients by offering luxury accommodations. Luxury rooms generate prestige for patients and funds for hospitals like Cedars Sinai, Los Angeles.

As of 2003, the U.S. government spends $1.7 trillion on health care. This translates into $1 out of every $6 or $7 of the U.S. budget going toward some type of government coverage for about half of all Americans. The other half of Americans are covered by employers, private insurance, or not at all.

In coming years, one of these sources of coverage will become dominant. If it is employer- or private-based coverage, the patient will become more responsible for the quality of his or her own health care. In some ways it will allow for more personal choice, and health care forecasters believe it will be just what take-charge baby boomers want. But for those who can't or do not have the resources to care for themselves, the future may mean no health care.

Despite the importance of the issue, experts fear a future of health care inaction. According to Robert J. Blendon and Catherine DesRoches of the Harvard School of Public Health, "Based on the experiences of the past decade, the biggest challenge facing the U.S. health care system . . . is the continued failure of decision makers to reach a consensus on how to address the major health care problems facing the country."

The Elusive Fountain of Youth

26 The 20th century was marked by exploration and expansion; the 21st century will be marked by contraction and preservation. For average Americans, that translates into figuring out how to extend their lives. For the baby boomers, and generations to follow, this means various approaches to living longer. Some of these approaches reflect contemporary scientific study and testing; some arise from long-accepted topical remedies. All are aimed at increasing the current American life span of seventy-seven years by as much as possible.

Yet, according to findings in a report by ScientificAmerican.com called "The Truth about Human Aging," the increase in life span in coming decades is likely to be limited to about fifteen years. This is because in the past century we have already discovered the scientific improvements such as childhood immunization and safer childbirth procedures that greatly increased human life span in developed countries from the 1900 norm of forty-seven. Still, although the chances for significant increase in life span are limited, Americans continue to engage in serious scientific research and various lifestyle practices to gain more time on Earth.

Research on life extension is somewhat hampered because scientists have not yet been able to find reliable methods for determining the processes that cause aging. Humans also cannot alter their own molecular constitution so that they can grow younger. The human train drives in one direction and it can't be stopped.

Despite this uncertainty, the antiaging industry is thriving. Its businesses comprise a multibillion-dollar force with many consumer tentacles. One wide-ranging set of goods now championed is products containing antioxidants. These components, naturally found in some fruits and vegetables, have been found to reduce the risk of diseases such as cataracts and macular degeneration. Consequently, food producers selling produce that is rich in antioxidants are experiencing an increase in sales. Sales are also high for antioxidant nutritional and vitamin supplements, even though there is no evidence that antioxidant supplements have a direct effect on curtailing aging.

The pharmaceutical industry will also continue to try to increase life spans through the development of drugs that moderate or control the course of chronic diseases. But while these drugs treat symptoms of diseases or actually cure them, they do not treat the body process of aging. Researchers will have to do more study of the physical manifestations of aging before drugs to combat it will be realized.

Aside from these accepted views and practices on aging, many more visionary advances have been developed. Most of them concern ways the human life span can be extended. But in large part, they have not proven applicable on a large scale. For example, while the idea of replacing older body parts with younger ones might increase a person's life, processes for cloning parts in large numbers are as yet unavailable. But variations are coming into use, such as replacing human tissue and some human organs through stem cell technology.

That leaves the most practical way to lengthen the life span: changing one's habits. In addition to personal lifestyle modifications, government and business will continue to try to increase the life span through educational programs. National health drives for issues including childhood immunization, decreased alcohol and illegal drug use, reducing tobacco use, and ending drunk driving have lengthened life spans as well as reduced the ailments associated with alcohol, tobacco, or drug use. Some national public health officials have also called for a national antiobesity initiative, as the percentage of overweight Americans has increased significantly over the past three decades.

So life goes on, but only for a while. Although the age of the oldest person in the world continues to increase, the chance for all humans to live into their 120s is unlikely. As ScientificAmerican.com reminds us, "genetic, environmental and lifestyle diversity"—that is, other things—will bring us down first. Scientists, social commentators, clergy members, and laypeople alike agree that there is no chance for immortality on Earth.

•

Everybody's Bionic

27 Cosmetic surgery is so 20th century. Bionic surgery is the wave of the future. Moving far beyond pacemakers, surgeons in the next few decades will be able to replace weakened or nonfunctioning body parts, such as hearts, eyes, lungs, kidneys, muscles, and even the brain. The Six Million Dollar Man and the Bionic Woman never had it so good.

Already, some health-related implants are used routinely. One is arthroplasty, or hip replacement surgery. Each year, according to ABC News, more than 400,000 people with hips disintegrated by arthritis or osteoporosis undergo hip replacement. By 2030, it is estimated that there will be 272,000 hip replacements done in the United States alone, due to the aging population

At the other end of the spectrum are replacement surgeries that would be more commonplace now if supply could match demand. These surgeries call for human organs of which there is limited availability. For example, according to findings in *BusinessWeek* Online, there is already a shortage of 100,000 hearts available for donation each year. As with other organ replacement, the demand for hearts is likely to grow more intense as the baby boomer generation gets old.

For the future, the search is on for workable human-made replacement parts, and in particular, for a heart. Thus far, many mechanical hearts have been designed and have become much more efficient than the pioneering Jarvik mechanical heart of the 1970s. Many of the latest versions have borrowed from technology used by NASA's space shuttle and have developed small turbines for pumping blood. While the turbine hearts are now used as bridge devices in operating rooms for patients awaiting transplant, scientists believe that the turbine heart will eventually be used for full heart replacement.

Other future improvements to implants may involve refinements in size and delivery. One is simplifying the implant's power supply. In the early 1990s, researchers developed what *BusinessWeek* Online terms a "so-called inductive system" that sends electrical power through the skin. It eliminates the need for an outside power source. This through-the-skin process also will be used for other types of implants, such as vision-enabling brain implants.

Within a few decades, some chronic medical conditions will be treated with computer chip implants. Implanted in the brain and spinal cord, the chips being developed are meant to ameliorate many nerve and muscle disorders, such as amyotrophic lateral sclerosis (ALS). At the University of New Mexico's Artificial Muscle Research Institute, scientists are developing polymer-metal composites for use as substitute muscles for patients with muscle-deteriorating diseases such as muscular dystrophy. Other products are also under development to repair bladder function in the incontinent, as are artificial parts including kidneys and blood vessels.

Restoring the senses is the goal of some implants. At Johns Hopkins University Medical Institutions and elsewhere, researchers are developing methods to restore vision and hearing to people. This technology involves restoring sight by implanting in people's eyes light-sensitive chips that yield a multiple-pixel image. Other vision systems, such as that developed at Dobelle Institute, Inc., in Commack, New York, send images by video camera to an electronic-circuit card inside a person's brain. As silicon chip technology increases chip power, artificial vision may eventually compare to that of the human eye, and one researcher suggests that artificial eyes may be workable by the 2020s.

Other physical conditions are being treated with artificial body parts, such as artificial hearing implants to restore hearing and electronic muscle stimulation for muscles in paralyzed arms and legs. Before the first quarter of the 21st century ends, researchers are also predicting the use of artificial kidneys and lungs. Also by that time, predict the British Telephone Labs, artificial brain cells should also be available. An artificial brain, however, is not projected to be developed until 2035.

In addition to developing new types of artificial parts and implants, researchers are creating "intelligent implants." According to Garth Ehrlich, executive director of the center for Genomic Sciences at the Allegheny-Singer Research Institute in Pittsburgh, interviewed for ABC News, researchers aim for the smart implants to reduce the possibility of dangerous infections. For example, an artificial hip embedded with MEMs, or microelectronic mechanical systems, is under development. The MEMs can detect the presence of destructive bacteria and trigger the release of antibodies stored within the implant. According to Ehrlich, implants such as these may be available within several years.

Amidst the development of artificial parts is much biomedical engineering research for devices that interact with the human body to ward off infection. Researchers at the University of Arizona Biomedical Engineering Program are developing medical devices that grow new replacement organs once implanted in the body. In one instance, they are using polymers to develop new blood vessels used during coronary artery bypass graft surgery that will work with the body's own defense system, which usually fights the implant as a foreign entity.

Because of stringent U.S. Food and Drug Administration policy, many of these implant systems and much ongoing research are done in Europe. In *BusinessWeek* Online, Dr. Bartley P. Griffith, director of Pittsburgh's McGowan Center for Artificial Organ Development, says, "The U.S. standard is that we're not going to use devices that might do harm, no matter how gravely ill the patient is." But some experts suggest that a reappraisal of European methods may lead to U.S. easing of current restrictions on implant devices.

In an age of bionic reconstruction, the phrase "100 percent natural" will lose its cachet. Instead, people will seek to be "100 percent functional," many of them with the help of artificial spare parts.

Female Physicians on the Rise

28 Watch out, the next woman you meet may be your doctor. For an increasing number of scientifically minded women, the medical profession is a stable, rewarding, flexible career choice. Since the late 20th century, the number of female doctors in the United States has risen substantially. From 1975 to 1995, the percentage of female physicians in the United States more than doubled. By 2010, analysts expect the number of female physicians to constitute 33 percent of the profession. Already in 2003, 45 percent of medical students are female.

The racial and ethnic breakdown of female doctors roughly reflects the makeup of the country. Of the 205,903 female physicians cataloged by the American Medical Association in 2001, 44 percent listed themselves as white. Four percent were black; 3.4 percent were Hispanic; and 11 percent were Asian. American Native/Alaskan Native accounted for .08 percent, and 3 percent noted themselves as "other." Thirty-four percent listed no race or ethnicity.

Not surprisingly, differences between male and female physicians have emerged. Studies have shown that female doctors are more likely to spend more time talking with patients than do their male counterparts. In part, the practice reflects differences in the way the sexes perceive the medical profession. In a poll of first-year medical students conducted by the American Psychiatric Press, women said that the most valuable quality a doctor could have was compassion, while male students said it was competence.

Female doctors are also more interested in reforming the health care system. For example, according to an American Medical Women's Association survey, 90 percent of its members approved of universal health coverage. This puts them at odds with the mainly male members of the American Medical Association. Female physicians have said they support change in the health care system even if it means a reduction in their earnings.

In addition, female physicians generally structure their careers in ways that more clearly reflect a need for balance between family and work. Over half of female physicians are employees, reports the American Medical Association. As such, they have more regular hours than self-employed physicians, most of whom are male. Females also tend to choose specialties that involve high contact with people and lower incidence of complicated surgeries. According to the *Journal of the American Medical Women's Association*, nearly two-thirds of those choosing to specialize do so in obstetrics/gynecology and pediatrics. Other specialties, many of which pay more but allow for limited interpersonal activity, attract a small number (20 percent) of females.

Owing to women's choices of specialization and their intent to balance family and profession, female physicians generally earn less money than their male counterparts. In the latest year for which it had figures, the Women's Physicians Congress reported that in 1997, the average salary for a female physician was $120,000. For a male physician, it was $175,000, or 31.4 percent higher.

For the future, the increased number of female doctors may result in many changes both subtle and obvious in the medical profession. As doctors seek ways to balance family and medicine, the number of part-time practitioners may increase. As the number of female physicians increases, communication between doctors and patients will improve, with one likely result a greater patient role in medical decision-making. Women doctors may also encourage a greater focus on women's health issues, both in their attention to women's health problems and by initiating more studies on women's diseases. More female doctors working as employees may invite the ownership of medical practices by big medical/business consortiums, which would further lessen doctors' control of their practice. Obstetrics/gynecology and pediatrics may become female-dominated specialties, while other specialties may become more male-dominated. Females may comprise a larger number of primary-care physicians, but because women are less likely to establish practice in rural areas (where school systems and housing are less favorable), the rural regions of the United States may be inadequately covered.

According to the Association of American Medical Colleges, the proportion of women medical residents increased from 28 percent of residents in 1988 to 38 percent in 1999. In 2003, 45 percent of all medical students are female. One outcome is certain: the number of women in the medical profession keeps increasing.

Gene-Based Drugs

29 Since time immemorial, pharmaceuticals have been discovered in roughly the same way: try out a little of this fungus, weed, or other strange substance and see what it does in the body. The prehistoric shaman experimenting on himself and the modern chemist experimenting on animals have both relied on this hit-and-miss method of drug discovery. Today, the first real challenger to this method has arrived: pharmacogenomics, or gene-based drugs.

Pharmacogenomics is the development of pharmaceuticals based on knowledge of the human genome, the entire set of human genes. In pharmacogenomics, drug discovery begins not with a fungus or weed, but with a human gene, preferably one that is known to be somehow associated with a disease. Once scientists pinpoint how the gene is linked to the disease, they can use that knowledge to develop a tailor-made remedy. For example, if the gene codes the manufacture of an important protein, but an individual is sick because he or she has a defective copy of that gene, scientists can use the gene in the lab to manufacture the protein that the patient is missing. That is a pharmacogenomic remedy: one based not on hit-and-miss searches for wonder drugs, but on rational development of treatments for diseases based on knowledge of the genome.

Another aspect of pharmacogenomics is developing drugs that are customized for patients who have a particular genotype, or set of gene variations. This is based on the premise that patients with one genotype may respond differently to therapies than patients with a different one. Genentech's drug Herceptin, for example, one of the first pharmacogenomic products, is designed to treat breast cancer in women who express the HER2 gene.

In ten years or so, scientists believe it will be possible for people to order fairly complete reports on their genetic makeup, giving them information on what medicines or foods can help them ward off the diseases. As of 2003, genetic tests were already available for about 930 diseases. When genetic knowledge becomes great enough, DNA scientist Leroy Hood told the *New York Times*, medicine will go from being one-size-fits-all to being "predictive, preventative, and personalized."

In some cases, pharmacogenomics may result in gene therapy treatments, in which patients receive a replacement gene or some other alteration in their genetic material as a remedy for disease. So far, progress in gene therapy in humans has been slow and unsatisfying, but if researchers can overcome technical obstacles, it may become an important part of pharmacogenomic treatment.

Completion of the Human Genome Project, with its mapping of the entire human genome, has been an important step forward for pharmacogenomics. Even while the project was still in process, academic and corporate research centers were lining up to analyze the data to find out what genes do in the body and how they do it. But don't expect to see your local pharmacy shelves flooded with pharmacogenomic products by tomorrow. The process of translating genomic data into drugs is slow, for several reasons. One is the misfit between the wealth of information and the speed with which scientists and pharmaceutical companies can apply it. Scott Morrison of Ernst & Young has said that as the information becomes more user-friendly, "[i]t will then turn into an engine that increases the quality and number of new drug targets and brings down drug development costs."

A bigger problem is whether the current business model for drug development is compatible with pharmacogenomic research. Right now, companies spend vast amounts on drug development, and to make a profit they count on big blockbuster drugs that reach lots of disease sufferers. But the kind of pharmacogenomic drug likely to be discovered in the short term will probably have a small market: patients who are made sick simply by having a missing or defective copy of some gene. More common diseases, like cancer, depression, or arthritis, are usually more complex in origin, involving several interacting genes, and the chances that they will be conquered soon by a pharmacogenomic wonder drug are slimmer. So drug companies may not want to bother with the kind of pharmacogenomic drugs that are doable now; and they may not want to wait for the lucrative kind that will be available later.

Eventually the day may come when patients will go to their doctor with all their genetic information on a chip and the doctor will examine the chip and prescribe appropriate gene-based remedies and preventive measures. For added convenience, consultant Roger Shamel has argued, the doctor may even have a "custom gene machine" in his office that churns out the remedies while the patient waits. We are probably still decades away from such scenarios, but other benefits of pharmacogenomics are already here, and picking up steam.

Generics Are Us

30 In the pharmaceutical industry, the big dollars and publicity campaigns go to new brand-name prescription drugs: Prozac in the 1980s; Viagra in the 1990s; and Nexium in the 2000s. Aggressively marketed to doctors and patients, these drugs quickly become omnipresent, displacing older remedies for the diseases they target. Because the new medicines are protected from competition by patents, their manufacturers can charge as high a price as the market will bear, and, since people will spend anything for their health, the market will usually bear a lot. So drug prices rise steadily, increasing the already bloated sum spent by Americans on health care.

Against this juggernaut expect to see a growing preference for generic drugs among everyone who has to pay for them: the federal government; private insurers; corporations that provide health benefits to employees; retail pharmacies (which earn a bigger profit margin on generics); and individual consumers. A generic drug is a medicine that has the same active ingredient as a given brand-name product, has been approved by the Food and Drug Administration (FDA) as being bioequivalent (achieving the same concentration in the blood), but is usually 30 to 80 percent cheaper. During a brand product's period of patent protection or market exclusivity (usually twenty years), no one is legally permitted to come out with a competing version of the same ingredient. But once that patent/exclusivity period lapses, all bets are off. Provided the FDA gives its approval, any manufacturer can make a generic version and slash the price to attract customers.

The power of generic competition has been increasing in recent years, and is likely to keep doing so. Already the rate at which brand companies lose market share to generics upon patent expiration "is greater than anything we've seen in the last fifteen years," Michael Yellen, senior portfolio manager for AIM Global Health Care Fund, San Francisco, told the trade magazine *Pharmacy Practice News*.

According to Yellin, "A branded company can lose 70 to 90 percent of revenue on a drug within the first three to six months." A case in point is the antidepression drug Prozac, which lost much of its market share when a generic version of its active ingredient became available early this century.

The public at large was once suspicious of generics, viewing them as inferior in quality as well as in price. That view is changing, in part due to a concerted effort—by insurers, pharmacy chains, and the generic drug industry itself—to spread the word that generics are just as good as the brand. Pharmacy chains are likely to promote the cost savings of generics through fliers and circulars; insurers typically offer lower copayments if patients use generics. Doctors, too, are more willing to prescribe generics: a study by ChangeWave Research reports that 76 percent of physicians are more willing to prescribe generics now than a year ago.

Companies that produce generic drugs, once rocked by price wars and poor business decisions, are now more likely to be stable corporations with healthy profit margins. They may offer not only no-name generics but generics with a recognizable trade name (so-called "branded generics") or "supergenerics," products that combine generic molecules with value-added features, such as an extended-release formulation.

Despite the attractiveness of generics to those who make them and buy them, they are extremely unattractive to one group: brand drug manufacturers. Brand manufacturers have long done everything possible to block generic competition: supporting legislation to extend patents; filing new patents on old drugs just before the old patents expire; mounting court battles and regulatory challenges; cutting deals that pay would-be generic competitors to keep their products off the market. Increasingly, these tactics are coming under fire from government officials, corporate lobbyists, and citizens' groups sick and tired of the high price of drugs.

The Federal Trade Commission (FTC) has cracked down on unlawful anticompetitive practices in the drug industry. The Schumer-McCain bill, a proposed piece of legislation to reduce the barriers to generic competition, has been working its way through Congress. In a high-profile case, Bristol-Myers Squibb recently settled a lawsuit with the Attorneys General of the fifty states, territories, and District of Columbia in which they alleged that the drug manufacturer illegally delayed generic competition to its cancer drug Taxol (generic name paclitaxel). In the settlement, Bristol-Myers Squibb agreed to pay $12.5 million to reimburse cancer patients overcharged for the drug from 1999 to 2003.

The brand drug industry will not go away; indeed, generic drugs couldn't exist if brand companies didn't create new products that will eventually lose patent protection. But brand companies will most likely have to focus more on innovating new products—aided by the discoveries of pharmacogenomic research—and less on blocking generic competition.

One irony of the increasing presence of generics is that their prices are rising; they are not as cheap as they were back when people didn't think they were any good. However, market forces will probably keep their prices from getting too high, since their whole appeal rests on being cheaper than the brand.

Less Stress in the Future

31 For decades, Americans have been conscious of how much stress they are under. Back in 1991, a Northwestern Mutual Life Insurance study concluded that 30 percent of adults experience high job stress everyday. That didn't even include standard life stresses—family, finances, lack of personal happiness. A 1993 study made the connection between stress and a host of illnesses, such as hypertension, heart attacks, diabetes, asthma, chronic pain, allergies, headache, backache, skin disorders, cancer, immune system weakness, and decreases in the number of white blood cells. For businesses, that

translates into $200 billion lost per year for stress-related ailments. But aside from chucking society, what's a person to do?

A lot. While some people require antistress or antianxiety medication, most rely on nonpharmacologic treatment. In recent years, one of the most effective techniques has involved refocusing the mind and body through yoga. It also has the benefit of being approved by the U.S. government. A report by the White House Commission on Complementary and Alternative Medicine Policy says, "CAM practices such as acupuncture, biofeedback, yoga, massage, and tai chi, as well as certain nutritional and stress reduction practices, may be useful in contributing to the achievement of the nation's health goals and objectives." The White House Commission even suggests the possibility of "teaching children in Head Start programs to breathe deeply as a relaxation technique" (particularly useful to tots before taking their government-mandated Head Start standardized tests).

All forms of stress control, in various ways, concern clearing the mind and focusing on experiencing life at the moment. For example, one of the simplest forms of stress reduction is to set aside five minutes per day to do nothing. Researchers have found that such regular focus away from oneself lowers blood pressure and slows heart rate, as well as increasing one's feeling of control over events. Laughing helps, too. Laughter can provide a day's worth of calming, increasing immunity to disease and reducing the stress hormones cortisol and epinephrine.

Other ways to lower stress include having soothing music in the background. This has been found to keep people's blood pressure and heartbeat level even when they have to accomplish a difficult task on a tight deadline. According to researchers, focusing for several seconds on the image of a loved one or a happy experience can bring extended periods of calm. Taking a short five- to ten-minute walk every day can also relieve stress, report researchers. Just breathing slowly and deliberately for five minutes can, over time, improve cardiovascular systems. Speaking more slowly also reduces stress and engenders a feeling of self-control. Being courteous does the same, and increases the overall level of calmness in one's life. Finally, researchers advise beginning and ending the day with five minutes of stretching to relax each part of the body, bottom to top. Known as progressive relaxation, this activity was found in tests at the University of Southern Missisippi to slow heart rates and lessen feelings of stress.

Various forms of stress-reducing meditation have become popular in the United States. Many involve the repetition of a prayer or mantra that fits one's religious beliefs, whether Buddhist, Christian, or other. A standard form of meditation is called mindfulness meditation. It involves bringing the mind into the finite experience of the present moment, with an extended attention to one's breathing. A structured form of secular meditation is to listen to audio recordings of music and environmental sounds; this practice is supposed to stimulate whole brain functioning and reduce chemicals associated with stress. Another approach is Holo-sync technology, which uses audio recordings to induce a deep meditative state.

Many studies on stress-reduction techniques have shown their effectiveness. According to the *AMA Medical Journal*, meditation is comparable to popular prescription drugs at controlling high blood pressure, and has none of drugs' side effects. In a University of Massachusetts study, it was found that those who meditate are able to reduce their chronic pain by more than 30 percent. Studies have also found that meditation can cut down on symptoms of PMS and may even slow aging. A study in the *Health News and Review* noted that people who had been meditating for more than five years were biologically twelve to fifteen years younger than those who don't meditate.

Finally, a dissent. Although Americans say they have been adversely affected by stress, they are generally able to operate with it. Stress management expert Dr. Donald Tubesing reports that most people handle 98 percent of their potentially stressful situations successfully.

But most researchers agree that it is those troublesome situations and the overall experience of a stressful life that have to be dealt with. It takes time, and Americans will most likely say they're too busy. According to Stanford University researcher and psychologist Frederic Luskin, "A lot of people say they're too busy to stop and deal with stress." He goes on to say, "But things you can do anywhere, and that don't have to take more than a few minutes, can stop the stress response before it goes out of control. The truth is, by learning to calm down, you can actually feel less busy."

Menopause in Flux

32 Holy hot flashes! With 36 million American women entering menopause over the next decade, health practitioners of all sorts have been formulating new treatments and attitudes to handle the end of childbearing. First, there is the new positive approach that is expected to continue for some time. Rather than being seen only as an end (the cessation of menses), menopause is being promoted as a natural phase in the midlife of a woman, a time of transformation and personal growth. In her book *The Menopausal Years: The Wise Woman Way*, herbalist and author Susun Weed called menopause "the years of transformation from potential mother to wise, whole crone." In less romantic terms, it is a call to accept the passage of time.

Greater changes have arisen and will arise to contain the physical symptoms that accompany menopause, which is a multipart process that can span decades. The average age for menopause is fifty-one. For years, a standard treatment for the discomfort and physical disruptions of menopause has been hormone replacement therapy. The most widely prescribed drug, Premarin, works by converting hormones in the body into the two estrogens that occur after menopause, estrone and estradiol. The therapy may run for months to years.

Since mid-2002, the therapy has declined in popularity for doctors and patients. At that time, hormone replacement therapy was put into question when a federally funded study, the Women's Health Initiative, was terminated. It was stopped in July 2002 when the random study cast doubts on the safety of hormone replacement therapy after it was found that women ingesting the estrogen-progestin drug Prempro rather than a placebo were more likely to have strokes, blood clots, heart disease, and breast cancer.

Still, many doctors tell women to continue the therapy for its effectiveness on the ongoing maladies of menopause, such as vaginal dryness, hot flashes, and bone loss. While the therapy has been shown to increase the chance of having blood clots, gall bladder disease, and breast cancer, its benefits are considered to outweigh the drawbacks. For many women, it also improves the appearance of the skin, making one's complexion look more youthful. Some doctors also cite laboratory and animal studies that suggest that hormone therapy may protect brain cells, which may forestall the progression of Alzheimer's disease.

Despite the popularity of hormone replacement therapy, many women will seek natural solutions. Women who do not wish to have their condition medicalized (that is, made part of the traditional medical system) prefer these remedies, which do not require medical supervision. In addition to wanting to handle the menopause as a natural occurrence rather than a medical condition, natural treatments are also likely to increase in popularity as the number of people covered by medical insurance declines and people need to take a more active role in their health care.

Among popular natural remedies are herbs that contain phytoestrogens. Common vitamins and food products have also been found to aid in reducing menopausal symptoms. For example, vitamin E has been found to reduce hot flashes, and calcium and magnesium have been found to promote bone density. Soy and tofu products are also reputed to have some benefit as they contain naturally occurring phytoestrogens that are similar in structure to human estrogens. Consumer food products have jumped on the bandwagon by creating products with menopause-helpful ingredients targeted directly to women.

Until more scientific studies are completed, the variety of claims that hormone replacement therapy can prevent cardiovascular disease and Alzheimer's disease will remain unsettled. Similarly, the debate about using custom-compounded estrogen products is up in the air. Until then, women will continue to handle the symptoms of menopause with hormone therapies, natural cures, and acceptance of the infirmities of getting older.

More Diabetes

33 In 2003, the U.S. government released good and bad statistics on the nation's health. In *Health United States, 2003*, a report prepared by the National Center for Health Statistics (NCHS) in the Centers for Disease Control and Prevention, the good news was that life expectancy had reached a new high for both males and females. Boys born in 2001 were expected to live 74.4 years, and girls born in 2001 would live 79.8 years.

The bad news is that we are finding more ways to complicate our health. Most dramatic is the rise of diabetes, particularly type 2 adult-onset diabetes. As of 2003, estimates show that 17 million Americans have diabetes in the United States. Rates for diabetes between 1997 and 2002 increased 27 percent. This means 6.2 percent of U.S. adults were diagnosed with diabetes (including gestational diabetes) by 2002, as compared to 5.1 percent in 1997. Across the country, diabetes has increased 50 percent over the past ten years, reports the Centers for Disease Control (CDC), and over 800,000 new cases are diagnosed each year. Further, the increases occurred across all sexes, ages, races, and levels of education.

Tied to the rise in diabetes is the increase in obesity. As the number of Americans with diabetes increased by millions, so did the number of obese Americans, who are those 20 percent or more above their normal weight. The rate of obesity in the United States increased by 74 percent since 1991, as measured by body mass index (BMI) by the CDC.

According to the National Council of Health Statistics, the percentage of obese Americans more than doubled between 1976 to 1980 and 1999 to 2000, from 15 percent to 31 percent of Americans. Currently, over 44 million Americans are now considered obese. Additionally, 65 percent of all Americans ages twenty to seventy-four were considered overweight in 1999 to 2000. Research has also found that 80 percent of people who develop type 2 diabetes are obese.

Diabetes mellitus is a disorder of metabolism, or how the body uses digested food to create energy. The disease is marked by the inability of the body's cells to take glucose from the body's blood, which it would normally do for growth and energy. Diabetes is the fifth leading cause of death in women, and the sixth leading cause of death in men. The disease is the leading cause of amputation, blindness, and kidney failure in adults.

Other troubling findings in the report include the discovery that 5 million more Americans have diabetes but are not aware of it. At least 16 million more Americans have prediabetes or impaired glucose metabolism, a condition that increases a person's risk for developing type 2 diabetes. There is also an increase in the numbers of children and adolescents with the disease.

There are simple ways to combat the onset of diabetes. A National Institutes of Health (NIH) study found that people with prediabetes who lost 5 to 7 percent of their body weight and ate and exercised moderately were able to forestall or prevent the onset of type 2 diabetes. A recent study presented by the Defeat Diabetes Foundation, Inc., suggests that a high intake of dietary fiber may promote enhanced insulin sensitivity and may help to prevent type 2 diabetes. Physicians and researchers at the CDC reiterate that a more healthful lifestyle is good prevention for diabetes.

Finally, a reduction in diabetes would save the nation money. According to the National Diabetes Information Clearinghouse (NDIC), the United States spent $132 billion in one year on treating diabetes, directly and indirectly. The costs included disability payments, time lost from work and premature death, hospitalization, treatment supplies, and medical care.

From an investor's standpoint, however, diabetes management is a moneymaking venture. "Diabetes is a great disease from a business perspective," David Kliff, publisher of *Diabetic Investor*, told the trade magazine *Retail Pharmacy News*.

Privacy, Please

34 New laws are trying to grant hospital and outpatients something they need along with treatment—privacy. In April 2003, the portion of the Health Insurance Portability and Accountability Act (HIPAA) affecting privacy was put into effect. The privacy regulations that became effective on December 28, 2000, had to be met by April 2003.

The act was passed by Congress in 1996 and was created to protect patients' medical records and develop standards for electronic transfer of their medical information. The new patient privacy regulations require hospitals, doctors, pharmacists, dentists, and other health care providers to inform patients of their right to privacy, which they began doing in writing in 2003. In hospitals and nursing homes, that means patients may choose to protect their privacy by not permitting to have themselves listed as patients. Doing so means that the hospital may not give out or sell any information about the patient's health or even his or her presence at the hospital. To provide access for family members, hospitals may give access codes to patients' families so the relatives can get basic information about the patient.

Other elements of the act include broadening patient access to his or her records by allowing them to request copies of their medical records from hospitals and doctors. To maintain the medical privacy of employees in the work setting, the act prohibits insurance companies from disclosing a worker's medical history to an employer. Says Janlori Goldman, director of the Washington-based advocacy group Health Privacy Project, "Most people . . . are worried about being discriminated against on the job [or that] they won't get a job or a promotion, so this will really go a long way toward protecting people in their jobs."

The privacy mandates also forced members of the medical profession to be retrained. Whether a pharmacist or doctor, the medical world had to be educated to comply with the new rules for privacy protection. Not only do providers require retraining, many have invested in security improvements to their office areas, such as hooded computers and consultation areas. To convey data electronically, others have installed e-mail firewall and secure-messaging improvements that filter, secure messages, and make other changes to comply with federal regulations.

Privacy will continue to be a patient concern in coming years, but so will criticism that the concern is overblown. Health care providers who find fault with the recent privacy legislation consider it hurtful for patients when a hospital or nursing home is prevented from discussing health conditions with relatives. One health care worker said, "What I see happening is the elderly being imprisoned in nursing homes or group homes because people won't tell what room they're in." In these cases, whether the patient wanted it or not, health care workers, not family, ended up making final decisions for the patient. What at first appears to be a clear-cut victory for patients' rights reveals itself to be a thorny question of balance between patients and the health care profession.

The Solar Threat

35 Sunshine and health have been linked for as long as parents have ordered their children to go out and get some sun. But that long association is coming to an end. Increasingly, sunshine will be seen not as a boon to health but as a threat.

With the degradation of the protective ozone layer of the atmosphere, the sun's ultraviolet rays have become more potent. As that trend continues, and as U.S. society ages, cases of skin cancer will increase. Already the number of new cases of melanoma, the most serious of skin cancers, has more than doubled since 1980. In 2000, over 50,000 new cases of melanoma were detected. By 2010, the American Academy of Dermatology projects that one in fifty Americans (or about 2.8 million) will develop some form of melanoma. In addition, there will be even more cases of less-threatening skin cancers such as squamous cell and basal cell cancer. In fact, throughout the Western countries, melanoma is the fastest-growing of all cancers. Additionally, although melanoma is already a leading cancer among young people, it is expected to become more prevalent among them in the future.

Given how treatable skin cancer is (it can be cured in 95 percent of cases), the medical community and consumer businesses will continue to develop medical and over-the-counter innovations to fight the disease. At both preventative and treatment levels, there is much money to be made in new developments.

As of now, prevention involves avoiding or limiting exposure to the sun to periods when the sun is less strong by wearing SPF (sun protection factor) sunscreen of 30 and protective clothing when in the sun. New standard practices to monitor the skin may include regular visits to the dermatologist, in which the doctor keeps a running photographic survey of a patient's skin; these may become as commonplace as mammograms and prostate exams. Do-it-yourself skin cancer tests and special mirrors for self-viewing may become popular, as they can detect potentially problematic spotting.

Consumer products serving the needs of potential cancer patients include clothing made from fabrics designed to shelter the body from sunrays. Such clothing is available today, but from limited outlets and aimed primarily at travelers. Over time, an increasing number of clothes for everyday wear will be made from UV-resistant material or will be treated by UV-resistant sprays. This will bring clothing up to par with eyeglasses and sunglasses that routinely have UV-screening properties ground into them. Self-tanning cosmetics will be even further refined to be more natural and less drying to the skin, and tanning salons may be reimagined so that they impart a suntan to the user without using techniques that damage the skin.

To answer growing medical needs, the numbers of plastic and reconstructive surgeons will increase, with many specializing in post–skin cancer reconstruction. In the public health arena, health classes along the lines of today's CPR sessions will train people to detect the differences between ordinary discolorations and skin cancers.

It is unlikely, but possible, that there may be a healthful cultural change. The next generations could adopt a preference for a nonsun-kissed look. The healthy, preferred look could be one's everyday coloring, even if pale, as long as it has no skin discolorations caused by the sun. In the 19th century, some women avoided the sun to maintain their pale beauty. Now everyone may avoid the sun for a longer life.

Telemedicine

36 In the 20th century, the doctor's house call died. In the 21st century, it returns—on the computer and videophone. Doctor-patient visits are just one type of the telemedicine trend that is revolutionizing the practice of medicine. For the average patient, telemedicine is an online consult with a doctor before approving a prescription to be filled online. For another patient just out of cancer surgery and already at her home, it is a video monitor that relays vital signs and images of the patient that allow a nurse at a medical center to monitor her progress. The nurse also uses the phone lines to check the patient's blood pressure and manage her pain levels.

Telemedicine services are particularly useful in regions that are medically underserved by physicians and hospitals. Rural and underpopulated regions where people have to travel long distances to doctors have been introduced to telemedical service, with success. As reported in *Pediatrics*, a study of a telemedicine program in rural California for children with special health care needs reported high levels of satisfaction in the teleconsultations. The pediatric subspecialists who consulted through a telemedicine program helped to cut down on medical errors and formed a link between specialists and the primary physician.

The ease of telemedicine also makes the practice appealing to any patient with travel difficulties, whether in rural or nonrural areas. Those facing long-term at-home rehabilitation are likely candidates for telemedical monitoring. Several companies, including HealthTech Services Corporation of Northbrook, Illinois, and Viterion TeleHealth, LLC, of Tarrytown, New York, produce telemonitors for use at home. These monitors allow physicians to track a patient's vital signs while also reducing the number of times a patient must visit the doctor's office.

Thus far, telemedicine has proven a good fit for physician and patient. Studies have shown that such telemonitoring reduces patients' visits to emergency rooms and also allows many people to keep living in their homes rather than transfer to a nursing home. Keeping patients from entering nursing homes will become increasingly important as the baby boom generation enters retirement years. At Journal-News.com, Craig Lehmann, dean and professor at the School of Health Technology and Management at Stony Brook University, said, "As the baby boomers reach that golden age when they fall under Medicare, you can't afford to be putting people in nursing homes and not managing them better, because it's going to break the bank."

Telepsychiatry has also grown widely over the past decade. According to a survey by *Telemedecine Today* (done in conjunction with the Association of Telemedicine Service Providers), there are twenty-five telemental programs in the United States. Those responding to the survey report an aggregate total of about 8,640 consultations per year. Compared to the number of consultations done in 1994, there was a tenfold increase.

Telemedical procedures with humans and robots are also becoming more common in medical practice. In addition to using robots in operating rooms to assist physicians, robots are being used to assist patients in long-term rehabilitation. A recent study using a robot developed at the Massachusetts Institute of Technology (MIT) showed promise in patients undergoing stroke rehabilitation.

According to *Telemedecine Today*, many hospitals and medical schools are using telemedicine to connect rural and urban physicians or to provide continuing education to physicians and health care professionals.

To maintain medical standards, state and national governments are proposing legislation and regulations for electronic medical practice. Governments and health care providers also have to make decisions on reimbursement rates. As of now, they are still under debate. While the first telemedical claims processed by the Department of Health Services in California were paid out in 1998, payment rates have not yet been regularized. At-home monitors that connect with hospitals are not yet always covered by health insurance. In addition, the rates for coverage of online medical consultations (much less their legal status in regard to privacy laws and malpractice suits) has yet to be determined.

Given the possibility that telemedicine may mean lower costs and increased medical attention, it is likely to be accepted as part of the health care system. In 1997, Dr. Rick Satava, professor of surgery at Yale University School of Medicine, in New Haven, Connecticut, told *General Surgery & Laparoscopy News*, "The barriers [to telemedicine] aren't technical any longer, but social." But with other elements of our social life becoming computerized, resistance is crumbling fast. If people can order a car and fall in love over the Internet, a telemedical doctor will be able to diagnose, rehabilitate, even operate on them. "It's clearly inevitable," said Dr. Satava.

Up with Health Care Costs

37 The dominant health care trend of the late 20th century will continue well into the 21st. Health care costs to consumers will rise markedly each year and larger numbers of Americans will be unable to afford traditional coverage. However, increases are likely to be in lower double-digit percentages than in the past several years. The Milliman Consultants and Actuaries twelfth annual HMO Intercompany Rate Survey projects a 2004 increase of 14 percent. While that number would mark the fifth year in a row of double-digit increases, the percentage increase, if it occurs as expected, would be 3 percentage points lower than last year's survey results. Whether this trend will continue is another matter.

Reasons behind the rise in health care costs, report the Milliman survey, include an aging population; rising rates of certain chronic or ongoing conditions, like obesity, diabetes, and asthma; the high cost of medical malpractice litigation; shortages in health care workers; reduced use of managed care; cost shifting from government to private insurers; costs of HIPAA compliance; and consumer demand for more performance-driven health care coverage. The American Association of Health Plans adds that increased government benefit mandates and duplicative regulations added $20 billion to overall health premiums.

In answer to cost increases, more varieties of partial coverage will be offered from untraditional sources. As unions dwindle and full-time employment with benefits lessens, the scope of traditional coverage will also be circumscribed. The days of the industrial worker with full Blue Cross/Blue Shield coverage are numbered.

Many consumer advocacy groups warn of the upcoming threats to the health care system. According to the United Food and Commercial Workers Union, the organization Communicating for Agriculture & the Self-Employed, and the National Coalition for Health Care, the year 2003 in health care was marked by the following:

- In the United States, 45 million Americans were uninsured, up from 38.7 million in 2000.
- About 3,000 people lose health insurance each day and 1 million lose it each year.
- By the end of the decade, 50 million Americans will have no health insurance.

Is this a problem for the United States? To some thinkers, it is not. Some public pundits (particularly some radio talk show hosts) have said that there should be no health insurance at all, and certainly none offered or regulated by the U.S. government. If a person cannot pay for services out of pocket, he or she should not receive them.

However, other groups are working with insurance companies and the government to expand possibilities for coverage and make it affordable for the uninsured. For example, the House of Representatives passed the Small Business Health Fairness Act (S. 545). It was designed to allow small business owners, who are increasingly unable to afford health coverage for their workers, to form national alliances through their trade or business associations that allow them to purchase national health care plans for themselves and their employees. Currently, these trade/business associations represent 80 million workers. Another group, Communicating for Agriculture & the Self-Employed, advises making it easier for individuals and small businesses to get coverage by increasing their bargaining power with insurers and health providers and making tax credits and vouchers available to low-income citizens. It also suggests expanding the types of coverage available, such as low-cost policies with limited coverage. Broadening the availability for coverage in high-risk pools would also allow people with serious pre-existing conditions to be covered, they say.

But the forces driving costs upward will continue and will hit providers hard. According to the Centers for Medicaid and Medicare Services, health insurance premiums and the medical expenses that drive consumer costs upward will continue to rise dramatically between now and 2010. Among the health services projected to have the highest increases are hospital care; physician services; outpatient prescription and over-the counter drugs; and nursing home and home health care. However, administrative costs of health insurance organizations increased at a slower rate than health insurance premiums since 1998. Administrative expenses increased on average by 6.2 percent, while the average insurance rate increased by 8.4 percent.

These increases are expected to affect both private and public health providers. For example, Medicare cost increases and spending are expected to rise from $252 billion in 2002 to $456 billion in 2010. State-run health programs will also be affected. In 2003, the Hawaii Medical Service Association (HMSA) asked for an average rate increase of 11.5 percent to cover increasing expenses. It was the largest increase for the state's most popular health plan in more than a decade. Other states face similar shortfalls.

Several forces will affect private providers as well. Among them is the underwriting cycle where health care premiums grow faster or slower than underlying health care costs. Because underpricing was standard in the mid-1990s, higher prices will ensue during the early century to regain profits for insurers. Another trend will be for private companies, which pay for employees' insurance coverage, to try to encourage employee health through incentives for healthy lifestyle improvements.

The rise of most quotidian elements of health care expenditures will bring the greatest increases for the largest number of Americans. One is prescription drugs. According to *Drug Cost Management Report*, the cost of prescription drug coverage will increase nearly 20 percent in 2003. This rise in drug costs will contribute to the projected increase for all plans to be at least 14 percent.

From all corners—the patient with coverage, the patient without coverage, public providers, and private providers—the call is the same: Help!

5

Lifestyles

Beyond Multitasking

38 Judging from how busy most Americans made themselves during the 20th century, it's clear that in the 21st, they won't have enough time to do all they have planned. To do more in less time, some will continue to use established methods of time management like delegating or hiring out work they once did themselves and multitasking, or doing several things at once. In the midst of all this activity, they will also return to traditional touchstones of time management. Instead of multitasking, they will set priorities and do one thing at a time. It might be called sequential tasking or some other catchphrase, but one way or another, it will be a return to a human pace.

According to Rob Brager, managing director of the law firm Beveridge Diamond, most people use some form of multitasking in their everyday work and home lives—writing e-mails while talking on the phone, or planning schedules during meetings. But others reject that as inefficient. Recent studies have found that for some people, multitasking invites them to escape their most important work. By making each task one of many, it removes the meaning from each discrete act. So people do many acts at once but do not concentrate on the single act they most needed to do. Even Dummies.com knows that people "don't have unlimited ability to pay attention to several things" at once and that with each new task, you "dilute your investment in each task."

While improving efficiency in old or new ways, Americans will also spend time trying to reflect on their life. Whether examining life or enduring a work crunch, the guiding idea is knowing when to juggle. As Dummies.com says, "[T]hese times may be fewer than you think." They add, "Your challenge is to know the difference between the times you have to multitask and the times that you don't." Most important, say time management experts, stop and take time to reflect on life. Says motivational speaker and InnerSelf.com author Sarano Kelley about the rush to live life, "Where are you rushing to? You really have only one clear destination—six feet under the ground. Why would you be in such a hurry to get there? Why are you moving so fast that you can't stop to see the enormity, beauty, and wonder of the world in front of you?"

Community-Building

39 Old-time science fiction often depicted the inhabitants of the future as living in isolation: Winston Smith, persecuted for being in love in *1984*; the astronauts hurtling far from earth in *2001: A Space Odyssey*; even George Jetson, who walked Astro on a little treadmill outside his lonely high-rise. But the real future that is now here is more characterized by community-building than by isolation. In real space and cyberspace, in ways large and small, people are bent on restoring, strengthening, and creating the human links that make for social connectedness.

The spread of gated communities—planned neighborhoods enclosed by walls or fences—is the most visible sign of the trend toward community-building. The number of gated communities nationwide has increased from about 2,000 in the 1970s to more than 50,000 in the early 2000s; according to one estimate, about one in eight Americans is now living in these settings. Desire for additional security is one driving factor, as is an interest in excluding outsiders of various sorts: Edward J. Blakely and Mary Gail Snyder, who analyze this trend in

Fortress America, call it "forting up." But the desire for a more close-knit community within the walls of the fortress is also at work. Ironically, says Setha Low, who analyzes gated communities in *Behind the Gates*, such settings are statistically no safer than other suburbs—so if security is what residents are looking for, they may not get as much as they would like.

Even if they are not behind gates, Americans are increasingly living in some kind of common interest housing developments, governed by homeowner's associations. Such developments can end with homeowners feeling oppressed by restrictive rules, but they can also foster feelings of community. Celebration, Florida, a small town famously founded by Disney near Disney World explicitly to promote a sense of community, continues to aim for what planners call a "spirit of neighborliness," with plenty of front porches, park benches, and communal events.

Even in New York City, legendary for its lack of neighborliness, greater numbers of people are turning their apartment buildings into small towns, with lots of sociable amenities, from gardens and recreation rooms to concerts and classes. One building, the St. Tropez at 340 East 64th Street, has a party room, movie nights, body-sculpting classes, and brunches. "We . . . want to keep a sense of cohesiveness," Robert Metz, editor of the building's newsletter, told the *New York Times*. In part, the still-potent memory of 9/11 has been driving the trend in New York City toward greater social connectedness, but it is part of a larger trend nationwide.

A less-common but more radical arrangement, the intentional community, has also been increasing. An intentional community is one in which people live together and work cooperatively to fulfill a common purpose or express a set of shared values, whether spiritual or secular. Though some people think this kind of development died out with the communes of the 1960s and the cults of the 1970s, their numbers have been rising since at least the 1990s.

In cities and towns of all kinds, a salon movement is growing, in which people meet at a prearranged time—in cafés, bookstores, houses, or churches—to converse on various topics. The Socrates Café network, which has fostered philosophical discussion since the mid-1990s, now has 200 salons operating nationwide. Political scientist David Niven told *Reader's Digest* that "thoughtful contact with others in a salon" is a way to fulfill the need for "a feeling of connection."

The Internet has made it easier for people to "meet up" in salons or other venues. In fact, *meetup* is now a term for a gathering that is prearranged online but takes place offline, in a real café or other public place. Meetup.com is a free service that organizes such gatherings on specific topics of interest—"about anything, anywhere." As of late 2003, nearly 700,000 people had used the service to sign up for meetups.

A weirder, more frivolous version of the same phenomenon is the "flash mob"—a large group of people who use the Internet to arrange to meet in some location, perform some brief action, then quickly disperse. The action is usually pointless but amusing—quacking like a duck, applauding loudly, and so forth. More serious is the "smart mob," a leaderless group of people who use technology (the Internet, cell phones, e-mail, Wi-Fi [Wireless Fidelity]) to maintain a community and/or organize and accomplish some purpose. (Howard Rheingold analyzes these groups extensively in *Smart Mobs: The Next Social Revolution*, 2002.) Not only are such groups increasingly important to election campaigns and political movements, but they are also building new forms of community, part virtual, part real.

Then there is the plethora of communities that are wholly virtual: people who have never met in person but who interact electronically on listserves, chatrooms, forums, multiplayer online games, and dozens of other virtual communities. The online auction site eBay, for example, is effectively a community in which people interact as if at a huge open-air flea market. Virtual communities even interact with other communities. In 2002, the *New York Times* reported that a check forger connected to a Macintosh sale on eBay was caught when the victim enlisted the help of Macintosh users through the close-knit world of Macintosh electronic bulletin boards. When the criminal was caught, one bulletin board message said: "I LOVE YOU GUYS!!! *group hug for mac users everywhere.*"

In some ways, virtual communities are even stronger than real ones. In *The Monochrome Society* (2001), Amitai Etzioni remarks, "If there is a snowstorm or you are sick with the flu, not very mobile, or afraid of the streets, you may not make it to your local country store or senior center. But you can always log on." Yet, virtual and real communities are not either-or. Increasingly, the growth of one is reinforcing that of the other—and both are part of a long-term trend toward stronger social connectedness.

Distance Learning Grows

40 In the 21st century, America will have more students of all ages. There will be the record enrollments of "echo boomers," the children of baby boomers, who were born between 1979 and 1994. There are the children of the millions of new immigrants. There are varieties of adults, from immigrants who want to learn languages and skills for employment to an entire generation of baby boomers who want to return to school.

Enrollment in public and private colleges and other institutes of higher education is expected to rise to 17.5 million by 2010. This represents a 20 percent increase since 1998. In addition, some states are expected to have heightened percentages of growth in enrollment. According to the Western Interstate Commission for Higher Education, statistics show that California, Arizona, Colorado, Washington, and Nevada will have enrollment increases of 25 to 35 percent by 2008. Enrollment in the University of California school system over the next ten years is expected to increase 43 percent.

Community college enrollment is set to increase greatly, particularly for older students. According to the National Center for Education

Statistics (NCES), the number of community college students over age twenty-five is expected to increase 9 percent between 1999 to 2010. Overall, NCES suggests that by 2010 the number of students over age twenty-five will be larger than the number of those under twenty-two.

The projected growth rates of enrollment reflect the exponential rate of college attendance over the past century. Since 1930, reports the Commission on National Investment in Higher Education, higher education enrollment in the United States increased seven times, while the overall population during the period only doubled. According to sources cited by the University of California public affairs office, 65 percent of all recent high school graduates enroll in college.

To accommodate the huge demand, among others, distance learning will become increasingly popular. Distance-learning expert David W. Butler says, "Distance or open learning . . . is in a strategic position to bring about the first overhaul of the teaching/learning process in 400 years, since the creation of the university concept in medieval Europe." According to Butler, distance learning is defined by the following: a student and instructor "geographically remote" from each other; the use of electronic and other "educational media"; and the use of "two-way communication between teacher and learner."

The number of students involved in distance learning has already increased greatly over the past decade. In 1998, 710,000 students were enrolled in distance-learning courses. In 2002, the number increased to 23 million. Fifteen percent of all higher-education students are taking distance-learning courses, which is an increase from 5 percent in 1998. As of mid-2003, the Distance Education Clearinghouse reports that more than a dozen states currently have virtual universities they are operating or have in development. There are also some regional virtual campuses in the United States. The International Data Corporation (IDC) projects that distance learning will grow by 33 percent during the first years of the 21st century.

According to experts in the field, distance learning will be particularly strong in some areas. It is highly applicable for training students in the career areas expected to grow in the early 21st century. According to the Federal Bureau of Labor Statistics, some of the areas of projected growth include teaching, computer-software engineering, nursing, accounting, and marketing.

All told, distance learning is set to revolutionize learning. From an abstract of a 2001 lecture by Dr. Michael G. Moore, director of the American Center for Study of Distance Education, "In the end . . . traditional education will co-exist with distance education, although the latter will be, in the near future, predominant in the field of professional, liberal and vocational lifelong learning."

Educational experts also believe that the general conception of distance learning will evolve and change. Formerly it was a synchronous learning experience of students and teacher at different sites experiencing a class at a certain time. Now the educational model is different. More likely the distance learning class is an asynchronous distance-learning system, where classes can be taken and participated in through computer and Internet access. Universities and colleges that offer distance learning will also have to redefine student classifications to include those who attend the school offsite.

Among the many online educational resources are the following:

- **Western Governors University**—an online university developed by a consortium of eighteen governors
- **University of Phoenix Online**—offers 100 percent of education via the Internet, including classes, registration, and book buying
- **Suffolk University**—offers MBAs online
- **Wayne Huizenga School**—offers Master of Accounting or MBA degrees
- **Other schools**—AIU Online; the University Alliance; the Art Institute Online; American Graduate School of Management; the University of Liverpool

Many states have established local support centers to encourage distance learning and offer counseling and technological aid. For example, Northern Arizona University allows students to attend lecture courses online and has a distributed learning program consisting of more than thirty degree programs with 900 courses and 4,700 students.

Other universities link with school systems to create joint-use facilities. In Nevada, for example, K-12 schools link with community college campuses in Reno and Las Vegas. Other school systems, such as Florida's, establish summer school sessions to serve the increasing population. In New York and elsewhere, students can make dual enrollment in high school and college. That way, they can earn college credit before attending college full-time.

Along with public and private colleges and universities, the U.S. government is also involved in distance learning. Acknowledging the growth of students seeking higher education in the 21st century, the government is supporting private-public partnerships that include college-level coursework. Through the U.S. Department of Education's Distance Education Demonstration Programs and the Learning Anytime Anywhere Partnerships program, distance education providers can offer increased federal aid because the restrictions placed on them are being reviewed and changed.

The U.S. military also uses distance learning. The current U.S. Army program earmarked about $55 million per year between 1998 and 2003 to establish distance-learning centers and develop courses. It was part of a long-term goal to establish a distance-learning system that will serve the army in the United States and overseas. By 2010 there will be 745 classrooms at more than 200 sites to teach 525 courses virtually at their home stations, according to Army LINK News.

Yet, since its growth in popularity, there has been criticism of the distance-learning process from educational groups. The National Education Association said that distance learning costs more than on-campus courses, and the College Board has said that distance learning would put students without computers at a disadvantage. Another education expert says, "Face-to-face with a talented professor in a classroom is still the best way to learn."

The experts may be right, but the reality is that face-to-face learning is simply not available to all those who want it, whether because of money or time. For these students, distance learning is another educational option. Former secretary of education Richard W. Riley has called education "the key civil right for the 21st century." For many, distance learning will help extend that right.

Duppies

41 As of mid-2003, the U.S. Bureau of Labor Statistics reported that 15 million Americans were unemployed or underemployed. Of that total, a sizable percentage of them are unhappy, highly educated, and comprise a new socioeconomic group. In the tradition of the young urban professionals, or yuppies of the 1980s, these workers constitute the depressed urban professionals or duppies.

According to the Word Spy, a Web site that charts newly coined words and phrases, *duppie* is defined as a person who once had a high-status job and must now work in a menial or lower-paying job. Whether the number of unemployed professionals levels off or increases, their high numbers already point to a shift in attitude for many: satisfaction in having discovered a simpler life. For others, the simpler life will be hard to bear. In current lingo, they may be afflicted by "affluenza," a form of excess materialism. Not just for the nouveau riche, affluenza can affect all social groups, from the multimillion-dollar executive who wants to make yet another $10 million to the average person who banks on winning the lottery.

But the reality of paying bills usually wins, and people change their work and their attitude toward it. As John Challenger, CEO of the outplacement firm Challenger, Gray & Christmas, says, "People who have been out for a while say, 'I've got to get back to work,' so they take downgraded jobs." In turn, this leads to the need to drastically alter one's economic life and eventually find different, less economically oriented sources of satisfaction. For those who got used to the material lifestyle a good job made possible, it means a less economically and socially secure life. One human resources executive became a marquee changer for a movie theater. She considers herself just another working person, no better than anyone else. Another woman, fired from a high-level job at Lucent, got work at a food store, but remains satisfied with her life. "I can live very, very cheaply," she says. A New York man, dropped over a year ago from his airline job of two decades and unable to find full-time work, will have to go to a homeless shelter if evicted. He still hopes he can meet his goal of finding enough work to pay his rent.

According to a survey on the online job board TrueCareers, because fewer high-paying jobs are being created, people are no longer looking primarily for salary compensation when they search for jobs. Now they are looking for once-standard benefits like health care coverage and perceived security in the job. According to Michael Caggiano, TrueCareers CEO, this represents a sea change in the aims of job seekers.

Downward mobility also affects how the United States sees itself. For a country used to each successive generation attaining greater wealth and social position, the move backward is disconcerting. How can the United States be the most productive country in the world with an exemplary standard of living when people can't get enough work? Will lower incomes have any effect on tax revenues and the overall economy?

While the term *duppie* may point to a worrisome social trend in the United States, the word means something different and much more menacing elsewhere. In Jamaica, a duppy is not a downward-bound worker but a ghost. According to Jamaican cultural experts, the duppy is an often fearful figure, who can cause personal injury and death. To ward off duppies, many Jamaicans mark their home with the blood of a white chicken. In the United States, duppies breed no such fear—yet.

The Lively Senior Lifestyle

42 By 2035, there will be twice as many senior citizens as there are today. While this may sound alarming, it is actually a natural progression of the growth in the United States population during the 20th century, as well as increased life span. The elderly population doubled before, between 1960 and 2003. What's more, with an elderly population that is, on the whole, healthier, wealthier, and better educated than any in U.S. history, many of them will find creative ways to maintain their familiar lifestyles. These activities will range from the psychological and political to the practical.

To begin with, tomorrow's older population will be well represented by advocacy groups of its own making. Over the next few decades look for the creation of many more public interest associations dedicated to seniors, as well as increased visibility for already powerful organizations like the American Association of Retired Persons and the National Council on the Aging. There will also be heightened demand on health organizations such as the American Heart Association and the American Cancer Society to promote further research directly related to aging adults.

In addition to staying as fixed on fitness as they had been since yuppiedom, aging seniors will establish an even greater world of preventative measures as they age. The U.S. government is likely to be involved, and has already indicated interest and earmarked funds through its Disease Prevention Initiative partnership within the department of Health and Human Services. The funds are aimed at funding health education and health promotion programs for older citizens.

One targeted health initiative will be increasing the rates for vaccination against diseases that affect older adults, such as influenza and pneumonia. Together, these two diseases comprise the fifth leading cause of death among senior citizens, yet can be deterred by vaccines. Currently, only about 67 percent of older people receive flu shots and only 54 percent receive pneumonia vaccines.

Other initiatives will be more broad-based. For example, the government, insurance companies, and health care providers will expand their training and education for helping older adults develop age-appropriate healthy lifestyles. These programs help older people live with chronic illnesses, which, according to recent research, affect almost 75 percent of Americans over age sixty-five. In addition to saving lives, these education programs will also have an economic purpose: to reduce health care payments for preventable or controllable diseases. This aim is part of a possible overarching restructuring of insurance for older people. In the future, private insurers may try to control mushrooming costs by downscaling or refusing coverage to the elderly in much greater numbers than they have in the past decades.

Family physicians are likely to alter their practice in coming years to accommodate the needs of a large older population. For example, family physicians are likely to take additional training to help middle-aged patients prepare for old age, and to more effectively treat the ongoing health losses that come with getting older.

During the next decades, older people will find various ways to redefine their state of advanced age. In addition to spending more money on antiaging skin treatments and getting plastic surgery, they will attempt to defy age by working to an older age. Even early in the 21st century, a sizable number of seniors envision never ending their work. The 102-year-old California man named in 2002 as the nation's oldest worker may not be such a rarity in the future.

On a practical level, older adults will find ways to live more safely. Technology will play a large role in this. One way it will be used is to make homes safe for older people, who have a higher incidence of household accidents (Currently, their rate of household accidents is higher than automobile accidents.). Among proposed technological solutions for the aged is a lifestyle monitor that records daily human movement. Studied by the National Institute of Advanced Industrial Science and Technology, the electronic sensors installed in the home monitor a person's body movement and vital signs during everyday activities, such as waking, bathing, eating, and dressing. The sensors may also monitor psychological changes such as mood swings. When mental or physical rates differ from established normal states, family and caregivers are notified.

Another technological aid for independent living may be the robot maid. Electronically programmed to the older person's day-to-day movements, the maid, in principle, could provide services in such activities as bathing, eating, relaxing, and preparing for sleep. Such a full-service robot maid is still a long way off, but household robo-gadgets are already on the market or in development.

In addition to adapting technology to their needs, the next generation of older people will make thrift a virtue. Conspicuous spending will be replaced by conspicuous saving. As boomers have less to spend, spending less will become the vogue.

Whether or not the next generation of older Americans will be happy remains to be seen. If they are like the current crop of senior citizens, they will run the gamut. Currently, adults over sixty-five account for the largest number of Americans calling themselves "very happy" (53 percent) and the largest number of those calling themselves "not too happy" (8 percent). Because senior boomers will probably have the same varied responses to aging as the past generation, they will do what they vowed they would never do: become like their parents.

The New Thrift, or Haute Penny-Pinching

43 In coming decades, the greatest generation of U.S. consumers will become tightwads—and proud of it. One reason why baby boomers and their children are becoming more thrifty is necessity. There is less money to go around now and for the future. Most salaries are not keeping pace with inflation, making for less discretionary income. In fact, the standard of living has declined steadily since 1970.

After adjusting for inflation, the median income of families with children and headed by adults under thirty dropped 32 percent between 1973 and 1990 alone.

Secure jobs are fewer; a high proportion of new jobs are in low-paying sectors, such as service, or are held on seasonal or contract terms. The costs of three major pulls on the family pocketbook—a new house, college, and health care—are growing at paces much faster than inflation. Today's pension plans are less generous than they were for workers entering the market fifty years ago, if they are available at all. This makes the current widespread stability of seniors seem less likely for the next generations.

Add to these elements the fact that the gap between rich and poor is growing. Not only is the salary of a major CEO over 400 times an average worker's salary ($36,000), it has grown much more over the past generation than a worker's salary. On average, an executive's salary is twenty times higher than it was in 1980, while the median salary of the average worker has doubled.

To live with these realities, young and middle-aged Americans will do what their parents and grandparents did from the start: make do with less. But they will do it in their own way. They will make it seem like it was their plan all along.

Those who consider saving money the center of a frugal lifestyle will take the way of the tightwad. Already there are movements to live frugally and several spokespeople who focus on introducing big spenders to a new life. For example, in her bestselling book *The Tightwad Gazette*, its sequel, *The Tightwad Gazette II*, and her newsletter, Amy Dacyczyn offers advice and pointers that show how to imitate the success she has had raising six children on her husband's $30,000 salary. In general, the advice centers on reusing or reimagining everything that might be discarded, or as she puts it, not "living stupidly." In different otherwise hard-nosed books, saving money takes on an aura of holiness, and becomes a way of simultaneously empowering oneself and serving God.

Another path to spending less is to embrace simplicity as an aesthetic. Such people may want to save money as much as the tightwad but will simply call their actions a movement toward simplifying. Magazines like *Real Simple* make the act of simplifying into a lifestyle choice and a sign of good taste. Features about women who have faced complications such as surgery or divorces show how to find peace through simplifying one's life. Tips for making household tasks less time-consuming and buying cheaper domestic goods address the practical side of simplifying, while advice on right and wrong responses to social situations addresses the moral component. Counselors offer advice on setting priorities, such as living on a budget. While mass-media endeavors like *Real Simple* may offer more attitude than practical solutions, they introduce the idea of living simply as a pleasurable choice.

While middle age and the years of senescence to follow may jolt people into a simpler lifestyle, frugal living clearly has appeal for younger adults as well. Signs of this interest are at least two major Web sites, each powered by trendy umbrella sites. Part of Yahoo! GeoCities is the Frugal House, a site filled with practical hints in subdivisions such as Skinflint Hints and the Frugal Chef. All Things Frugal, a Web site that is part of the Yahoo! Frugal Living Club, contains the Pennypincher E-Zine and Tightwad Tidbits Daily. The online tastemaker Salon.com also weighs in to support thrift. As part of its intellectual and socially relevant fare, Salon.com's Well online community offers a "Thrift as a Way of Life" conference.

In the early 21st century, living simply remains an alternative lifestyle, but it will become a mainstream practice over time, when it has to. By the third decade of the 21st century, a frugal way of life will become widely practiced and accepted. By then, millions of baby boomer senior citizens will have to find ways to live without some of the financial safety nets they had expected, and younger generations will find that acquiring consumables is not all it's cracked up to be.

Omni-Connectedness

44 A generation ago, a phone company jingle sang, "We're all connected." Now there's no excuse not to be connected to the telephone, e-mail, video mail, digital moviemaking, and on-demand TV and movie watching. There are numerous varieties of ways people can be connected to their TV, computer, and telephone. Like flavors of latte, there seems to be no end in sight. Americans like the control of connectivity and are willing to pay for it.

Over 90 percent of Americans still have landlines, but that number may decrease as a larger chunk of Americans (already over 50 percent) carry cell phones. In one upscale New York suburban elementary school, cell phones were spotted in kindergarten backpacks.

Considered a luxury fifty years ago, the long-distance telephone call is now a standard part of telephone use. Many smaller phone services have already introduced long-distance services that cost one or two cents per minute. But competition, particularly from Internet providers, is driving costs down to even lower levels (a.k.a. free). In some cases, Internet providers offer software for users who download it to make free long-distance calls. The technology is called VoIP, or voice over Internet protocol.

Then there is the cable or satellite hookup for entertainment. It's not your father's cable guy anymore. As of mid-2003, the *New York Times* reported that about 70 million American households have cable service. That number has been steady over the past few years. What has changed is the growing integration of additional services. Among them are additional services that cable companies offer, like the digital video recorder and integrated devices such as the set-top box that has a digital video recorder integrated into the cable system the household already uses. Twenty million households are projected to have digital video recorders by 2006, according to the Yankee Group. Similarly, families can get extraconnected from their phone companies, which will sell packages of television, high-speed Internet access, and home and wireless phone service. In the end, families will have at their disposal such niceties as VOD (video on demand), a DVR (digital video recorder), and HDTV (high-definition television). That should satisfy the family until the MPEG-4, a new satellite compression technology, appears in a couple of years.

No discussion of America's obsession with connectivity would be complete without mentioning the Internet. Once the tool of the academic community, it is now in over half (54 percent) of American households. With it comes the need for speed. Eschewing the old dial-up Internet format, more and more households want high-speed Internet access, provided by cable, digital subscriber lines, or satellite. Called broadband, the faster service reached about 16 million houses in 2002, with more increases expected throughout the decade. Since 2002, subscription to dial-up Internet service has been on the decline.

Among practical uses, people will bow to corporate wooing and pay their bills online. Already millions pay bills online directly to companies, such as phone, utility, credit card. But increasingly, banks themselves will offer incentives for consumers to pay all their month's bills through an online service sponsored by the bank where you have your checking account or by an outside bill-paying service.

The computer that connects with the Internet will also have to be wired for wireless connections away from home. The Wi-Fi connection is already offered at airports and coffeehouses, but is likely to become standard at any public place where people pause (and spend money). In short, it will become a necessary convenience for consumers and a cash cow for businesses. In a *New York Times* article, one Starbucks marketing executive said, "We know it [Wi-Fi] keeps them in the store, and perhaps long enough to buy that second cup of coffee."

For many, the humble cell phone will (or already has) become a phone-television or phone-video recorder. As of 2004, cell phone–TV service offers good sound quality but only a limited number of channel selections, and limited number of frames per second. The cell phone camcorder allows recording of several video clips of up to fifteen seconds each, with sound. The video clip is then sent by e-mail, where it entertains as written letters and personal presence used to do.

Finally, there's also something for the person who still listens to radio. To get favorite faraway stations, listeners will increasingly subscribe to satellite radio. Particularly useful in the car, it offers many varieties of music and talk, and never loses its signal. It will make pay radio as natural as pay TV.

But for some people, complete connectivity has its drawbacks. Not only does it make the omniwired person always available for work, it also erodes good manners. Time itself has been redefined. The new designation is called *soft time*, or the inexact period between the time two parties have agreed to meet and the time they do. It is marked by cell phone calls detailing where the caller is each step of the way, allowing the caller freedom to dawdle.

There is no sign that the movement toward omni-connectedness will end. Scientists keep increasing the speed of Internet data transfer; in fact, they doubled the world speed record in October 2003. At that time, scientists at the CERN particle physics laboratory in Switzerland sent 1.1 terabytes of data to fellow scientists at the California Institute of Technology in less than thirty minutes. In everyday terms, the transmission went at a speed more than 20,000 times faster than an average home broadband setup. Oliver Martin, head of external networking at CERN, commented, "This new record marks another major milestone towards our final goal of abolishing distances."

American households are also abolishing distances, in their own way. According to research done in 2003 for the *New York Times*, U.S. families would welcome additional forms of connectedness and are willing to pay for them. Currently, the outside limit for monthly charges is about $500. That's a twenty-five-fold increase over the cost of being connected in 1960—through a telephone party line. Back then, entertainment was listening in on the other calls on your party line; now, it is listening in on the other calls in your video store line.

The People's Environmentalism

45 While federal proenvironment programs and regulations either are unchanged or are being reduced during the early 21st century, national interest in preserving the environment remains high and is expected to continue. A recent national poll said three-fourths of Americans responding named the environment as a "high priority" issue. Four of five respondents considered themselves environmentalist or sympathetic to environmentalism. The language of environmentalist issues, from global warming to recycling, has become second nature to most Americans.

Private involvement in environmentalist causes is also booming. The number of environmental groups has grown from a few hundred in 1970 to more than 8,000 in the early 21st century. These groups also receive significant financial support. According to the National Center for Charitable Statistics, which monitors nonprofit fundraising, individuals, companies, and foundations gave an average of just under $10 million per day to environmental groups in 1999.

As in politics, the groups that form to make environmental statements are varied. Activists will continue to have divergent political views and religions, but will unite under a shared cause. Already active are partnerships between secular environmentalists and religious institutions. According to Worldwatch Research Director Gary Gardner, "This collaboration could change the world. . . . Environmentalists have a strong grounding in science. Religious institutions enjoy moral authority and a grassroots presence that shape the world views and lifestyles of billions of people." Together, he believes, they have force in changing public policy. Among pairings of scientists and religious institutions in the name of environmentalism are the Episcopal Power & Light that allows U.S. customers to buy renewable energy electricity and the Interfaith Coffee Program, which sells coffee grown under environmentally sound conditions to its congregants.

Individual items will continue to be focal points for activists of all sorts. For example, hybrid cars that run on a combination of gas and electric power have gained popularity, thanks to a mix of film celebrities, business leaders, politicians, and religious communities who bought the car. Buyers included movie stars Leonardo DiCaprio and Cameron Diaz, the New York City government, and Republican Utah Senator Robert F. Bennett. Environmental causes for the purchase range from decreasing dependence on finite natural resources to fighting terrorism.

Activist organizations will continue, each serving the purposes of the environment differently. Greenpeace will continue its activist techniques to warn the industrialized world of its dangers to the environment. Among the conditions it protests are toxic waste, acid rain, and uranium mining.

Since the 1970s, the long-range "deep ecology" movement has been active, attempting to broaden the way people think about the environment. Begun by Norwegian philosopher and mountaineer Arne Naess, the deep ecology movement is contrasted with what Naess describes as the practical, short-term results-oriented "shallow ecology" movement. In its statement, the deep ecology movement "involves redesigning our whole systems based on values and methods that truly preserve the ecological and cultural diversity of natural systems." Its leaders accept all human models but reject the "industrial technology model" of human convenience and comfort and instead support common harmony with other beings and other cultures. Among the many environmentalists affected by this philosophy have been former vice president and author of *Earth in the Balance* Al Gore.

Greenspirit, a government and industry consultancy started by Greenpeace founder Patrick Moore, promotes what Moore calls a "rational" environmental policy for the 21st century. Moving toward an economy of sustainable energy, managing the world population, controlling urban sprawl, and stabilizing or reversing deforestation are among its aims.

Along with environmental groups that wish to change a nation's thinking about the earth, there are groups that will try to convince the public about the shared advantages of conservation. For example, the Nature Conservancy uses hands-on conservation programs to study and preserve nearby geographic areas. In one of its projects, at California's Cosumnes River Preserve, thousands of schoolchildren collect natural artifacts and plant trees. Other groups, like the Malpai Borderlands Group, an Arizona- and New Mexico–based group of ranchers, enter into ranching and open space partnerships that preserve wildlife and ranches. Matt Magoffin, a member of the group, points out that "environmentalists are fighting with ranchers, but we both want the same goals."

In the 21st century, conservationists may turn more to corporate donations. Increasingly, corporate donations are looked on favorably, particularly as major companies like beverage giant Starbucks have become involved in conservation projects and funding initiatives. To the charge that corporate money is somehow tainted, a National Audubon Society executive remembered what someone told him: "'The only thing wrong with tainted money is there t'aint enough of it.'"

While the grass-roots environmentalism will continue and grow throughout the early 21st century, so will professional forecasters. Public policy institutions will project and promote environmental changes for the future. In 2003 the Pew Center on Global Climate Change released a report called "U.S. Energy Scenarios for the 21st Century," which outlined possible avenues for U.S. energy supply and use from 2000 and 2035. It pointed to the need for new public policy, increased investments, and the immediate action to achieve long-term goals—in short, a complete climate change policy.

All these avenues for environmental activism, from practical initiatives between big businesses and activists to buyers of hybrid cars, will mark the 21st century. It's because people will see their environment changing and they will want to do something about it, with or without government involvement.

The Pricing-Out of College

46   According to the College Board, people who have a college degree make $1 million more during their lifetime than high school graduates. So in the 21st century, most people will continue to try to attend college. But the costs are already astronomical and are expected to increase. For those able to save, $12,000 is the yearly sum needed to send nine-year-old Junior off to college in less than a decade. For those starting with a newborn, it's $279,000 divided by eighteen. And for the eighteen-year-old entering college in the fall, the four-year price tag is $120,000. Because an increasing number of Americans will not be able to foot the entire college bill themselves, the coming decades will see people borrowing more money, demanding creative financing programs from colleges, attending nontraditional educational outlets, and dropping the stigma from not attending college and skipping the ordeal entirely.

For years, college costs have risen at rates that are higher than inflation or other economic indicators. For example, according to the National Center for Public Policy and Education, tuition at four-year public colleges and universities during the years 1992 through 2001 rose faster than family income in forty-one states. And while federal and state governments have increased their support of student financial aid, the increases have not kept pace with the costs of attending college.

Further, other traditional sources of aid have not matched increases in costs. For example, Pell Grants, a long-standing source of need-based funding, now covers a smaller portion of tuition at four-year colleges and universities than it did in the mid-1980s. And while institutional aid (from the colleges) amounts to $13 billion each year, an increasing amount is being awarded on a nonneed basis. In 1981, 91 percent of state financial aid went to students on a need-and-academic performance basis; in 1999, only 78 percent of state aid used those criteria.

State aid, in particular, has been greatly affected by recessionary periods. In most cases, states compensate for recession-driven shortfalls in their budgets by raising tuition. Over the past years, this has occurred widely across the United States and is expected to continue.

To compensate for these increased costs now and in the future, many parents will borrow more money. Students themselves will also rack up more college debt. From 1989 to 1999, the average cumulative debt by seniors at public colleges and universities increased greatly among all income groups, and in particular within the lowest income quartile. For students, debt grew from $7,629 to $12,888.

For those who want another road to education, more students in the future will seek alternative learning sources. For example, millions will seek a degree education online, where colleges specialize in subjects that can be taught by distance—that is, without great classroom involvement. Two-year college enrollment is also expected to increase, as are many forms of practical training, such as paralegal training or various types of computer training. But whatever the path is to improvement, the numbers don't lie. Parents will continue to have a larger and larger portion of their budget earmarked for education because they think it is worth it. Whether it is or not, college will take a higher percentage of the family's current take-home pay and the student's future earnings upon graduation. The lifetime of education promised by college may yield a lifetime of promissory notes.

Read the Animals Their Rights

47 Once upon a time, it was easy to exploit animals. Eating meat was as American as apple pie, furs were glamorous, and lab rats were out of sight and out of mind. But over the past few decades, animal rights, once the concern of a small minority with the distinct image of being zealots, has become mainstream.

The modern animal rights movement had its genesis in 1975, with the publication of *Animal Liberation* by Australian philosopher Peter Singer. Since then, animal rights has become a powerhouse: inspiring academic discussion, spurring activist groups such as People for the Ethical Treatment of Animals (PETA), and influencing governments and corporations. As of 2003, twenty-five U.S. law schools offered courses in animal rights law. Major corporations such as McDonald's and Burger King have applied pressure on the meat industry to slaughter animals more humanely. Some beauty and cosmetics companies, such as the Body Shop, have marketed their products as being "cruelty-free"—i.e., not tested on animals. During the rise of animal rights, fur lost some of its panache, vegetarianism became more popular, meatless dishes found their way into supermarkets and restaurants, and celebrities got on the bandwagon.

Though usually thought of as a left-wing cause, animal protection has been broadening its constituency to include some prominent right-wingers. Matthew Scully, a former speechwriter for President George W. Bush, argues in his book *Dominion: The Power of Man, the Suffering of Animals, and the Call to Mercy* (2002) that even though animals do not have rights per se, people should treat them mercifully and eat vegetarian.

Where there is a movement, there is usually a backlash, and animal rights is no exception. Many have taken issue with the sometimes violent tactics of groups such as the Animal Liberation Front and the Earth Liberation Front. The Southern Poverty Law Center, for example, has decried the bombings, beatings, vandalism, and other terror tactics of some animal rights activists. Patients hoping that animal research will bring new cures and treatments for their diseases have little patience with animal rights activists trying to put a stop to animal research. "I wish they'd use their creative talent for a cure instead of rodent rights," one AIDS activist told Reuters NewsMedia about a 1996 animal rights protest against experimental baboon marrow transplants for AIDS sufferers. Companies and individuals targeted by animal rights activists have resorted to the courts to protect them from criminal acts. In Britain in 2003, for example, Huntingdon Life Sciences won restraining orders against the group Stop Huntingdon Animal Cruelty.

Many private individuals and organized groups have argued in letters-to-the-editor and Web sites against the presuppositions of animal rights activists—everyone from circus fans defending the use of animals in circuses to wildlife trappers defending the humaneness of leg traps. Groups concerned with animal welfare, but not committed to animal rights, have squared off with more zealous activists committed to nothing less than an end to animal husbandry. In a November 10, 2002, article in the *New York Times Magazine*, Michael Pollan argued that it is acceptable to eat "free-farmed" meat—meat from animals raised on small farms where they can live pleasant lives and are slaughtered humanely. "I don't have a catchy name for it yet (humanocarnivore?)," he wrote, "but this is the only sort of meat eating I feel comfortable with these days."

Backlash or not, the animal rights movement has set the terms of the debate. They can no longer be ignored, but must either be accepted or confronted—a process that will be going on for some time.

Relaxed Parenting

48 As humorist Joe Queenan outlined in his book *Balsamic Dreams*, the ideal child of baby boomers is scheduled for self-improvement and parental self-gratification every minute of his waking day. Excessive parental management may lead to an obsessive child who seeks to meet the high expectations she and everyone else has for herself. This means balancing a life of homework deadlines, work, and extracurricular activities—but little enjoyment. This striving for perfection is hard on the child and the parent. In a *Boston Globe Magazine* article "How to Raise a Perfect Child," one parent said, "I'm overwhelmed. . . . I feel like I could devote my life to figuring out what to play with my kids."

In the 21st century, however, views on child rearing may be changing. The trend is toward more relaxed parenting. This means child rearing that is less concerned with constantly living up to set ideals for achievement and social status that the parent and child feel compelled to meet. Instead, as Tim Smith proposes in his book *The Relaxed Parent: Helping Your Kids Do More As You Do Less*, parents will seek to counter what David Elkind cites in *The Hurried Child* as the push for children to take on the "new freedoms" of adulthood too quickly, without the experience of age or adult guidance. In addition, relaxed parents live by and instill in their children what Smith calls "timeless principles" that guide them throughout life.

One reason to restrain the micromanagement is that it will not ensure a better behaved, happier, smarter, or socially integrated child. While most child experts do not fully discount the importance of parental involvement in a child's life, many doubt their long-term effects. In her 1998 book, *The Nurture Assumption: Why Children Turn Out the Way They Do*, Judith Rich Harris debunks the idea that "what influences children's development . . . is the way their parents bring them up." Instead, she claims that while caring treatment of children is important because it is humane, it does not determine future behavior. Instead, children are shaped, she says, by their genetic makeup and their life with their peers, particularly the peers encountered in the elementary school years.

Further, it makes sense over the long term for children to look to their peers for guidance in how to navigate the world. For the world will be theirs, not their parents'. As cited in Malcolm Gladwell's article "Do Parents Matter?," Boston College psychologist Peter Gray points to the evolutionary need for children to learn from their peers. He says, "[W]e tend, egocentrically, to believe that it is the relationship between us and our children that is important. But just look at them. Whom do they want to please? . . . And, from an evolutionary perspective, who should they be paying attention to? Their parents—the members of the previous generation—or their peers, who will be their future mates and future collaborators? It would be more adaptive for them to be better attuned to the nuances of their peers' behavior."

But even as parents stop trying to micromanage their children's lives into an Ivy league–bound ideal, there is little guarantee that the parents' lives will be any more relaxed. They will still be the parents. They will still worry. They will still want their children to live a better life than they had. And no matter how relaxed their parenting, they will still feel an emptiness in their lives once their children have gone and wonder if the children would have turned out better if they had heard Chopin around the house instead of Cher.

The Security Imperative

49 Since the attacks of September 11, 2001, America has been protecting itself. Within U.S. borders, this means watching its citizens. At airports, passengers are being screened and classified for degrees of security risk by U.S. Homeland Security workers. Those who want a faster check-in can be part of a prescreening that allows the airlines to check them against profiles in state and federal databases, or have their information shared with the FBI or the federal passenger identification system. In everyday terms, the quest for airport security means there is more waiting in line, removing shoes, and emptying suitcases. And it is just one of many levels of security.

Of far greater importance is the U.S. cabinet department that contains airport security programs—the Department of Homeland Security. Founded after 9/11, the homeland security department was meant to indicate the nation's attention to national security. Its $40 billion budget is aimed at devising and implementing various initiatives to fight terror.

Among these initiatives are color-coded alert levels, training for airport security employees, and intensified surveillance systems. To critics, the security measures have impinged on personal liberties. For example, in

2003, the FBI was found to have assembled information on the organization and practices of antiwar groups in the United States, reported the *New York Times*. FBI officials said the surveillance was intended as information gathering, while others considered it an attack on civil disobedience.

The Patriot Act, passed in 2001, was designed to protect Americans from its enemies by increasing the government's abilities to gather information on citizens in order to fight terrorism. Again, some citizen critics see the Act as an intrusion on their privacy. Among them are retailers who do not wish to be forced to share personal information on their customers with the government. To show their opposition to the Act, some merchants have by choice ceased to collect such information, which retailers could use to increase business.

Another outgrowth of 9/11 is the Joint Operations Command Center (JOCC). This surveillance facility is affiliated with several U.S. agencies, including the Secret Service and the Department of Defense. Its purpose is to link the closed-circuit cameras in various U.S. public facilities, like shopping malls and schools, if needed.

Aside from Homeland Security programs and airport security mandates, security measures are profligate and growing in everyday life. Americans maintain many of them on themselves and their neighbors, in forms such as home electronic fences, alarm systems, and for the socially insecure, gated communities. There are also the military-style sport utility vehicles, Jeeps, and Hummers.

Greater security moves are possible and could be implemented within a couple of years. They may include electronic identification cards that have various types of personal information encoded in them. These digital cards could include a person's driver's license, national identification number, or thumbprint. The electronic monitor within the card, which could be used for public transit or bridge-and-tunnel fares, could also track a person's travel path over an indefinite period of time (as New York's E-Z Pass does now for tunnel and bridge crossings). Otherwise, hand-held identification and weapon-seeking systems could be used by security guards and police stationed at public entrances. With such precautions, even the everyday errand of food or mall shopping would be made safer but more time consuming. Coats, car trunks, and packages may be checked by security guards as shoppers enter and exit.

To keep terrorists from coming near enough to a power plant or other source of widespread damage, there might also be various types of buffers. They could range from infrared cameras to heat sensors to physical barricades. According to the *New York Times*, a variation of this round-the-clock patrol system, USHomeGuard, has been proposed by Priceline.com founder Jay Walker. It uses Web technology and human monitors to track the nearly 50,000 strategic public facilities.

To further monitor individuals, the government may be able to use satellite technology to track everyone's e-mail and phone calls, or at least those who arouse national suspicion. It is also possible that it may create a domestic security agency, to track U.S. citizens suspected of terrorist actions.

But how much of the national budget is the government willing to approve? ($100 billion per year is one government-insider estimate.) Citizens may not approve a security tax increase, given current antitax sentiment. Champions of civil liberties have already voiced disapproval of the relaxing of surveillance laws under the Patriot Act. Other perceived intrusions on civil rights, such as a national identification card or national driver's license, may be fought from the grass-roots level.

In the name of security, 21st-century America has become a world of biometrics, government car monitoring, and business and government electronic databases. The days when a neighborhood cop provided protection are now an eon away.

Spam Wars

50 Once, e-mail was a breakthrough in communication. Now, because of spam, it is more of a breakdown. The electronic in-boxes of computer users everywhere are overloaded daily with unwanted ads for

pills, pornography, sex aids, debt relief programs, and get-rich-quick schemes. These unsolicited commercial e-mails, sent in bulk from mysterious sources, are spam—and a war is on to stop them.

Nearly 60 percent of all e-mail is now spam, according to the research firm Gartner Group. Though each individual spam message uses only tiny bits of computing power and time spent in hitting the delete key, the costs add up when multiplied by millions of e-mail users. Ferris Research estimates the total annual cost in productivity at $9 billion. Never mind the intangible costs—the assault to the sensibilities of prim grandmothers faced with risqué ads and the frustration of automatically deleting what you think is a spam message, only to find out it was an important business message.

The war to stop spam has begun and is likely to heat up in coming years. It is a war with many twists and turns—in fact, a series of wars. Every time the antispam forces add a new weapon, spammers find a way to evade it, if the weapon doesn't backfire first. Meanwhile, spammers develop their own new weapons to spread spam, prompting antispammers to develop new defenses.

Spam filter software is available that sifts through incoming e-mail and blocks spam. These programs typically work by looking for certain words, addresses, or other telltale signs of spam. But the filters have a bad habit of blocking some legitimate messages, and spammers have learned to evade filters by changing their messages—using subject lines, for example, that sound like they could be legitimate.

Another approach is a system that requires ID or proof before admitting an e-mail into one's in-box. An example is a challenge/response system, in which only mail from people in your address book is admitted directly into your in-box; other mail requires senders to solve a simple puzzle to verify that they are human beings and not computers. Unfortunately, this approach can block some legitimate mail, since computers sometimes issue mail that people want to receive, such as bank notices. A more long-term approach now under development by Internet standard-setting bodies, is to revise mail delivery codes so that Internet service providers (ISPs) can verify the source of incoming e-mail. That would probably take years to implement, and in the meantime spammers might develop ways around the new system.

Organizations exist that track down the worst perpetrators of spam and alert ISPs about them. The Spamhaus Project, for example, keeps dossiers on the 200 most prolific spammers and their addresses, and makes the information available to ISPs so they can screen out spam. But spammers have become adept at hiding their addresses, going so far as to disseminate viruses that can hijack the PCs of e-mail recipients, turning them into bulk e-mail generators operated by remote control. These zombie drones, or spam zombies, are a growing problem. In November 2003, *Newsweek* reported that in one semester Texas Christian University had four instances when its network was hijacked to send out mass quantities of spam. Such virus attacks are illegal, and antispammers can respond by bringing in law enforcement. But because of the difficulty of tracing the sources of the attacks, successful prosecution is unlikely.

Other battlefields of the spam wars include civil lawsuits and state and federal legislation. In one such lawsuit in 2002, spammer Alan Ralsky settled with Verizon for an undisclosed sum and agreed to stop spamming its customers. But suits often have limited success, because spammers can move on, changing their names and addresses to evade penalties and ducking to new jurisdictions around the world. Numerous states have enacted various kinds of bans on spam, but enforcement is difficult, and the laws are often vulnerable to constitutional challenge on grounds of interfering with free speech or interstate commerce. In 2003, the U.S. Congress passed its own antispam measure, but critics say the law was weakened by industry lobbying to the point where it will probably have little effect.

With collective antispam efforts so far unsuccessful, it's still every user for himself. Individual users try numerous tactics to avoid spam, from extreme wariness about giving out their e-mail address to using disposable e-mail addresses. Some people are going so far as to shift to communicating via a more primitive technology: the telephone. Yet, as long as people want to use e-mail, spammers will probably find ways to get to them. The spam wars roll on.

6

Marketing

Child Shoppers

51 The millennium generation may be young, but they are already shaping buying decisions. Also known as the echo boomers or the Y generation, they are currently nine to twenty-four years old. Not only are they not in their prime earning years, but most of them are minors who live with their parents as well. Yet, over the past several years, these children and young adults have come to strongly influence the spending of billions of dollars in nearly all areas of the economy. Some children spend their families' money directly: one-tenth of American children even have credit cards. In all, the market for American children from four to twelve years old is responsible for about $30 billion in spending annually, with the spending power of "'tweens," or eight- to twelve-year-olds, increasing the most dramatically.

The influence of American child shoppers on parents' purchases has been going on for decades, and according to the Web site Global Issues That Affect Everyone *(http://globalissues.org)*, the rate of that influence has grown rapidly since the mid-1980s. In 1984, it was worth about $50 billion; in 1990, it was $132 billion; in 1997, it was about $188 billion. Partly for that reason, advertisers spend about $2 billion per year advertising to young consumers, with food ads making up about half of all advertising aimed at kids.

Overall, according to the Center for a New American Dream, U.S. spending for advertising in 2002 was more than $230 billion. That meant advertisers spent an average of $2,190 per year to reach a household.

Much of it is on television, which, according to the American Medical Association, is watched by children for 12,000 to 18,000 hours during their childhood and teenage years. In all, children see about 20,000 TV commercials per year, or about one hour of commercials for every five hours of television watched, according to the Center for Media Education. As the amount of television a child watches increases, the more likely he or she is to believe advertising claims.

Having children pay attention to advertising is important to advertisers because they represent such a fruitful market. According to the nonprofit Center for Media Literacy, children comprise three markets in one. One is a current market that spends $4.2 billion per year of their own money. Another is a future market that can be pursued now. Finally, they are also a source of influence, leading adults to make purchases.

Because a child has so many lives as a consumer, major companies have made concerted efforts to teach children brand loyalty. One reason is that studies have shown that promoting brands to children when they are young works. Findings indicate that children begin to recognize product brands at about eighteen months of age. So companies like McDonald's that engage consumers at a young age and keep them for life prove the staying power of brands. Even brands for items children will not purchase until adulthood, such as Dell Computers or Cheerios, become commonly known and trusted in childhood. As noted by Richard Lutz, professor of marketing at the University of Florida, children often follow their parents' product preferences.

Increasingly, companies target part of their product lines to children. Among the many dozens of companies trolling for children with targeted products are Heinz with green and purple ketchup, baby clothes from Harley-Davidson, and children's biographies from the Arts & Entertainment channel. Publishers have also appealed to the youth market with young people's editions of magazines such as *Time, Sports Illustrated*, and *People*. General Motors, for example, is gauging the desires of future drivers by inviting schoolchildren to their showrooms for opinion-gathering sessions on what they think about GM cars.

Companies also try to reach children through schools, even preschools. They sponsor textbooks and field trips, and supply school lunch food, thus insinuating themselves into children's lives. Science-oriented companies sponsor science classes that introduce their brand-name products. Companies that have sponsored classes or field trips include Toys "R" Us, Sports Authority, and Oral-B.

Countering this media deluge are independent nonprofit educational watchdog groups such as the Center for Media Literacy. One of the Center's goals is to "help citizens, especially the young, develop critical thinking and [other] skills needed to live . . . in the 21st century media culture." Among its programs are studies of the messages of modern culture.

The result of this advertising overload in children is a sophisticated product awareness and increased desire for consumption. Dan Cook, assistant professor of advertising and sociology at the University of Illinois, believes that "The children's market works because it lives off of deeply-held beliefs about self-expression and freedom of choice." He adds, "Kids not only want things, but have acquired the socially sanctioned right to want. . . . Childhood makes capitalism hum over the long haul."

In 1929, President Herbert Hoover sponsored a White House Conference on Child Health and Protection. The conference reported that children were independent beings with interests of their own, and that children should be given their own items and furniture to form a sense of self-definition. Nearly a century later, millions of children spend billions of dollars creating what President Hoover called their "self-definition."

Comfort Brands

52 As change comes even more quickly in the 21st century, some Americans will seek solace in the familiar. Especially for aging consumers (read baby boomers and generation X), this means products that were well known in their youth. Because some of these brands have already died a natural death, savvy businesspeople have and will continue to resuscitate the brand. In some cases, the relaunched products are reimagined as they once were; in other cases, they are repackaged in new forms that match current packaging preferences. But the taste, texture, or original label elements are left unchanged. These elements are what distinguish the product and allow them to conjure up an unfettered youth.

The brand-revival process has been going on for over a decade, as baby boomers saw their youth slipping away. Brands that were reborn in the 1990s included the Volkswagen Beetle and Burma-Shave shaving cream; resurrected icons included Starkist Tuna's Charlie the Tuna and the hourglass-shaped Coca-Cola bottle (but in plastic rather than glass). Similarly, General Motors's Buick line of automobiles has been reimagined for the 21st century (but the Oldsmobile, the nation's oldest car, has been discontinued). Says futurist Watts Wacker, coauthor of *The 500-Year Delta*, "We . . . don't know what's going to happen. So we need some warm fuzzies from our past."

One entrepreneur, Jeffrey Himmel, has resurrected several lost brands to great success. Jeffrey Himmel has saturated the market with inexpensive advertisements that bring back memories and has reintroduced products including Gold Bond medicated powder and Ovaltine chocolate drink mix, the antacid Bromo-Seltzer, and Breck shampoo.

Rescuing old brands extends further than lunch-box food and beauty aids. It extends to alcoholic beverages. Some long-established beers have been revived by entirely new demographic groups than the ones that made them famous. Old Milwaukee, Pabst Blue Ribbon, and Falls City Beer were once low-cost blue-collar choices in their cities or regions. Now they are embraced by young adults who view them as unpretentious and anticommercial. Like their fellow frugal drinkers of past decades, the hip crowd who rediscovered the beers now drink them because they are cheap.

Retro-based toys will continue to have appeal, particularly for adults. For example, in 2002, over 25 percent of holiday sales of Star Wars toys were for adults. Similarly, high percentages of adult sales are common for some types of Barbie dolls and the Magic-8 ball. And once-familiar regional brands like Moxie, Bubble Up, and Nehi are available to adults through specialized Web sites like www.realsoda.com. At high-toned but cozy retro-candy stores in shopping malls and big cities, familiar candies such as Pixy Stix and bubble gum cigarettes are taking a growing portion of the multimillion-dollar candy market: "It brings back memories of being a kid," said one Midwestern candy store customer.

But all is not well on Memory Lane. Says James Lileks, syndicated columnist and author of *The Gallery of Regrettable Food*, Americans may run through their memorable brands faster than they can relive them: "If contemporary pop culture becomes so saturated with retro references that they become the dominant cultural signifier today, what will we be nostalgic about in 20 years?" Look to the Brand Lab, a University of Illinois think tank that specializes in the study of resuscitating old brands. It says that there are five criteria that designate whether a product is ready for revival, including uniqueness, reputation, and strong brand equity. Then it takes the right entrepreneur to take it under the wing and a public that still wants to relive its happy past.

Diversity Marketing

53 In the 1990s, corporate market planners refined the strategy of selling to an array of markets according to lifestyles. This could mean everything from age to sex to college affiliation to political preference. In the early 21st century and in the foreseeable future, the standard for segmented marketing is diversity marketing, or selling to ethnic segments.

A main goal for the 21st century is reaching the African-American, Hispanic, and Asian populations, which grew nearly four times as fast as the white population in the 1980s and 1990s, and whose combined buying power is $1 trillion.

Retailers and other businesses know that Asian-Americans, African-Americans, Hispanic-Americans, and other groups have billions to spend, and will do so if they are reached in the right way. To the marketer, it means understanding the basic beliefs the groups hold dear and translating them to how they present and sell their products, many of which are basic commodities like homes, clothing, and automobiles.

Each of the three groups differs in their shopping preferences according to demographics and their attitudes toward shopping. These differences in shopping preferences define the groups as consumers more than does race. While each group may favor certain types of items or stores, they make their overarching choices according to age and economics.

Hispanics

Already the largest minority in the United States, Hispanics represented one in eight of U.S. inhabitants in 2000 and are projected to be one of three by 2100. Their spending power is immense. According to the University of Georgia's Selig Center for Economic Growth, Hispanics control about $580 billion in spending power. This amount is projected to grow to $1 trillion within five years. According to the 2002 U.S. Census, the Hispanic community in the United States is the fastest-growing demographic group in the country. By 2007, the numbers of Hispanics in the United States is expected to reach 44.1 million, or 14.6 percent of the population.

Hispanics extend across the social spectrum, from U.S.-born Hispanics who are completely familiar with the English language to Hispanics born outside the United States who primarily speak Spanish. A 2003 CBS News study noted that U.S.-born Hispanics overwhelmingly listen to mostly English broadcasts (81 percent), while most foreign-born Hispanics (56 percent) listen to mostly Spanish TV and radio.

To reach these various groups, marketers offer sales materials in Spanish and English, depending on the economic level of consumers they want to reach. Many businesses including major insurers such as Blue Cross and Blue Shield and Humana, Inc., offer materials in both languages. Health care companies also hire Hispanic representatives to sell health insurance to Hispanics.

Hispanics have also greatly increased their home ownership in the past decades and have become a prime market for real estate sellers. Hispanic home ownership rates increased from 42 percent in 1990 to 46 percent in 2000. Realtors have spoken of drawing on what they perceive as feelings of devotion to family to establish working relationships marked by closeness and loyalty.

Family closeness is also a consideration for pharmaceutical firms marketing to Hispanics. Given that Hispanic children are often involved in the medical care of parents, pharmaceutical executives speak of a multigenerational reach with drug sales.

Simpler elements of everyday life are being retooled for the Hispanic market. Avon has created new color schemes, McDonald's has Spanish-language advertisements, and Häagen-Dazs has created its own version of the Spanish ice cream flavor favorite, *dulce de leche*.

African-Americans

African-Americans, who represent 12 percent of the U.S. population, have $300 billion spending power and an increasing representation in the middle class. As of 1999 Census numbers, 25.2 percent of married African-Americans nationwide had incomes between $50,000 and $74,999; 22.6 percent of the married couples had incomes over $75,000.

According to the U.S. Bureau of Labor Statistics, African-Americans currently have greater representation in professions including accounting, engineering, computer programming, law, medicine, journalism, and management. They buy 21 percent of automobiles and watch more television than the general population.

Marketers also wish to increase African-American use of computer technology and the Internet, which now accounts for 10 percent of computer users with home computers. "If you're wired today, you can get the juice to control your destiny," said musician and composer Quincy Jones at a 2002 national technology conference in Chicago.

Asian-Americans

According to the handbook published by the Asian American Journalists Association called "All American: How to Cover Asian America," Asian-Americans have been viewed in media coverage as the eternal outsider. Yet, according to the 2000 Census, Asian-Americans are a highly desired marketing target. Census findings indicate that as a group they are better educated than average Americans and will account for the fastest increase in buying power from 1990 to 2007, at 287 percent. This places its projected growth much higher than the United States as a whole, which is 131 percent. Already the 2000 Census notes that Asian-Americans and Pacific Islanders had a median income of $55,521 as compared to $42,148 for all races. Further, according to a 2003 study by Forester Research, Asian-Americans are a highly desired market group because of the youth and wealth of its buyers. Currently, they represent the leading ethnic group for online shopping. On average, they make six purchases per year, while Hispanic-Americans make three online purchases per year and African-Americans 1.8 purchases per year.

Every ethnic group has its preferences, but all are part of the great U.S. marketing machine, and businesses and advertising firms will become more adept at reaching these markets. They have what businesses want—money to spend.

Personal Advertising, or Mass Customization

54 As technological advances allow American consumers to control how they get their goods and culture, advertisers try to stay a step ahead. On the Internet and on television, advertisers will tailor their ads to match their target audiences, much as some cable TV outlets do already. Soon Internet and television outlets will be able to amass enough information to individualize their pitches to each subscriber. For consumers, these electronic advertisers will do the grunt work: they consult a client's list of needs and offer customized items. A personalized advertiser can look over a client's shoulder and shop for him or her. Personalized advertising represents a new way to build a business. One home-furnishings executive called the amassing of personal information a way to create a "customer relationship management system . . . a set of policies and procedures that guides all the interactions between the store staff and the customers or the prospects."

Each form of electronic communication uses a different approach to reach consumers, and much of it is in use in some form already. For example, advertisers on cable TV access customers through the set-top box or the video-on-demand server. Their software is placed in the server and collects information on the income and composition of the household subscriber. Using this information, advertisers can adjust the images and message of an advertisement to match the subscriber's level of interest in a product.

On the Internet, companies will use a variety of one-to-one Web applications to reach desired customers. One software technology allows cable and satellite operators to profile and deliver individually targeted commercial advertisements. The software will identify individuals the advertisers wants to reach based on specific demographic, psychographic, and purchasing habits that the advertiser wants to capitalize on. It will then organize the viewers into groups that will get certain commercials according to the desires of the advertiser.

Through software applications, companies will be able to build personalized communities online to which they can send specialized content and advertisements. Some companies, such as Amazon.com, already use individualized audience targeting to increase sales. Banks and other financial institutions are introducing a new sales medium to automatic teller machines (ATMs). It collects data on the user's holdings and navigation practices on the Web to offer product recommendations during the screen time once marked "Please wait . . ." Another e-mail personalization application uses a rules-based "personalization engine" and the company's Web content management system to target individuals and assess the content of e-mail messages. This procedure helps marketers and advertisers create e-mail newsletters and promotions.

Technology to deliver personalized advertisements over wireless telephones is also being introduced. According to mobic.com, the technology "is expected to enhance the consumer experience by giving users more control over the advertising and offers they receive."

All of these personalized online advertising techniques adhere to basic concepts of advertising. As outlined by online advertising company Avenue A, they involve using the marketing to drive sales online and offline, advertising along all digital channels, continuously updating campaigns, building the brand being sold, and understanding how consumer attitudes and choices are intertwined.

While these technological changes redefine marketing, consumer groups and the government will counter with measures to protect consumers' privacy. But even as laws may be implemented, the consumer world is likely to be besotted with personalized electronic advertisements and entreaties. The view, according to forecasters, is likely to resemble that of Steven Spielberg's movie *Minority Report*, where talking billboards call out personalized messages as you walk by. That's e-novation. It's the personalized marketing that Rob Carscadden, president and chief operating officer of the marketing technology company Zaq Interactive Solutions, Inc., calls a shift in advertising away from mass media toward "a personalized direct marketing model."

Selling to Venus and Mars

55 Men and women may be as different as Venus and Mars, but they have at least one common thread: they buy things. Yet the game is no longer as simple as selling men powerful cars and women pretty-colored ones. Now both sexes have independent interests and separate sources of money. Learning how the genders buy and how to reach them will continue as one of the major areas of interest for ever-eager sellers.

As the 21st century began, marketing visionaries saw the future in selling to women. In her book (with Lys Marigold) *EVEolution: The Eight Truths of Marketing to Women*, marketing guru Faith Popcorn said that selling to women should not just constitute a niche interest. It should be, as she wrote in *USA Today* in 2000, "a benchmark for virtually all business decisions made today." Supporting her position were the findings that women either buy or influence the purchase of 80 percent of all consumer goods, purchase half of all cars and personal computers, and account for nearly half of stock owners. They also buy 75 percent of all over-the-counter drugs and influence even more (80 percent) of health care decisions. It was time, Popcorn suggests, to rise above fears of gender stereotyping and sell to women what they want to buy and how they want to buy it. Business futurist Tom Peters concurred. He said that beginning in the late 1990s, "[w]omen are Opportunity Number One for the foreseeable future."

To sell to women successfully, Popcorn suggests understanding the ways women buy differently from men. It means developing an all-encompassing sales approach that fits a woman's multilayered life. It means picking up on a woman's ability to juggle various elements of life and do various tasks at once. Other marketers point to another factor that drives women's buying patterns: saving time. "Women aren't just busy—they are time starved," says Martha Barletta, president of Trend-Sight Group. Because the majority of women ages twenty-five to fifty-four are expected to be employed, they will seek everyday services that allow them to save time. In a supermarket, for example, this approach includes features that streamline the grocery-pharmacy experience, such as pharmacy-like health testing, wider selections of organic foods, in-store prepared meals, and an all-day fruit/salad/homemade smoothie bar. The time-starved, stressed-out female consumer also desires such conveniences as the incorporation of mini-massage parlors, banks, and mailing centers in supermarkets.

Online, women browse more than men and tend to build relation-ships via online chats with sales staff and customer service at favorite sites. Men, on the other hand, reports Bernadette Tracy, president and founder of NetSmart America, are more likely to survey entertainment, business listings, and news. For online shopping, they are more likely to target and buy a desired item rather than shop at several sites for a variety of choices.

According to various sales performance experts, male consumers seek a direct sale from a salesperson who shows credentials and exudes confidence in and knowledge of the product. Most male buyers want a salesperson who gets to the point quickly, with little emotion and some humor. The male buyer who becomes impatient because of the store, online site, or salesperson, leaves and does not buy.

Yet, reports of the vast gulf between male and female shoppers may be exaggerated, at least for the younger generation. According to a study done by WSL Strategic Retail, a global marketing and retailing consulting firm, there is no longer a gender-based difference in the way men and women ages eighteen and thirty-four shop. The WSL Strategic Retail study "How America Shops 2002" detailed the similarities between men and women who are under thirty-five, such as younger men and women making nearly the same amount of shopping trips per week (3.6 for men, 4.1 for women). Perhaps most surprisingly, more young men than women are going to department stores—22 percent of men versus 16 percent of women—and 29 percent of men versus 18 percent of women go to malls.

The WSL report suggests that this newfound male familiarity with shopping is fueled by a generation of liberated mothers who expected their sons to learn to shop for themselves. In so doing, they learned to navigate the malls, grocery stores, and brand names of everything from cereals to jeans. The result is a generation of men who are involved consumers. To marketers, says WSL, young men are "the new generation of untapped shoppers." In Faith Popcorn–speak, it is Hevolution.

The Supersized Life

56 Thanks to the nation's bounty, Americans are living the supersized life. Big Gulps, big agriculture, and big food companies have changed the American diet. Big price tags on big cars and exotic goods let the rich or rich wannabes live the supersized consumer life. Small is not beautiful.

First and foremost, America has embraced the supersize diet. Supersized food portions of all types have changed the caloric standard across America. One reason for this situation is the superfast lifestyle. Working families with heavy social and business commitments don't have time to prepare meals at home from scratch. To save time, fast food comes to the rescue. In the 21st century, fast food, which is supersized in many ways— big portions, packed with fat and calories, and supereasy to eat—has become standard fare for working families. Further, there is perceived added value in purchasing fast-food outlet combination meals (such as the McDonald's Extra Value Meal) or upgrading the size of the soft drink.

While the increase in price may be slight, the increase in calories is steep. What's more, when there is more to eat, people comply. Larger portions show up in more calories consumed per person. Since 1977, the average daily calorie intake of Americans has increased by more than 10 percent. That means about 200 more calories per person per day, which translates (for those who don't expend extra energy to burn the calories up) to an additional twenty-one pounds per year.

The additional pounds lead to weight-related health problems such as heart problems and diabetes. Not only do these ailments affect life span, their treatment often ends up being paid by American taxpayers, who subsidize or pay for parts of the health system. According to a recent World Health Organization (WHO) report, health care costs due to obesity have reached $75 billion—and U.S. taxpayers picked up about half of the bill. If the trend toward supersizing continues to increase, the costs will also grow. In *USA Today*, Anne Wolf of the University of Virginia Medical School says, "As the population ages and the prevalence of obesity continues to rise, Medicare is going to be picking up the health care tab for these people." Already the annual medical spending attributable to weight-related health problems is about 9.1 percent of national medical costs.

Where does the low-cost, high-fat fast food come from? Its source, at least in part, is subsidized farming. According to an article for the *New York Times Magazine*, Michael Pollan says that the underlying problem of too much processed food is "agricultural overproduction." He says the government is "doing its best to make matters even worse, by recklessly . . . [subsidizing] . . . farmers to produce even more unneeded food."

Countering this seemingly unstoppable expansion are several forces, some large-scale, some personal. Michael Pollan suggests employing farm subsidies for their original use, which was to "solve the problem of overproduction." As Pollan noted, farm subsidies introduced under President Franklin Roosevelt in the 1930s were meant to control production and thus keep the farm market from collapsing. At the time, surplus grain was kept off the market. Such a program, Pollan posits, could be used to stem American overproduction.

The courts are also emerging as a battleground against supersizing of foods, particularly of those high in fat and calories. Although, according to Fox News online, a federal judge dismissed the class action lawsuit filed on behalf of New York children claiming McDonald's food caused health problems such as diabetes, high blood pressure, and obesity, McDonald's itself suggested dangers in the supersized food. During the proceedings, McDonald's said that processing (often with crops produced in supersize quantities) "creates an entirely different and more dangerous food."

Meanwhile, the supersized consumer lifestyle beyond food is also going strong. Retail analysts reported that for the 2003 holiday season, discount stores' sales lagged, while high-end retailers like Tiffany's surged. Even as the economy was not fully recovered, buyers bought supersized luxury items like South Sea pearls, Hummers, and $1,000 champagne. Maybe their luxury shopping is subsidized by low-cost supersizing at supermarket and fast-food stops—not to mention bulk buying at the big box stores along the five-lane highway. The supersized life is built on excess, of which there is no end.

Teleshopping for Everything

57 First it was catalog ordering by phone. Then it was buying online. Shopping outside the box (be it a mall or department store) has become mainstream. And it is growing. According to Forrester Research, some 63 million U.S. households will buy online by 2008, which is double the 34 million households buying online in 2002. Global Internet shopping has grown massively as well. According to a Drexel University study, it has increased by over 100 percent annually, from $35 billion in 1998 to over $3 trillion in 2003. The trend is so deep and transformative that Internet experts and authors of *The Age of E-Tail: Conquering the New World of Electronic Shopping*, Philipp Gerbet, Dick Schneider, and Alex Birch, call the age of Web retailing a golden period of exploration comparable to the Age of Discovery in the 15th century.

Reasons for the popularity of Internet shopping and the behaviors it generates are ongoing subjects of interest. According to a study by the London Business School and the University of California, Irvine, working women are likely to turn to electronic shopping as a way to make more time for maintenance and discretionary activities—activities they can't or don't want to do online, usually done away from home. For while electronic shoppers may order food and other necessities online, they are likely to continue to travel outside the home for maintenance activities such as children's school-related programs or medical visits. The overall rate of shopping is also likely to increase, says the report, despite the time-saving electronic shopping. People will still shop for escape and for entertainment, which is how people traditionally viewed the act of shopping.

In the future, grocery buying on the Internet will become commonplace, say researchers. Currently, it is more of a novelty than a standard practice, with delivery systems and lack of availability getting in the way. But according to a study by the Institute for Horticultural Development in Victoria, Australia, the baby boomers' hectic family schedule resulting in an inability to balance work and leisure schedules, followed by a senior lifestyle marked by isolation and lack of transportation will result in higher home food deliveries. According to the study, "The growth in electronic communications services linked to new food categories such as 'home meal replacements' are expected to also contribute to the growth in home shopping in the U.S."

Some attempts at online "shopping" have been aimed at the improvement of society. For example, at the turn of the century, Santa Monica, California, leaders attempted to increase voter participation with an interactive computer terminal system that allowed citizens to discuss public affairs online with each other and with elected officials. Over the first few years, the system has not been widely used, yet those who did use it may have had an effect on city policy on homelessness. More study with such systems is needed to improve their appeal to a wider citizenry.

Public and private Internet shopping sources are faced with the same concern: how to reach the audience. This need will prompt Internet marketing improvements. The aim will be to make the experience as similar as possible to an in-store encounter with a knowledgeable salesperson. To that end, various softwares are available to companies to create online stores, with product displays and demonstrations similar to a store. An increasing number of sites even offer real-time human assistance. To do that, online sites have had to develop varied examples of customer models, from inexperienced to highly knowledgeable; fast downloading of information; and forms of interaction that reflect the customers' interests. According to the Drexel University study, such refinements in the shopping experience will allow online shopping eventually to overtake traditional on-site shopping. "[T]he dominance of electronic purchasing is inevitable," the study says, and retailers have to change to fit it. "Internet marketing," it says, "must be like a smart-missile that can anticipate and intercept the consumer's product searches." In all, the dominance of e-retailing is supposed to make us partake in a "new e-lifestyle age that will enable people to be more social, recreational, and fulfilled."

In the age of at-home Internet shopping, one product that has been a perennial flop might finally take off. It is the videophone, which allows the receiving and transmitting of either live or recorded audio and video signals. With it, you and the Lands' End operator, for example, can look at each other while placing an order, thus restoring the social interaction that at-home Internet shopping might have taken away.

7

Politics

Asymmetrical Warfare

58 At the height of the Cold War, Americans had no problem picturing what a direct attack on the United States would look like. A roughly comparable superpower—the Soviet Union—would strike us with intercontinental ballistic missiles more or less as sophisticated as ours. This would have been symmetrical warfare, in which the enemy would have been essentially a mirror image of us. But when a direct attack on the United States finally came on September 11, 2001, the enemy turned out to be radically asymmetrical: nineteen hijackers armed with knives and box cutters. With such low-tech instruments our own technology (passenger airplanes) was turned against us, killing 3,000 individuals on American soil in a single day. Americans had entered the Age of Asymmetrical Warfare.

In one sense, asymmetrical warfare is as ancient as history. It has been at work anytime a force of insurgents or raiders has used crude weapons and guerrilla tactics to harass and undermine a more numerous and better-equipped enemy. What is different about the Age of Asymmetrical Warfare is that unconventional tactics, whose effectiveness was once limited to regional or civil conflicts, are now being used by foreign enemies to challenge the world's greatest powers on their own turf. Those enemies range from "rogue" states such as North Korea and Iran, who refuse to play by the rules of the present-day international system, to shadowy nonstate organizations such as Al Qaeda, which launch terrorist attacks against civilian and military targets. Despite being far weaker in population, wealth, and technology than their First World adversaries, they inspire fear and influence policy by being determined, ruthless, inventive, and hard to destroy. Asymmetrical warfare is also known as fourth-generation warfare, or 4GW, according to a theory of how it has succeeded three previous stages of combat: classical, industrial, and maneuver warfare.

Present-day asymmetrical forces are hard to counter for a variety of reasons. Some leaders of rogue states, because of their insularity and peculiar ideologies, seem bizarrely deaf to the appeals to rational self-interest that deter other regimes—for example, promises of aid and threats of sanctions. Even when invaded, such regimes have proven capable of surviving in insurgent form to make life miserable for the invading armies—as Saddam Hussein loyalists did after the United States invaded Iraq. Some asymmetrical forces, such as Al Qaeda, might be organizations that have no single homeland that can be invaded, thus they are able to hide effectively from the militaries or police forces pursuing them. And some are fanatics, like the suicidal 9/11 hijackers associated with Al Qaeda, who actively seek death in service to their cause.

Whatever the reasons, asymmetrical forces are hard to wipe out and are increasingly more dangerous. Every technological advance the developed world creates—from nuclear weapons to shoulder-launched missiles to poison gas to weaponized anthrax—is one more weapon that asymmetrical forces can turn against it. Even the fast-moving circuits of the Internet may become a terrorist weapon, if hackers succeed in sabotaging vital systems. The damage from such a "cyberwar" or "e-jihad" may range from a day's inconvenience to global apocalypse.

The Age of Asymmetrical Warfare is driving government policy worldwide, and nowhere more than in the United States. It has already sparked two U.S. wars: the 2001 invasion of Afghanistan in search of Osama bin Laden and other perpetrators of 9/11; and the 2003 invasion of Iraq to overthrow Saddam's regime on the theory that it might be developing weapons of mass destruction and might have links to Al Qaeda. The military itself is changing in response to the Asymmetrical Age. Los Alamos National Laboratory's *Research Quarterly* reports that asymmetrical warfare has fueled a transition to a "lighter, more-flexible military, one that relies less on overwhelming numbers . . . and more on stealth, rapid response, and precision weaponry."

Asymmetrical warfare has also shaped foreign policy, driving the formulation of the Bush Doctrine, with its proviso permitting the United States to launch pre-emptive wars. It has also led to stronger links with Britain and weaker ones with France and Germany, on account of their respective stances toward the Iraq war. At home, the Age of Asymmetrical Warfare gave birth to a new cabinet department of Homeland Security and the Patriot Act, with its controversial curbs on civil liberties and numerous security measures, from federalization of airport security to a color-coded system of terrorist alerts.

For the most part, the United States is conducting asymmetrical warfare the way a big power might be expected to, by using all the advantages of its size and wealth. But even big powers can benefit from fielding their own asymmetrical forces. In Afghanistan and Iraq, U.S. Special Forces crept in small numbers behind enemy lines to play important roles: advising and supporting indigenous rebels; gathering intelligence; capturing or killing enemy leaders; and calling in surgical air strikes to take out targets.

Of course, many voices have been critical of how the United States is adapting to the Age of Asymmetrical Warfare. According to some of these schools of thought, the United States should combat terrorism through means such as international police investigations and being a good global neighbor rather than full-scale war. This kind of debate is likely to continue for some time—as will the Age of Asymmetrical Warfare that sparked the debate.

China Rising

59 The rise of China is "perhaps the most important long-term trend in the world," *New York Times* columnist Nicholas D. Kristof wrote in 2002. It has been a trend long in coming: twenty years earlier,

John Naisbitt in *Megatrends* (1982) noted "the recent emergence of China as a new contender in manufacturing." Today, China is the world's sixth largest economy, the scheduled host of the 2008 Olympics, and, after a long campaign, a member of the World Trade Organization. China, although not yet a superpower, is rapidly advancing in the wealth, capabilities, and prestige that make for elite status.

China's strength stems partly from its population, which, at 1.3 billion, is the world's largest. It also stems from a dedication to free enterprise that has been growing for a quarter-century, ever since Deng Xiaoping came to power in the late 1970s. Although China's leadership is nominally Communist, its commitment to market reforms has helped put the nation's economy in overdrive. China's annual output is growing at a double-digit pace, faster than any other major economy. Foreign investors are flocking in. The country has far outstripped India, its similarly sized neighbor and once-close economic rival. According to the World Bank, in 2002, the average Chinese citizen earned $890 a year, compared to $460 for the average Indian. The profits from all that growth are distributed unequally, with the urban coastal areas reaping the most from the boom, yet the standard of living is rising even in the rural interior.

China's newfound power is also rooted in a commitment to science and technology that is evident in the background of its president, Hu Jintao, trained as a hydrologist. China has had nuclear weapons for nearly four decades, and also has satellites and intercontinental ballistic missiles. But it is growing scientifically in other ways. Its space program, which launched a man into space in 2003, is valued for its military and industrial potential as well as scientific aspects. In addition, it is developing a biotechnology sector, partly thanks to its willingness to permit experiments forbidden by U.S. regulation.

Despite all its progress, China does not yet rank as a global behemoth on the level of the United States, which has been the world's sole superpower since the collapse of the Soviet Union. It is a regional power, jockeying with Japan for influence in East Asia. It recovered Hong Kong from Great Britain in 1997 and Macao from Portugal in 1999, and is perennially looking to regain complete sovereignty over Taiwan.

Yet, it has one major weakness: the mismatch between its authoritarian system of government, inherited from Communism, and the freedom and openness associated with Western-style economic growth.

As the standard of living rises in China and people grow used to competing on the global market, the Chinese people are increasingly prone to be frustrated with the pace of political change and to view their Communist leaders as irrelevant. The gap between rich and poor is growing, and social services are woefully inadequate, increasing the potential for unrest. The government tends to be secretive and slow to respond to popular needs, as notable in its handling of both the AIDS and SARS epidemics. Despite popular frustration, full-scale democratization remains elusive. China's leadership showed in the Tiananmen Square massacre of 1989 that it would crack down when faced with the possibility of overthrow, and it has remained ruthless with dissidents ever since. It is also as ready as ever to restrict the flow of information: as recently as 2003, China unilaterally edited Hillary Clinton's memoir, *Living History*, to remove unflattering passages.

However, in many ways, the opening of China's society is already underway. The Internet and global communications make it possible for news of the real world to reach China. A poll in 2002 revealed that 80 percent of Chinese want to elect their officials directly. Faced with growing discontent, in 2003 the Communist Party pledged more help for the poor and further market reforms.

Provided that political instability does not derail China's economic growth, it will continue to climb in global stature. As China becomes more powerful, it will increasingly come into conflict with the world's only superpower, the United States. China will increasingly try to increase its influence in East Asia not only commercially, but militarily as well—for example, by developing a modern navy with regional and global reach. This trend, too, has been long in coming. According to a 1997 Defense Department report, "China's long-term goal is to become one of the world's great powers. Its leaders envision that, at some point during the first half of the twenty-first century, China will be securely established as the leading . . . political power in East Asia."

There have been numerous moments of tension between the United States and China in recent years: the accidental NATO bombing of the Chinese embassy in Belgrade, Yugoslavia; the alleged Chinese stealing of U.S. nuclear secrets; the forcing down of a U.S. spy plane in China. Yet, hot war between China and the United States is unlikely: both have nuclear weapons and would stand to lose too much in a nuclear exchange. A prolonged cold war, like the one that prevailed for decades between the United States and the Soviet Union, is a possibility, but unlikely given the integration of both countries into the global market. There will be mutual suspicion, jockeying for power, perhaps even saber rattling. But in the end, the desire to make money from each other is likely to keep China and the United States at peace with each other—especially if China's government succeeds in becoming more open and responsive to its people.

Disunited Europe

60 Europe has been heading in the direction of greater union since shortly after the Second World War. But recent events have raised roadblocks on the path to union. The power of globalization will keep propelling the integration of Europe's economy, but policy divisions will probably keep Europe more politically splintered than was once expected.

The European Union (EU) emerged in 1993 from the European Community, which in turn had its origins in the post–World War II restructuring of western Europe. The vision of the European Union was to cooperate not only in advancing free trade, but in a number of other areas, including a common currency, shared foreign and security policies, and domestic and justice matters. With the addition of new members in the 1990s, the European Union represented fifteen countries, forming an economic behemoth with a larger population and larger total output of goods and services than the United States.

The most prominent symbol of European unity is the euro, which became the common currency of twelve countries on January 1, 2002. But the euro is also a symbol of the disunity that persists despite the grandiose dreams of United Europe, because three European Union members—the United Kingdom, Denmark, and Sweden—have chosen not to use the new currency. Even those who do use it don't always follow the economic rules: France and Germany have been criticized for maintaining larger budget deficits than permitted under EU rules. In general, hard times breed dissension, and times have been somewhat hard in the EU. Since 2000, the economy of the twelve countries using the euro has averaged growth of only about 1 percent a year.

Another sign of continuing disunity was the split over whether to support U.S. military intervention in Iraq in 2003. Britain supported the United States; France and Germany opposed—and no amount of talk could bridge the two sides. The issue was not only whether to support this particular war, but what the role of Europe should be in the post–Cold War world. France and Germany were determined to lead Europe into striking an independent stance from the United States, whereas Britain was sticking to the old Anglo-American alliance. Meanwhile, the United States was further dividing Europe by signing up support from eastern European nations—countries that want to be part of the European Union but also want to stay on the Americans' good side.

Yet another sign of trouble was the failure at a summit on December 13, 2003, to settle on a constitution for the European Union. Again, there were substantial divisions between the bloc of states organized around France and Germany versus those aligned with the United States. The picture presented was of a Europe not of unity but subcommunities, in which some cliques agree to do things one way while others go another way.

None of these signs of disunity are indications that the European Union is in danger of ending. Ten new members are joining on May 1, 2004, raising the number of members to twenty-five. The economic benefits of a European free-trade zone remain great, as does the economic muscle that results from common action. In December 2003, threats of economic sanctions by the European Union persuaded the Bush administration to abandon disputed steel tariffs. Economically, Europe will continue to strive for unity. Politically, disunity is likely to continue.

Exurban Voters

61 On the suburban frontier lie the exurban voters, and they are changing the country. Not only are they exploding the population in once rural, lightly populated areas like Frederick County, Maryland, and Douglas County, Colorado, they have also established new voting allegiances and are determining elections. As of the early 21st century, they and the Republican Party are singing the same song. Both are calling, "Cut taxes and don't mess with my SUV."

The exurbs have been growing since the 1980s, after international businesses began moving some of their offices outside the city. Before the 1980s, reports Robert Lang, a demographer at Virginia Tech, only one-fourth of businesses were established away from the city. But in the 1990s, it became commonplace to see office parks and other business headquarters being built in far suburban areas. As companies built the exurban work sites, their employees followed and set up shop in nearby towns.

Exurbanites are distinguished, says demographer Lang (in the *New York Times*), by a populace that does not have to commute to, live in, or visit the city. Because they work in an office park in New Jersey, Maryland, or Colorado, they don't have the exposure to the usual urban concerns (crime, need to maintain old infrastructure, constant demand for social services) that city dwellers or even commuters do.

Instead, their concerns revolve around comfort and space, and how to maintain them. Generally, exurbanites want to keep their towns from becoming too crowded, as they have seen happen in suburbs closer to the city, but they don't mind the benefits that strip-mall development (especially with national brand-stores) can bring. One government expenditure they approve of is roads so they can travel to work faster. But they don't want higher taxes to get it.

In the 21st century, these middle-class desires for maintenance rather than change have been answered by the Republican Party. The effects of exurban voters to swing close elections to Republicans in 2002 is proof of the Republicans' appeal. In Maryland, Democratic candidate for governor Kathleen Kennedy Townsend lost to Republican Bob Ehrlich largely due to his command of the outlying exurban Harford and Frederick counties. Similarly, in Georgia, incumbent Democrat Max Cleland lost to Republican Saxby Chambliss for the Senate seat in Georgia when Chambliss swept the exurban Forsyth and Gwinnett counties. Similar Republican wins occurred in Colorado and elsewhere.

Because of demographic shifts, an increase in population, and the forcing of the suburban limit ever outward, exurban voters are sure to build their power base. But, according to some prognosticators, eventually the Democratic Party will overrun the Republican Party in these geographic areas. In their book, *The Emerging Democratic Majority*, Ruy Teixeira and John B. Judis determine that social and demographic changes over the next few years will shift voters toward the Democratic Party. The new Democratic Party will be different from its New Deal and Great Society incarnations, which centered its energies on serving workers in an industrial economy. Instead, according to Teixeira, it will be more heterogeneous and in tune with the needs of the service economy. It will be "the party of the post-industrial future."

The Democratic Party will draw its support from workers in what Teixeira calls "ideopolises," which are the cities and suburbs "organized around the production of ideas and services." These areas are peopled by lawyers, other professional workers, low-level service and information workers, nurses, teachers, and union members, as opposed to the urban wage and assembly-line workers of the 20th century industrial era. Demographically, the party will contain high numbers of women, minorities, and immigrants. But much of the Democratic Party's constituency also will be comprised of exurban voters, who will place domestic issues above that of national security and will want progressive political leadership to effect change. Issues will extend far beyond Social Security and prescription drug benefits, and to handle these problems, voters will turn to the Democratic Party.

Though it may be hard to believe given the Republican dominance in the White House and Capitol Hill, Teixeira believes the shift to the Democratic Party will come soon. In an article for TomPaine.com, he says, "Before the decade is over, the Democrats are likely to complete this journey, and the country will move from a conservative Republican majority to a progressive Democrat one."

Hipublicans

62 Some diehard Rush-lovers, Hillary-haters, and plain registered Republicans are cool. They are the Hipublicans, and they are increasing in number to support conservative political thinking and fight liberalism wherever it appears. Given that the number of American voters who consider themselves Republicans has increased over the past few decades until it nearly equals that of those who call themselves Democrats, it stands to reason that some of those new to the cause are young and forward-thinking.

But what exactly are Hipublicans? They're young, well-financed, and, as John Colapinto writes in the *New York Times Magazine*, "poised to inherit the responsibility of shaping the Republican Party in the years to come." In fact, the term *Hipublican* came to public notice in Colapinto's 2003 article, "The Young Hipublicans," where he detailed the mix of middle-class sensibilities, academic seriousness, and conservative political ideology that make up most of the Hipublicans he profiled. They are also fiercely committed to their aim, which is, as Colapinto says, "bringing out the unacknowledged conservatism in other students," not to persuade students to accept a new ideology but "awaken them to the fact that they already embody it."

Rather than standard-bearers like Trent Lott, Hipublicans are shaped by many young conservative thinkers including Ann Coulter and Karl Rove. But according to Suzanne Fields, writing for townhall.com, a formative voice for many college-aged Hipublicans is free speech champion Dinesh D'Souza. His book, *Letters to a Conservative,* is standard reading for young conservatives. D'Souza speaks the language of Hipublican. Said one Bucknell University conservative, "I'm not a Pat Buchanan conservative. I'm a D'Souza conservative." Generally, they are also highly influenced by former President Ronald Reagan, as leader and as icon.

Many Hipublicans have employed various types of activism to promote the conservative ideology. Sometimes the activism is homegrown, as with the students who establish on-campus conservatives clubs. Other forms of activism are at least partly funded by conservative interest groups, such as the Young Americans for Freedom and the Collegiate Network, among others. They help conservative students to set up publishing ventures and bring well-known conservative speakers to the campuses.

But the strength of the Hipublicans is their fierceness of conviction and their ability to work at such a young age with Washington Beltway insiders. They have also brought together a demographic group that is often downplayed today in favor of more flamboyant types. They unite the largely white, middle-class young men and women who support freedom and democracy but not the way the Left sells it.

Given their track record, Hipublicans are sure to become more prominent on the political scene as campaigners, fundraisers, and office holders. When they do, marketers will have to think about packaging them to the public. What if some Hipublicans became more stylishly dressed? They'd be yet another cultural subgroup, the Metropublicans.

Independence Day (From Political Parties)

63 Party politics in the early 21st century may tell the story of the ascendancy of the Republican Party. For in 2003, according to a Harris Poll, the lead of those who identify themselves as Democrats has hit a historic low. Only 34 percent consider themselves as Democrats, while 31 percent consider themselves Republicans, with numbers rising annually.

Yet, in recent national and local elections, the majority of party-affiliated voters split their votes, and only a minority followed one party. In so doing, they were demonstrating a greater voting trend: the growing disassociation from strict party affiliation and turn toward independent voting.

In 2002, a *USA Today*/Gallup poll announced that 35 percent of Americans call themselves politically independent. It and other findings suggest that independents are the fastest-growing political constituency in the United States. This marks a grand shift from past political party identification in the United States.

Now, for various reasons, U.S. voters do not want to be affiliated with either of the two major political parties; yet, because independents by their nature have not banded together in a party affiliation, they lack power as a group to influence public policy on a large scale. As a result, they are pursued by Democrats and Republicans according to individual issues, such as campaign reform, environmentalism, or tax cuts.

Still, the power of unaffiliated voters remains strong, particularly in affecting national elections. In 2000, self-proclaimed independents split their votes between Democrat Al Gore and Republican George Bush: each got 44 percent of independents' vote. But the 3 percent national showing by Ralph Nader may have tilted the outcome of the election toward Bush. And in 1992, Ross Perot won 14 percent of the vote for president as a member of the United We Stand Party, which may have helped to elect Democratic candidate Bill Clinton.

To solidify the power of independents, various interest groups want to build consensus and define independents as a political and social force. Activists for the cause believe that independents would carry more weight to promote independent-minded candidates of any party and to shape policy. One group, the Committee for a Unified Independent Party, states its goal as "building the independent movement" in order to "take on the corruption of the two parties" and "end political corruption and the influence of special interests." This independent action group calls for political reform from both parties that will make the democratic process more open to ordinary people.

Despite gathering together under the name of "independent," there is little as yet in the early 21st century to mark them as a political power. One characteristic of independents, reports surveys by ABC, the Henry J. Kaiser Family Foundation, and Harvard University, is that voters who call themselves independent often lean toward established party policy. "You scratch independent leaners and you will find closet partisans," says political scientist David Magleby, dean at Brigham Young University. Added Magleby, "One of the reasons people resonate to the term 'independent' is because of their hostility to parties and institutions. They want to be more neutral and they don't want to be tainted by a negative term that makes it seem you are captured by a party."

For example, *Washington Post*–ABC News polls on 2002 elections indicated that 85 percent of the Democratic-leaning voters would vote for the Democrat, and 68 percent of Republican-leaning independents would vote for the Republican candidate. As for the small percentage (less than 10 percent) of independents who are truly independent, often they decide not to vote, says Magleby. "Pure independents do march to their own beat. They are volatile. They have the lowest rates of turnout." This leaning toward a party is echoed in the 1992 book *The Myth of the Independent Voter* by Bruce Keith and others.

But whether there are more independents or party-affiliated voters, the problem that remains is a declining voting rate. In 1960, 60 percent of the nation's adults voted in the presidential election. In 2002, turnout was 39 percent. Thomas E. Patterson, Bradlee Professor of Government and the Press at Harvard University John F. Kennedy School of Government, believes that one reason is lack of party loyalty. "Americans who today have a party loyalty and an awareness of the parties have a voting rate more than twice that of those who call themselves independents and who cannot find words with which to describe the parties," he says.

India Prospering

64 "India" and "poverty" have long been words that go together. But on the world business front, India is becoming known as something else: a thriving place for investment and opportunity. India's economy is now the second fastest growing in the world, after China. In years to come, it will probably prosper as never before.

India's economic renaissance began in 1991, when the government started liberalizing an economy that had been heavily subject to state planning. Since then, India has dismantled numerous regulations, lifted restrictions on foreign investment, and generally cut red tape. New industries, such as software development companies and service centers for financial institutions, have been allowed the freedom to grow with minimal state controls. They have been so successful at persuading U.S. companies to "outsource" software and services work that a political backlash has been growing in America about the export of jobs to India. Bangalore and Hyderabad have become particularly prosperous as a result of these high-tech industries.

Just as important to India's prospering has been a cultural change away from a traditional antipathy to materialism and spending, and toward a Western-style consumer society. As prosperity fuels the growth of India's middle class, more of them look for material treats that go with that status. Demographically, India is a young country—half its people are under age twenty-five—and its youths are increasingly likely to enjoy buying stuff. "Consumerism as a term is no longer seen as a bad word," Yogesh Samat, head of the growing Indian coffee-bar chain

Barista Coffee, told the *New York Times*. Starting with no shopping malls in 1998, India now has 150 of them. A taste for mobile phones has helped make India the world's fastest-growing telecommunications market. And there is plenty of room for growth in selling consumer products to Indians: in 2001, only 32 percent of Indian households had a television. That's a lot of TV sets waiting to be sold.

There are also thorns in this rosy picture. Twenty-six percent of the Indian population is still living in poverty. India's neighbor and rival China is enjoying even greater growth. Bureaucracy and poor infrastructure (bad roads, unreliable electricity) continue to hamper growth in many places. With 70 percent of the work force employed in agriculture, the Indian economy can still be severely hurt by a bad monsoon season. Then there is always the danger of war with neighbor Pakistan, which, like India, is nuclear equipped. Indeed, among the people most interested in selling to India are arms merchants, vying with each other to sell fighter jets and radar systems to the booming Indian defense market. In the coming decade, India is expected to be the world's largest importer of arms. As long as it doesn't destroy itself with war, India is likely to survive its other problems to become one of the economic success stories of this century.

Islamic Flashpoints

65 The terror attacks of September 11, 2001, brought more global attention to the Islamic world than it had received in years. Now the question is, where next? What Islamic countries might be the next flashpoints for terrorism, war, or revolutionary change? What trends might affect the Islamic world at large?

It is difficult to generalize about the Islamic world, which comprises 1.5 billion people in many different parts of the globe. Still, one notable trend is an increased suspicion and hostility toward the United States as a result of the war in Iraq. Polls in 2003 showed that majorities in seven of eight predominantly Muslim nations said they were worried that the United States might threaten their countries. The occupation of Iraq by American troops has revived feelings of humiliation that still rankle from the colonial past. This has aided the recruitment efforts of Al Qaeda and other Islamist terrorist groups; even the buildup to the war aided recruitment. In March 2003, on the eve of the war, one American official told the *New York Times* that Iraq had already become "a battle cry" for Al Qaeda recruiters.

Perhaps alarmingly for the West, there are signs that the appeal of Islamism, a political ideology rooted in Islam, is spreading. However, here too the picture is complex. Though the best-known brand of Islamism (the brand of Al Qaeda and the Taliban) is an anti-Western theocratic fundamentalism, it exists in varied forms. In all cases, it is a studied response to the modern world, and often a postmodern blending of elements. It may have Marxist echoes in its critique of Western economic imperialism. It may be prone to conspiracy theories, including anti-Semitic ones. The radical or militant versions of Islamism advocate using violence and terrorism to establish a totalitarian theocratic regime. But there are also liberal versions of Islamism, which seek to synthesize religious and liberal principles. These kinds of Islamism may be conducive to peace between the West and the Islamic world.

However one tries to understand the Islamic world, it is important to realize that the term *Islamic world* can be misleading, suggesting a homogeneity that does not exist. Each country with a Muslim majority has a different history and a different set of problems. Turkey is predominantly Muslim but has a strong pro-Western, secular tradition. Even so, its Parliament voted against the Bush administration's request to use Turkey as a staging ground for the Iraq war. Ironically, the fight in favor of Bush's request was led by a devout Muslim from an Islamist background, Prime Minister Recep Tayyip Erdogan. Whether in the Islamic world or outside it, politics makes strange bedfellows.

One closely watched potential Islamic flashpoint is Pakistan. Even though the country is an American ally that aided the U.S. war in Afghanistan, it is believed to be harboring terrorists and is politically unstable, with the potential of becoming an Islamic theocracy. Its current leader, Pervez Musharraf, took power in a coup, and the country has no strong democratic tradition. Of greatest concern internationally is the fact that it has nuclear weapons. In January 2004, some tension was abated when Pakistan and India agreed to resume formal peace talks, easing fears of a nuclear war between the two powers. But in December 2003, Musharraf barely dodged two assassination attempts by Islamist groups, raising fears of nuclear weapons finding their way into radical Islamic hands.

Crises with international repercussions may erupt anywhere in the Islamic world. In Saudi Arabia, Islamist militants late in 2003 tried to assassinate security officials, perhaps in an effort to destabilize the pro-American government. Al Qaeda members on the run from Afghanistan are believed to have established new bases of operation in the Caucasus, including the breakaway Russian republic of Chechnya. For the foreseeable future, the only constant in the world of Islamic flashpoints will be flux.

Mini-Nukes

66 Just when you thought it was safe to stop ducking and covering, the people who brought you the last nuclear age are moving on to a new one. The idea is to develop a new generation of small, light nuclear weapons that are more useful on the battlefield than the old enormous, bulky ones. Critics charge that this notion brings us one step closer to a world where nuclear devastation is acceptable. But already the tide may have turned in favor of mini-nukes.

In the Cold War world, where the United States and the Soviet Union reigned supreme as antagonistic nuclear superpowers, the doctrine of "Mutual Assured Destruction"(or MAD) governed nuclear policy: build enough weapons and make them sufficiently large and secure, so that if either side struck first, both sides would be assured of complete destruction—thereby deterring either side from striking first. Now the picture of nuclear war is changing. There are no longer two matched superpowers, but one superpower, the United States, facing a complex world with a bewildering variety of threats. Nuclear war may consist of a suicide bomber from a shadowy terrorist network exploding one small atomic bomb on an American street, with no Soviet-style monolithic enemy to fear the consequences of an American counterattack. In addition, more nations are trying to develop nuclear arms, and some of them—such as Pakistan and North Korea—are poor enough that they might be inclined to use their atomic arsenal rather than resort to more costly deployment of conventional forces.

The advantage of the post–Cold War world, from a military standpoint, is that the United States has more freedom to exercise its nuclear muscle without fearing annihilation from a rival superpower. This is attractive to some military planners because of the proliferation of deep underground bunkers that house enemy military operations and are difficult to reach with conventional munitions. To combat these so-called hard and deeply buried targets (HDBT), the Bush administration is pressing for research on small nuclear weapons that can dig deep into the earth and destroy such bunkers.

The Pentagon is not necessarily asking for a bigger strategic nuclear arsenal; in fact, the report foresees a reduction over the next few years to between 1,700 and 2,200 active warheads. But the Pentagon does want more flexibility in its arsenal, including "variable and reduced yields" (i.e., a smaller bang) to "limit collateral damage" in case the weapons have to be used.

A chorus of critics have opposed the Pentagon's plans for mini-nukes, arguing that it undermines U.S. efforts to stop nuclear proliferation, and that even small nuclear weapons would likely cause unacceptable casualties and fallout. Further, critics say, the administration's position brings the world closer to nuclear war. However, defenders of administration policy say that the U.S. capacity to deter and respond to real-world threats will suffer if the weapons are not developed.

In 2003, Congress refused to fund the contentious research to the extent the administration wanted, but Defense Department planners regrouped at a United States Strategic Command meeting later that year to refine its plans in preparation for trying again. There is reason to think they will eventually get their way. Lawmakers are politically reluctant to appear weak on defense, and past administrations have succeeded in pushing through controversial research on projects like "Star Wars" missile defense. Mini-nukes are like miniskirts: despite perennial criticism, they will probably not go away for long.

Remembering the Forgotten Continent

67 Africa has long been known as the forgotten continent. North America and Europe shine on the world stage because of their rich and powerful nations. In Asia, Japan has long been prominent, and other countries, such as China and India, are rising as economic and political powers. South America has had its troubles, but it is increasingly part of an integrated and prosperous Western Hemisphere. Africa alone has been left out of world affairs. Only now is Africa beginning to be remembered.

Africa's woes began with the indignity of colonization by Europe in the 19th century. Nationalist movements won independence in the 1950s and 1960s, but the new countries were unstable, with disputed boundaries, leaders who were often corrupt and incompetent, and factions that plunged African nations time and again into civil war.

Famines periodically wracked the continent, disturbing the world's conscience and bringing in emergency help until the crisis subsided, after which the world looked away again. During the Cold War, the two superpowers, the United States and the Soviet Union, each maintained one principal interest in Africa: preserving its own influence. The superpowers poured large sums in foreign aid into Africa, chiefly to fund their own client states and entice them from switching to the other side. The effect was to prop up tin-pot dictators and prolong regional wars.

After the Cold War was over, there was no more Soviet Union, and the United States was much more reluctant to extend foreign aid. The continent was left more or less on its own. Some of the results have been calamitous, others promising.

The worst calamity has been AIDS. In sub-Saharan Africa, 28.5 million people were infected with the HIV virus as of 2001, the highest incidence in the world, and the region is projected to have the greatest continuing growth of infection. In addition, many countries have continued to suffer from brutal dictators, such as Robert Mugabe of Zimbabwe, who stole the 2002 presidential election to maintain his ruinous grip on that country. Civil wars and regional wars have continued to ravage the continent, sometimes prompting intervention from outside: for example, U.S. forces were sent to Liberia in 2003 to enforce a cease-fire. In the Democratic Republic of Congo, the death toll from a prolonged civil war and related causes was 3.3 million as of late 2002,

The promising developments have come about precisely because Africa is no longer the plaything of rival superpowers. Rather, Africa now has to compete, like all other regions, for the attention of global investors and multinational firms looking to make a profit. The bad news is that it has a long way to go before it can build the infrastructure of a first-world power, or even of a developing one such as Thailand or Singapore. The good news is that if it develops the habits that investors like—stable government, low government spending, low inflation, privatized economy—it has the potential to attract the investment capital that can drive development.

Africa has the resources to be attractive to investors, if African countries would only stay stable enough to make ongoing business possible. The oil reserves in Nigeria's Niger Delta attracted several multinational oil companies, but they had to shut down operations temporarily in 2003 on account of ethnic fighting.

Several African countries have been striving to show themselves worthy of investment. Even Libya, once a global pariah, renounced terrorism and weapons of mass destruction in 2003, setting the stage for an end to international sanctions. For other countries, the road to the world's good graces is as short as a balanced budget. According to allAfrica.com, Ugandan president Yoweri Museveni has made his country one of several African nations with balanced budgets and strong protection of property rights.

South Africa is another country that is trying to promote growth. This is a nation that only recently, in the 1990s, emerged from apartheid and built a multiracial democracy. Now, according to Reuters, South Africa is aiming to copy the miracle that built Asia's "tiger" economies by building a combination duty-free industrial development zone and deep-water port. Known as the Coega Industrial Development Zone, it is modeled on the similar zones in countries such as Singapore and China that helped propel economic growth.

In addition to stimulating private initiatives, some African countries have been supporting their native industries by demanding fair treatment at world trade conferences. For example, they have sought elimination of agricultural subsidies in the developed world that block their farmers from competing. The 2003 Cancún meeting of the World Trade Organization collapsed in large part because of this contentious issue.

All this African activity has been jogging the memories of the developed world, enticing world leaders and deep-pocketed businesspeople to visit Africa. According to the International Monetary Fund, since 1994 the economies of the sub-Saharan African countries have been growing an average of 5 percent a year. Still, there are skeptics about Africa's reliance on the capitalist bandwagon. In Cairo's *Al-Ahram Weekly On-Line,* scholars Rita Abrahamsen and Ray Bush wrote, "The manner of Africa's integration into the world economy serves primarily to ensure the further extraction of profit by Northern countries." On the other hand, Africans seem to be ready to have some profit extracted by northern countries so long as some hope for a reasonable livelihood is left for the southern ones. For the time being, Africans are no longer willing to remain forgotten.

The Rise of Gerontocracy

68 According to the *Merriam-Webster Dictionary*, *gerontocracy* means "rule by elders; specifically: a form of social organization in which a group of old men or a council of elders dominates or exercises control." Nineteenth-century British political leader William Gladstone called it simply "government by old men."

In the 21st-century United States, control by the aged will involve more than governmental control. With the aging of the baby boomers (along with the aging between-the-wars generation and generation X), the overall age of the United States is rising and, for a variety of reasons, the work force it comprises will not retire. We are headed for what in 1999 Christopher Shea on Salon.com deemed an "American Gerontocracy." But in the 21st century, American elder rule will be much broader in scope. It will span all occupations that don't have an automatic cessation date.

Part of the reason behind holding on to jobs will be necessity. But part of it will be the will to power. It's possible that the members of the gerontocracy will even build popular support for their job tenure. In their book *Gerontocracy, Retirement, and Social Security*, Casey B. Mulligan and Xavier Sala-i-Martin detail, among other points, how the elderly have been more successful than other age and social groups in lobbying their causes in the political arena. Older people may use the approaches to make their continued presence in the work force acceptable.

Nonetheless, business forecasters view the coming gerontocracy as a challenge. According to interbiznet.com, a gerontocracy-based business world is apt to be "risk averse and slow to grow," offering few incentives to young (generation Y and beyond) generations of workers. The delicacy needed to manage the upcoming gerontocracy and its successors will be huge, according to interbiznet.com. It counsels, "Figuring out how to manage a rapidly aging workforce may be the most immediate problem. Figuring out how to make that same environment exciting for the young will be number 2."

The battle between the young and the old generations is powerful; it will probably never end. For all those baby boomers who, as gerontocrats, will be holding on to their jobs when it's time to go, remember that yours was the generation that once said, "Don't trust anyone over thirty."

Starve the Beast

69 The fiscal 2004 budget projects a deficit of $521 billion. That's $507 billion more than the Bush administration projected for 2004 just two years ago. After critics noted that only a few years ago under President Clinton there was a budget surplus, talk turned to how to increase revenues and cut government spending. But over the next several months, revenues decreased. Under the 2003 Bush tax cut and business incentives, revenues in 2003 were reduced. In 2000, the federal government took in 20 percent of the GDP (gross domestic product) in taxes. In fiscal 2004, it is projected to be only 15.7 percent of the GDP. If the tax cuts become permanent, as the Bush administration hopes, revenues will continue to be lower.

So the answer seems to lie in cutting government spending. Yet, Bush's proposed 2004 national budget is the biggest in history and includes not only greatly increased funding for defense and security but a new presidential plan for Medicare prescription drug coverage that has increased in projected cost by one-third (that is, $134 billion) within a few days of its creation.

Determining what is important for the national government to pay for will be the ongoing debate of the early 21st century. What the president and Congress determine is important will in some form survive. Given the high cost of government, what's left will not be fully funded and will wither. As economist and columnist Paul Krugman (and others) has said, it is a way to "starve the beast"—and the beast is the domestic arm of the government.

One way to reduce the size of the government (or beast) is to reduce the number of federal employees and other federal employee entitlements. To an extent, the Bush administration was successful in this regard. It proposed moving up to half the federal civilian work force to private companies and largely controlling the hiring and movement of the 170,000 employees of the Department of Homeland Security. Critics of these moves say that fewer federal jobs will disproportionately affect women and minorities, for whom federal employment has traditionally offered strong opportunities. And during the war in Iraq, the Bush administration also oversaw what the *Army Times* discussed as substantial cuts to "key family services" that include curbing growth "in pay and benefits, including basic pay, combat pay, health-care benefits and the death gratuity for survivors of active-duty troops." Another way to reduce domestic spending is to shift it to defense or security needs. For that in 2004, discretionary security-related spending rose to 4.7 percent, from 3.4 percent of the GDP.

To pay for this and other increases in defense spending, and to dent the deficit, more than keeping domestic costs down will be needed. For that, it will be necessary to substantially cut Medicare and Social Security, according to some public policymakers. Yet, others think that making corporations pay their taxes will help to feed national revenues and cut the deficit. According to Krugman, eliminating such tax loopholes could yield $200 billion per year.

But none of these changes in the tax system or the drastic restructuring of now accepted social programs such as Medicare and Social Security are likely to occur soon. In the meantime, the United States will have, what Krugman calls in the *New York Times Magazine*, "a fundamental mismatch between the benefits Americans expect to receive from the government and the revenues government collects." He warns, "If taxes stay as low as they are now, government as we know it cannot be maintained."

Unabashed Imperialism

70 There was a time when only leftists called the United States an empire or its wars imperialist. But in recent years, even conservatives and middle-of-the-roaders have become comfortable with the notion of an American empire. This unabashed imperialism, which has been flourishing since the terrorist attacks of 9/11, steeled many Americans into a willingness to do anything necessary to prevent a recurrence of that day. But its roots lie before 9/11, in the formation of a group of neoconservatives who formulated what might be called neoimperialism. Members of that group now exercise strong influence in the Bush White House, and their views—already enshrined in policy and war—are likely to influence international events for years to come.

The history of neoimperialism dates from 1992, just after the Gulf War, when Paul Wolfowitz, then undersecretary of defense for policy for the first President Bush, wrote the Defense Policy Guidance, a draft set of military guidelines calling for a new conception of American power. During the Cold War, the United States had followed a policy of containment—using its military to hold back but not offensively attack the Soviet Union. But the Soviet Union had vanished in 1991, and the United States was left as the world's sole superpower, vastly superior to all rivals in wealth, influence, and military might. Wolfowitz argued that containment was now obsolete and that the United States should attack pre-emptively and alone when necessary to maintain U.S pre-eminence and to prevent the rise of a great power rival.

In 1997, Wolfowitz and other neoconservatives, including Donald Rumsfeld, William Kristol, Richard Perle, John Bolton, and I. Lewis "Scooter" Libby, formed the Project for a New American Century. In 2000, they released a report, "Rebuilding America's Defenses," that built on the basic principles of the earlier Defense Policy Guidance, saying that America should preserve and extend the "American peace," or Pax Americana. For historians of empire, Pax Americana is a clear allusion to empire: the Roman Empire was known as the Pax Romana and the British as the Pax Britannica.

With the election of George W. Bush as president in 2000, Wolfowitz and his fellow neoimperialists came out of the wilderness: he, Bolton, and Libby became high-ranking members of the Bush administration, while Rumsfeld became secretary of defense. Even though Bush, as presidential candidate, had advocated less "nation-building" and greater "humility" in U.S. foreign policy, Bush as president gave free rein to the hawkish neoimperialists, especially after the terrorist attacks of September 11, 2001. In September 2002, he issued the National Security Strategy, which essentially ratified the neoimperialists' views. It articulated what became known as the Bush Doctrine: that the United States should not permit the development of a challenge to its global military supremacy; that it should strike pre-emptively when necessary; and that it should act alone if other countries were not willing to join such an effort. The Bush Doctrine was realized the following year when, without United Nations support, the United States and several allies overthrew the government of Saddam Hussein in Iraq, purportedly to prevent his development of weapons of mass destruction.

Before, during, and after the Iraq war, American empire became a hot topic. Critics of intervention in Iraq were more likely than supporters to use the once-inflammatory term *empire*, but even conservatives were less likely to resist it. Kristol said on Fox News in Spring 2003: "We need to err on the side of being strong. And if people want to say we're an imperial power, fine." Some people dispute the terminology on technical grounds. Historian Paul Schroeder pointed out that the United States does not have an empire; rather, it has hegemony: "clear, acknowledged leadership and dominant influence by one unit within a community of units not under a single authority." The latter relationship, says Schroeder, best describes the international system that prevails today, where even long-time allies like France and Germany managed to oppose the United States in its quest for UN approval of the Iraq war.

Even greater than the disputes about terminology are the disputes about the vision of American power articulated in the Bush Doctrine. Foreign critics, in Europe and elsewhere, accuse the United States of arrogance and bullylike behavior. Domestic opponents predict that it will lead the United States into a weaker, not stronger, position. They say that it will leave us more vulnerable to terrorism by distracting us with unnecessary wars and alienating allies who might be able to help; that it is morally reprehensible because of the bloodshed and conquest it entails; that it will encourage enemies to build nuclear weapons faster to deter us from attacking them; and that it sets a precedent for other nations to launch pre-emptive (read "aggressive") wars against their own enemies.

The fiscally conscious complain that neoimperialism will bankrupt the country. Hard-headed foreign policy "realists" argue that it is unrealistic to expect other nations to sit tight while one nation tries to lord it over all of them permanently. The more the United States tries that strategy, say the realists, the more other nations will tend to band against it as a threat to their security. Greater security will be found in working cooperatively with other nations in an internationalist arrangement.

Against all such criticism, neoimperialists ask a fundamental question: Is it better for the United States, and the world, if America keeps the position of global pre-eminence it now has, or becomes weaker relative to other countries? If American pre-eminence is better (as the neoimperialists argue), then, for as long as possible, the United States should not allow itself to become weaker.

At least for the present, given the Bush Doctrine, the United States will probably become increasingly neoimperial. In the long term, it is hard to say what will happen, because there is no good historical precedent for the current moment—one in which there is so vast a gulf of power between one nation and all the others. Whether neoimperialism will have a long run, or is as doomed to failure as old-fashioned imperialism, remains to be seen.

Webocracy

71 During the 2004 presidential election, Web power began with a short note on the Weblog for Howard Dean in July 2003. Hundreds of volunteers answered, and the Dean campaign began. On Wednesdays in late 2003, New England college students who met on the Internet gathered to plan the election campaign of the former Vermont governor. Ultimately they were part of the Dean team that raised $25 million for his early campaign. Not only were these students important because they represented a grass-roots movement that injected youth into presidential politics, but also because they brought the Internet with them. In coming years, masters of the Internet universe will wield an increasingly large amount of political power. They will create a Webocracy.

Developing political power online begins with forming online communities. For example, in 2003, after meeting and doing some campaign planning, the Dean supporters linked with campaign strategists and learned to fundraise. They learned to solicit small amounts of money online and at in-person gatherings of friends and family. They also held neighborhood Dean awareness events called "meetups." Combined with larger, traditional contributions, Dean set a record for one-quarter fundraising in late 2003, when his third-quarter donations totaled almost $15 million.

In addition to direct personal involvement in the campaign, Internet-based political supporters generally engage in ongoing verbal interaction with a campaign. As a result of interaction online with a political staff, Internet supporters become active in shaping the fundamental ideas of the campaign.

Another way Internet supporters interact with the campaign is to contribute to the Weblog. There, supporters are updated on the latest developments and offer ideas for improving the campaign. They also set fundraising goals for one another, and donate in small amounts to continuously add to the coffers.

How Internet supporters make their connection known will determine their level of power now and in the future. For example, both Dean and Wesley Clark supporters raised the millions of dollars online that they needed to make their candidates active players in the campaign.

Overall, these political groups are part of an even larger move to create Web groups with shared interests called "smart mobs." They use cyberspace to pursue common goals, such as a political campaign, or, as was done in 2002, to build a crime-fighting online group and track down a criminal and turn him over to authorities. In politics, law enforcement, and more, the harnessing of Web power is just beginning.

8

Religion and Spirituality

Christianity: Decline and Rise

72 An old story about Christianity is that it is on the wane, in decline, soon to be defunct. There is some evidence to back up this claim, but not enough to tell the whole story. The real future of Christianity looks more complicated.

In Europe, cradle of Christian civilization, Christian belief and church attendance have reached relatively low levels. According to the Gallup International Millennium Survey, only 48 percent of European respondents say that God is very important to them, and 48 percent of western Europeans and 44 percent of eastern Europeans almost never go to church at all. The European Union made a conspicuous point in 2003 of not including mention of Christianity in its charter, despite the urging of the pope. A survey by *Opinion Research Business* in Britain in 1999 reported that fewer than 50 percent "believe in Christ."

The United States has a reputation among developed countries for being relatively more religious than Europe. According to the Gallup poll, the percentage of Americans who believe in God or a universal spirit has stayed stable in the 90s for years. But specifically Christian belief is another story. According to the American Religious Identification Survey, the proportion of Christians in the United States declined from 86 percent in 1990 to 77 percent in 2001. And even among avowed Christians, there is much disagreement with certain traditional Christian doctrines. A Barna Research Group study found that among mainline Protestant denominations such as Lutherans, Episcopalians, Methodists, and Presbyterians, only 27 percent accepted the traditional Christian view that man does not earn his way to heaven by good works. Among both Catholic and mainline Protestant Church members, only 17 and 20 percent respectively think Satan is real.

Evidence like this has led to predictions that Christianity as we once knew it has had its day. Episcopal bishop John Shelby Spong, an advocate of liberalized doctrine, even wrote a book with the title *Why Christianity Must Change or Die*. And it is true that in the developed world, Christianity increasingly must compete with other forms of religious belief and nonbelief, both new and old—everything from neoagnosticism to Islam.

Yet, it is unlikely that traditional Christianity will simply wither away any time soon. Setting aside the question of whether there are divine guarantees that Christianity will prevail, there are three factors that probably ensure its continuing strength: the mission fields of the developing world; the renewed popularity of orthodoxy; and the attractiveness of fundamentalism.

In Africa and Asia, the number of Christians has risen dramatically in recent years, to about 360 million in Africa and 313 million in Asia in 2000, according to the *Encyclopedia Britannica Book of the Year*. Of those, 9 million were added in Africa and 23 million in Asia in just the three years from 1997 to 2000. Christianity is flourishing in, of all places, China, despite lack of a historical link to Christianity and despite years of persecution and suppression by its atheistic communist rulers. The global spread of Christianity is likely to continue, driven in part by the same forces that are making English a global language and pushing sales of Western products and popular culture throughout the world: namely, the starting advantages possessed by Western businesses (and churches) in an increasingly borderless world market. The Druze might wish to establish missions in every corner of the world, but unless they can get capitalized by donors from wealthy countries, as Christian missionaries are, they are unlikely to get their wish.

Even within the developing world, orthodoxy shows no signs of yielding quietly to critics like Bishop Spong. Instead, a pro-orthodoxy movement is developing in many denominations. Methodist theologian Thomas Oden, a former advocate of liberal doctrine who has turned into a defender of orthodoxy, argues in *The Rebirth of Orthodoxy: Signs of New Life in Christianity* that the era we have entered is not post-Christian but postsecular. Says Oden, "God is at work in grassroots Christianity, awakening a ground swell of longing for classical ecumenical teaching in all communions." Orthodox belief has proven resistant to change in several high-profile cases. The Catholic Church maintained its ban on clerical marriage and ordination of women despite the opposition campaigns that arose in the wake of the church's pedophilia scandal. And conservative Episcopalians have threatened to split that denomination in half in protest against the ordination of a gay bishop.

Supporting the groundswell of orthodoxy is the growth of fundamentalism. An increasing number of Christians are Evangelicals, Pentecostals, or members of other groups whose faith tends toward the conservative, fervent, and evangelizing. Sociological factors that might help account for this trend include a yearning for simple explanations in a complex world—the same yearning that is driving the spread of Islamic fundamentalism. The adherence of Evangelicals/Pentecostals to traditional Christian doctrine is markedly stronger than for mainline Protestant groups: for example, according to Barna, 55 to 73 percent of Evangelical and Pentecostal groups accept that Christ was without sin, as compared to 28 to 33 percent of mainline Protestant groups. Another Barna study shows that people who evangelize or share their faith with others are more likely than nonevangelizers to hold traditional Christian views such as that Christ was without sin and that every word of the Bible is true. Since these are the people who are spreading the Christian message on the streets and in workplaces, the Christianity of converts now and for the foreseeable future is likely to be traditional in character. That factor will add ballast to the long-term persistence of Christianity despite the persistent rumors of its imminent demise.

Friendly Agnosticism

73 Asked to comment on how she regarded her Christian friends, a young Jewish girl in 2000 told the *New York Times*, "Nobody knows whose religion is right, so be accepting of everyone who is out there." This was a pithy formulation of what is increasingly the national religion of America. Shared by many people of all faiths—Christian, Jewish, or other—this doctrine holds that no matter what we believe, no one knows what is true, so all religions are equally acceptable. When theologians talk this way, they are espousing a doctrine called theological pluralism, religious relativism, or religious indifferentism. But when laypeople talk this way, it might better be called Friendly Agnosticism: friendly because it strives to be generous to people of other persuasions; agnosticism because it assumes that we cannot know the truth about the issues upon which religions disagree.

Friendly Agnosticism is anathema to traditional believers who don't agree that all religions are equally acceptable. But it is also anathema to many believers in logical thought, because, logically, the position as it is frequently formulated appears to be self-contradictory. Take, for example, a Christian who claims (while praying in church) that Jesus is the son of God, but who also claims (while mingling with non-Christians in the office) that it is impossible to know what is true about the matter. Such a Friendly Agnostic affirms both that Jesus is the son of God and that it is impossible to affirm that Jesus is the son of God. This is incoherent—yet the Friendly Agnostic puts up with the incoherence for the sake of being friendly. Similarly, the Friendly Agnostic who says (as many do) that all religions lead to God leaves unclear how he can know that all religions lead to God if he doesn't know what is true about God. Again, the motive is friendliness but the logic is fuzzy. However, even the friendliness is fuzzy, because he is still disagreeing with anyone who affirms, as many traditional believers do, that it is possible to know what is true about God. It may be that the only people to whom Friendly Agnosticism is really friendly are other Friendly Agnostics.

Even in established churches with strong traditions of orthodox doctrine, many lay followers practice Friendly Agnosticism. In 2000, the Vatican declaration *Dominus Iesus* met with a storm of protest from American Catholics for condemning theological pluralism—which is to say, Friendly Agnosticism. That same year, in the Presbyterian Church in the United States, Reverend Dirk Ficca ignited a storm of controversy when he suggested at a Church conference that Jesus Christ might not be the only way to salvation. The present-day propensity to say "Happy Holidays" rather than "Merry Christmas" or "Happy Hanukkah" may be another symptom of the force that drives Friendly Agnosticism: a fear of appearing unfriendly if one clearly states one's own religious views. On the level of individual houses of worship, Friendly Agnosticism is increasingly in vogue. "[I]n a typical Bible study, anyone can say any ol' incorrect thing, and everyone just nods their heads in agreement," says computer scientist Troy DeJongh.

In part, Friendly Agnosticism stems from a more generalized relativism about truth that is commonly called postmodern. In part, it is the result of living in a society that stresses religious liberty. The founding fathers' decision to separate church and state was originally undertaken for practical purposes, to avoid religious wars and prevent any one sect from oppressing the others. But over time, this spirit of civil tolerance has seeped into religious beliefs themselves, partly through the public school system. Stephen Macedo in *Diversity and Distrust: Civic Education in a Multicultural Democracy* (2000) writes: "It may well be that a public school program that teaches civil tolerance will have the effect of indirectly promoting religious tolerance"—where "religious tolerance" amounts to the Friendly Agnostic claim that "all religions are merely different roads to God."

Despite its avowed antipathy to orthodoxy, Friendly Agnosticism has itself become the reigning orthodoxy. It may be contributing to the growing number of people who abandon religion altogether to become brights (atheists and agnostics), or who blend agnostic belief with spiritual quest in the brew called neoagnosticism. It may also encourage a readiness to shop for new beliefs and mix and match doctrines in the shopping mall of religion. Like any orthodoxy, Friendly Agnosticism is a ripe target for subversive attacks; already a backlash is in process in the form of various movements for a return to traditional Christian doctrine. Even so, one can expect that Friendly Agnosticism will continue to hold sway over many people for some time.

Islam Evolving

74   Islam is in the news nearly every day, what with terrorist attacks by Islamist militants and war in Muslim countries. But less publicized is the change that is occurring within the religion of Islam as a result of its peaceful contacts with the modern world. What is currently playing out is no less than the evolution of liberal Islam.

Playing a large role in this evolution are the millions of Muslims who now live not in Islamic countries but in the secular democracies of the developed world. In the United States alone, the *World Almanac 2004* estimates that there are now about 5 to 6 million Muslims, and more are coming, through immigration, birth, or conversion. In Europe, there are now more Muslims (32 million) than there are Anglicans (27 million). By some estimates, early in the 21st century Islam will surpass Judaism as the second largest religion in the United States, after Christianity.

There are signs already that the new generation of Western Muslims is different from their forebears. Asma Gull Hasan, as she describes herself in *American Muslims: The New Generation* (2000), is hip, twenty-something, feminist, and Muslim. The American-born daughter of Pakistani immigrants, she feels her generation is at the vanguard of a "de facto Reform Islam." Far from corrupting Islam, she considers American Islam to be more religiously pure than Islam in other countries precisely because it lacks the cultural baggage found else-where: it is "a return to the Qur'an without the influence of pre-Islamic Arab culture."

The new generation of Muslims is, of course, Internet-savvy, and they are giving birth to a whole world of CyberIslam. This includes Liberal Islam Web sites, even one *(www.liberalislam.net)* whose sources of wisdom encompass that great desert philosopher Ben Kenobi in the *Star Wars* films.

As social change takes place, scholars are making their own contributions by identifying theological justifications for liberal Islam. M. A. Muqtedar Khan, in *American Muslims: Bridging Faith and Freedom* (2002), defends the compatibility of Islam and democracy. Charles Kurzman, in *Liberal Islam: A Source-Book* (1998), argues that liberal Islam is a thriving tradition currently undergoing a revival, and that it includes such concerns as democracy, separation of church and state, women's rights, minority rights, and freedom of thought. Scholars at the Middle East Institute's 56th Annual Conference on October 11, 2002, in Washington, D.C., argued that democracy and liberalism are concepts found in Islam and need not be derived from Western civilization. According to law professor Aziza Al-Hibri, Thomas Jefferson himself once used the Koran as a source for his statement, "There is no coercion in religion."

The emergence of a new kind of Muslim is perhaps seen best in Shazia Mirza, a British-born child of Pakistani immigrants who has gotten international attention as a standup comic. A devout Muslim, she wears the hijab, the Muslim female head covering, but is incongruously modern in her style and references—incongruously only because of her audience's preconceptions of what a Muslim is like. After 9/11, she broke the ice with audiences by saying, "My name is Shazia Mirza. At least that's what it says on my pilot's license." Some might find Mirza's humor offensive. But the huge laughs that followed that joke were a sign that the convergence of Islam and the modern world might be not only possible, but entertaining as well.

Look on the Brights' Side

75 Back in the prehistoric 1960s, *The Flintstones* theme song proclaimed "We'll have a gay old time!" Today, a cartoon series with that tag line might seem to promise an evening of homosexuality. That is how the word *gay* changed meaning over just a few decades: from an adjective meaning "merry" to a noun meaning "a person of homosexual orientation," or an adjective related to such persons. Now a different minority is trying to transform another common modifier. They are the brights, and they are defined not by their sexual but religious preference—or rather, their preference not to be religious.

According to the Web site of the brights *(www.the-brights.net)*, a bright is a person who has a naturalistic worldview—that is, whose set of beliefs is "free of supernatural or mystical deities, forces, and entities." No ghosts, goblins, good fairies for brights—and certainly no gods or God. A more old-fashioned term for a bright is an atheist or agnostic, though they have also been known to call themselves freethinkers, humanists, rationalists, secular humanists, nontheists, and skeptics—and to disagree freely among themselves about why and in what way they don't believe in exactly what. Brights also include people who are just not religious, without giving the issue much thought.

The new meaning of "bright" was coined by Paul Geisert, a bright in Sacramento, California. The idea is to improve the image of people who don't believe in God or other supernatural entities, but who may encounter public scorn when they call themselves atheists or agnostics. A 2003 study by the Pew Forum on Religion & Public Life indicates they have an uphill struggle: more than half (52 percent) of Americans have an unfavorable view of atheists, while the unfavorable rating for, say, Protestants is only 10 percent. Present attitudes being what they are, the election of an openly atheist president is probably farther off than the election of an African-American or female one. But a president who is openly a bright, brights hope, might be more palatable than one who is openly an atheist. They also hope that if the new meaning of "bright" comes into more widespread use, it might encourage timid nonbelievers to come out of the closet, and perhaps make it easier for nonbrights to defend the civil rights of brights.

At this moment, it is impossible to say whether the proposed usage for "bright" will become a permanent part of the language. But if it doesn't, it won't be for lack of initial publicity. Philosopher Daniel Dennett and scientist Richard Dawkins wrote articles in the mainstream press in 2003 promoting the brights, and mathematician John Allen Paulos commented on the movement for ABCNews.com. According to the Brights' Web site, there are potentially 29 million brights in the United States; if that figure is correct, and just 10 percent start speaking of themselves as brights, that will be nearly 3 million people selling the new usage. By signing up to be counted on the Web site, and through other avenues such as water-cooler discussions and Web-organized meetups (an "International Brights Meetup Day" was scheduled for November 2003), those 3 million might be a lever to change the language.

On the other hand, there is reason to be gloomy about the prospects of the term *brights*. For one thing, the analogy to "gay" is flawed. *Gay* meaning "homosexual" did not originate in a conscious decision by one person to introduce a new term, but in the normal, murky, chaotic give-and-take by which language evolves. Most deliberate efforts to coin new terms are as doomed to oblivion as George Costanza's effort on *Seinfeld* to coin himself the nickname "T-Bone." Further, as Paulos points out, self-identification by the nonreligious as "bright" will tend to appear "smug, ridiculous, and arrogant" to many people. (One disgruntled nonbeliever on an Internet forum wrote: "[T]his sort of campaign makes us nontheists look like dweebs.") As a matter of logical implication, and as much as brights vehemently deny it, the choice of the term *bright* for "nonreligious person" entails that only nonreligious people are bright (with a connotation of intelligent), while religious people must be dim (with a connotation of stupid). Insulting one's opponents is not a likely way to gain their favor.

The brights movement may not succeed in changing the language, but it does point to one current trend: rejection of belief in God is increasingly likely to be voiced publicly rather than kept private. Science writer Natalie Angier came out of the closet as an atheist in "Confessions of a Lonely Atheist" in the *New York Times Magazine* in 2001, and Dennett and Dawkins, in their writings, have demonstrated a proatheism zeal that is virtually evangelical. This phenomenon of open atheism, or public nonbelief in God, conforms to a more general trend among politicians, entertainers, MFA-graduates, blog writers, and others toward confessional statements about their private lives, often with an effort to include themselves in an oppressed minority in the hope of gaining sympathy. (In point of fact, brights in certain areas of public life, such as academia and science, are likely to encounter little oppression for being brights; nontheism is widely practiced in those arenas, and openly religious people are the ones more likely to suffer discrimination.) Open atheism is also rooted in the tendency of the contemporary religious scene to look more and more like a shopping mall or political campaign, in which competing sects lock horns publicly using sophisticated, techno-savvy PR strategies. For these reasons, open atheism is likely to continue as a trend, though the prospects of the new term *bright* are cloudy.

Neoagnosticism

76 Agnosticism has always been the middle ground between belief and disbelief in God. Where theism affirms that God exists, and atheism denies it, agnosticism says, "I don't know." However, in practice, agnostics since Thomas Huxley (the English biologist who coined the term in the 19th century) have usually allied themselves with the atheists. The traditional agnostic says, "I don't know if God exists, so I

will withhold belief in him and carry on as if there were no such thing"—making such a person a de facto atheist. This tradition is now breaking down. At least some contemporary agnostics most definitely carry on as if there were such a thing as God—even if it is not exactly God. These are the neoagnostics.

Winifred Gallagher, who numbers herself in this group and coined this term in her 1999 book *Working on God*, defines neoagnostics as "well-educated skeptics who have inexplicable metaphysical feelings." They are not sure there is a God, but they hunger for higher meaning and search for it by trying out different forms of religious belief and practice. They distrust what they call "organized religion," that is, any spiritual institution that requires its members to believe and do certain things, such as go to church on Sunday. In keeping with their advanced education, neoagnostics are disproportionately upscale; as Gallagher says, "They are everywhere, especially at the top." They are also disproportionately young and hip. "Now it's becoming the in thing to be spiritual," Buddhist teacher Jagad Guru Paramahamsa told *Christianity Today* in 1999. "It's more cool, modern, and progressive to be spiritual. But without God," says Paramahamsa.

Neoagnostics tend to agree with remarks such as "I believe in spirituality, not religion" or "I don't believe in a personal God, but I do think there is a sacred or transcendent dimension to life." The link between advanced education and this kind of spirituality without a traditional God is supported by a number of studies. For example, the 1998 General Social Survey found that people with more than four years of college are more than twice as likely (17.2 percent) as people with only a high school education (7.4 percent) to believe in a "higher power but not a personal God." The Gallup International Millennium Survey, which surveyed sixty countries on five continents, found that more educated people tend to "prefer the idea of [God as a] 'force' or flatly reject the notion of a superior being."

The personal spiritual quest Gallagher describes in *Working on God* is a good example of the neoagnostic's eclectic search for meaning through the world's numerous religions, mythologies, and mystical traditions. Gallagher sampled Zen Buddhism, Judaism, and Christianity, trying out their practices, asking skeptical questions, and ultimately stirring together her own personal spiritual brew.

As neoagnostics struggle to construct their personal spiritualities, a booming industry has sprung up to cater to them: books, religious goods (everything from candles to kachina dolls to Wiccan pentagrams), retreats, lecture series. Some traditional religions are more adept than others at attracting neoagnostics. Tibetan Buddhism, for example, is a highly organized and dogmatic tradition, but its leader, the Dalai Lama, is a master at presenting its more accessible teachings to nonbelievers in a genial and nondemanding way. Many neoagnostics are interested in the movement broadly known as New Age, which emphasizes occult and paranormal phenomena and the teachings of the East (as transmitted by way of California), but neoagnostics tend to sift New Age claims as skeptically as any other claims. The Internet, with its computerized search engines, has proven, so to speak, a godsend to neoagnostic spiritual searchers. At this writing, Google responds to the phrase "spiritual search" with 4,350,000 results.

Many neoagnostics are scientific materialists at heart, tending to believe that the natural world, produced through evolutionary processes, is all there is: no afterlife, no choirs of angels. But, buoyed by research findings showing that medical benefits accrue to those who meditate and pray, and by brain studies showing neurological changes during meditation and prayer, they believe that something good is going on when one feels spiritual, even if there are no spirits as such. Biologist Ursula Goodenough, in her book *The Sacred Depths of Nature*, writes: "As a non-theist, I find I can only think about these [mystical] experiences as wondrous mental phenomena. But in the end it doesn't matter: All of us are transformed by their power." Other neoagnostics are not committed to absolute materialism, and are willing to accept the possibility that there is something spiritual or transcendent over and above nature. They don't know what it is, and suspect they can't know what it is, but want to tap into its power just the same.

Neoagnosticism has its critics: religious people who say that it shows a dilettantish unwillingness to commit to one tradition; atheists who say that it shows a muddle-headed refusal to accept the consequences of there being no God. The brights movement, which calls for a worldview free of supernaturalism, has no patience with the supernatural dabblings of neoagnostics, while the movement for a return to Christian orthodoxy has no patience with their heterodox spirit. Nevertheless, neoagnosticism is likely to remain an important movement because of its balance between two conflicting factors in 21st-century society: the hegemony of modern scientific culture, with its denial of the supernatural, versus the persistent human hunger for the supernatural. It will probably flourish so long as democratic capitalism flourishes, because of its optimal use of what democratic capitalism provides: religious liberty and a marketplace to provide for every need, including spiritual ones.

Pray Your Way to Health

77 Without announcing it, many Americans link religion and health. In a 2003 *Newsweek* poll, 70 percent of Americans asked said they prayed often for the health of a family member—which was substantially less than the 27 percent who pray for their own financial or career success. The impact of religious belief on health and the place of faith in the practice of medicine are becoming an area of intense research and controversy among medical practitioners.

Interest in the link between religion and health has been spurred by dozens of recent studies on the subject. A survey of about 150 investigations on religion and health pointed in some cases to the positive effects of religion. The strongest link was a study offering persuasive evidence that church or service attendance promotes longer life. This study also provided moderate evidence to support the hypotheses that religion or spirituality can protect against cardiovascular disease and that being prayed for improves one's physical recovery from an acute illness.

In a 2003 *American Psychologist* finding reported in *Vibrant Life*, forty studies revealed that over the time the studies covered, regular attendees of public religious services had a 29 percent lower death rate than those who did not or rarely practiced. This study also took into account other factors aligned with church attendance that could improve health. For instance, the study considered the idea that attending religious services promotes the building of social support systems, and that actively religious people tend to take better care of themselves than those who do not attend services regularly.

Among other things, the findings in these studies have spurred many medical schools to understand and acknowledge the force of religion in patients' lives. As of late 2003, more than half of U.S. medical schools offer courses in spirituality and medicine. The courses, far from teaching faith healing, focus on understanding the importance of religion and spirituality to patients and how it may affect a patient's state of health.

A leading researcher in the link between faith and health, Dr. Harold Koenig, MD, MHSc, founding director of the Center for the Study of Religion/Spirituality and Health at Duke University Medical Center, believes that the studies validate the claims for religion and health. Speaking at a conference on Spirituality and Healing in Medicine, Dr. Koenig said, "At least six studies in the past two years have found a relationship between . . . a religious community and longer survival. Religious beliefs and activities [correlate] with better mental and physical health in the vast majority of the studies."

Further, Dr. Koenig has been involved in studies at Duke University Medical Center that found that people who prayed and attended religious services regularly had lower blood pressure than their counterparts who did not pray or attend services. Put simply, Dr. Koenig told BBC News online, "Participating in religious services is associated with significant health benefits in elderly people, even when you take into account the fact that the religious people tend to start out with better health practices and more social support."

Some researchers even point to the possibility of a "God gene," or a group of genes linked with belief, in humans. In support of this possibility, researchers quoted in the *Telegraph* point to the usefulness of a moralizing god to effect social cohesiveness and perpetuate life, particularly among larger societies. Says John Burn, medical director of the Institute of Human Genetics at the University of Newcastle (England), "A willingness to live, and if necessary, die, for a belief is a powerful selective advantage. I think there is a genetic propensity for us to believe."

Countering research on the health benefits of religious belief is research published in the *Lancet*. Researchers at the College of Physicians and Surgeons at Columbia University found little empirical support for the claim that good physical health is promoted by religious or spiritual belief. Lead author Richard P. Sloan, Ph.D., professor of behavioral medicine at Columbia University, noted that the research did not identify other variables that could account for a link between health and religion, and did not refine their definitions of religious activity.

Further, the researchers suggest that even if a rigorous study identified causal links between religion and health, medical practitioners should not attempt to integrate religion into medical treatment. Dr. Sloan said, "[W]e would never expect a doctor to say, 'There is compelling evidence that marriage is beneficial to health. My advice is to get married.' That would be regarded as an outrageous intrusion. It is even more so for religion than marriage."

Whether gaining an awareness of a patient's spirituality becomes standard operating procedure for physicians, it is likely that Americans will continue to access their God during health crises. As Dr. Koenig said in *Newsweek*, "[O]lder adults in America today are a very religious population."

RELIGION AND SPIRITUALITY

The Religion Shopping Mall

78 Say what you will about consumer culture, it is not closed-minded. Americans are always open to shopping around, considering alternative brands, and trying out the new-and-improved. This is just as true if the commodity in question is not detergent or jeans but religion. Americans are open-minded about religion, and America has turned into one big religion shopping mall.

True, there are some Americans who view their religious convictions as immovable, and would not ever consider altering them. But in our consumer society, such a stance is itself a choice, like unstinting loyalty to Maytags. Many other Americans, even if raised in a certain religion, are likely to shop around once they are let loose from the home, looking for the best possible fit for their own spiritual style. Some Americans are not raised in any religion, and are even more likely to consider a multitude of faiths should they feel a spiritual quest coming on.

Two broader trends feed this tendency. One is the omnipresence of consumer culture, which tends to color everything in its own free-market hue. Especially since the collapse of Communism and the end of the Cold War, it seems that the laws of supply and demand can do no wrong, so it seems fitting that religions should have to compete for consumers' faith commitments on the open market. Another motivating factor is the likelihood that each of us will come into contact on a daily basis with people of different faiths. Gone are the days when everyone the average Methodist met was another Methodist. Now cable and satellite television transmits a variety of religious talking heads into our homes, from Buddhist monks to Catholic nuns to Protestant televangelists. Recent news events rooted in the Islamic world have driven high sales of books about Islam. Immigration is constantly complicating the religious demographics of America. At one time, a book on American religion was published with the title *Protestant-Catholic-Jew*. Now it

193

would have to include the country's 5 to 6 million Muslims, 2 to 3 million Buddhists, 1 million Hindus, and 250,000 Sikhs. The subtitle of Diana Eck's *A New Religious America* (2002) says it all: *How a "Christian Country" Has Become the World's Most Religiously Diverse Nation.*

There is not literally a religion shopping mall—a brick-and-mortar mall with each religion occupying a separate storefront. But the Internet comes close. Many denominations and even individual houses of worship have Web sites inviting people to join. In addition, there are multifaith Web sites such as Beliefnet and Faith.com, which cater to every spiritual need and provide information on virtually every religion. Beliefnet even includes a Belief-o-Matic, which will analyze your responses to a quiz and "tell you what religion (if any) you practice . . . or ought to consider practicing."

The religion sections of bookstores are also versions of the religion shopping mall. Even in the Bible Belt, bookstores offer not only Bibles but books by the Dalai Lama, works on the occult, and tomes on "earth-based religion," such as Wicca and paganism. There are also books about the religion shopping mall itself—the intertwining of the consumer mentality with religion—such as *Spiritual Marketplace* (2001) by Wade Clark Roof and *Shopping for Faith* (2002) by Richard Cimino and Don Lattin.

Just as consumer culture has changed the way believers act in searching for religion, it has also changed the way religions or houses of worship act in trying to attract believers. Houses of worship are more apt to be image-conscious and consumer-friendly—whether by literally setting up shop in a shopping strip, offering swank vacations at retreat centers, or packing in believers in giant megachurches. Denominations may mount professional PR or advertising campaigns, and try to field attractive spokespeople on talk shows. Some religions may alter their doctrine, or at least their presentation of doctrine, to make it more palatable to consumers. For example, most Christian churches still have the doctrine of hell in their body of dogma, but many priests and ministers rarely if ever teach it from their pulpits, in part because of fear that churchgoers won't like it—and will vote with their feet by going elsewhere.

Indeed, one characteristic of the religion shopping mall, as of consumer culture in general, is consumer mobility. Believers who feel free to shop among religions feel free to go back and forth among different religions, and to mix and match. They may accessorize an underlying Episcopalianism, for example, with a dash of teaching from the Dalai Lama and a few prayers from the Upanishads. They may thoroughly mix traditions to form what Cimino and Lattin, in *Shopping for Faith*, call hybrid religions. They may adopt the practices of a certain faith while de-emphasizing belief in its doctrines—a position similar to that of Elaine Pagels in *Beyond Belief* (2003). They may even be neoagnostics, who are not sure there is a God but nevertheless want to build their own personal spirituality.

There are still stick-in-the-mud believers who insist the important question is not whether a religion caters to one's "spiritual needs" but whether it teaches the truth. As C. S. Lewis wrote in *Mere Christianity*, "the question should never be: 'Do I like that kind of service?' but 'Are these doctrines true.'" Such an austere position will probably always attract some people, but it does not change the existence of the religion shopping mall; rather, it is one of the options available in the mall.

9

Science and Technology

Back to Space

79 In 1972, when the last American left the moon, the heart seemed to go out of the nation's space program. In the decades that followed, there were still accomplishments—unmanned probes to the planets, Skylab, the space shuttle, the Hubble Space Telescope—but these were far less glamorous than the lunar achievement. Before, we had reached for the moon; now, we used a space truck to install satellites in a parking orbit. We had gone from adventurers to glorified cable installers. Recently, however, space has become an area of interest again—not just to the United States, but to countries around the world as well. It may be that a Second Space Age is beginning.

Part of the reason for the decline of the First Space Age was the waning of the Cold War. The American quest for the moon was undertaken as part of a space race with the Soviet Union that had started when the Soviets launched the satellite *Sputnik* in 1957. In those days, it seemed that U.S. prestige and security were tied up in beating the Soviet Union on the high ground of space. As the Soviet Union deteriorated and finally, in 1991, passed out of existence, the U.S. space program's raison d'être died with it. Two fatal space shuttle disasters—the *Challenger* in 1986 and the *Columbia* in 2003—gave a black eye to the once proud National Aeronautics and Space Administration (NASA) and led many people to argue that the United States should get out of the space business altogether.

But the tide is turning back to space, driven this time not by a bipolar superpower rivalry but a multipolar international competition. On October 15, 2003, China asserted its growing prestige by becoming the third country to launch a man into space. Later that year, the European Space Agency managed to put a probe into orbit around Mars, although the landing craft it sought to place on the planet, Britain's *Beagle 2*, failed to establish contact with Earth. In the first days of 2004, NASA recovered from the *Columbia* disaster with two unmanned-spacecraft successes: *Stardust* scooped up samples from the nucleus of the comet Wild 2, while the *Spirit* rover landed on Mars and beamed spectacular pictures back to Earth.

Several countries have announced ambitious plans for space missions. China plans to establish a lunar orbital station. France has developed a commercial satellite launching service. Russia and the United States maintain a continuous space presence on the International Space Station. The U.S. spacecraft *Cassini* is set to reach Titan, a moon of Saturn, in July. President Bush proposed to send astronauts back to the moon by 2020 and eventually build a lunar base to use as a launching pad to Mars. He also proposed a successor to the space shuttle—a new spacecraft with more varied capabilities called a crew exploration vehicle.

Proposing a plan is not the same as following through. The first President Bush called for lunar colonies and a Mars mission back in 1989, but the plan went nowhere. This time, a changed, more competitive international scene might provide the drive needed to follow through on the plan. However, technical obstacles still remain. Going to Mars is not the same as going to the moon: the journey is considerably longer, exposing astronauts to much greater risks of radiation exposure. Replacing the shuttle is not as easy as it sounds. Numerous ideas are still being discussed for a replacement that will be cheaper, safer, and more versatile than the shuttle. Should the vehicle be vertically launched or horizontally launched? Should it be fully reusable or include disposable booster rockets? Or should a radically different method of reaching space be used? One such method would be the space elevator, a long, thin, strong

THE 100 BEST TRENDS, 2005

cable stretching directly from a location on Earth to a satellite that always hovers in a geosynchronous orbit over that location. Nanotubes, a product of nanotechnology, might be used in building such a cable.

A bigger obstacle is lack of public interest in space exploration. Polls show that interest in space has been low since the early 1990s, and has never been as high as it was around the time of the first moon landing, in 1969. The one thing that might raise public interest is if ordinary people are able to go to space commercially. At present, only the very rich have been able to buy their way into space, by signing up with the cash-strapped Russian space program. But it is just possible that in the coming years a commercially viable scramjet, a lightweight supersonic-combustion engine, will be developed. Operating at several times the speed of sound, it could fly from New York to Paris in an hour and could make space accessible to a wider clientele. At the moment, several nations, including the United States, are competing to build a viable scramjet. In 2002, an Australian team succeeded in sending a scramjet prototype 195 miles over Earth, at speeds of up to 1.5 miles per second. Commercial scramjet travel might be fifty years away, but space agencies may be using them much sooner than that. In a world where adventure tourists are willing to pay large sums for African safaris, the prospect of seeing space firsthand might be the best way to interest people in contributing to the Second Space Age.

Globally Warmer

80 Despite record cold and snow in some parts of the country, global warming has not gone away. Even President Bush's skepticism about the issue—a skepticism not shared by most climate scientists—has not made it go away. Here is a weather report on what we can expect on this issue in the next few years.

We can expect continued accumulation of evidence that global warming is occurring, and that it is being caused by rising levels of greenhouse gases. These are substances such as carbon dioxide that are known as greenhouse gases because of their heat-trapping properties. These gases are emitted by the world's factories, automobiles, and other fossil-fuel-burning machines. Evidence for global warming and the greenhouse effect comes from many quarters, and it should continue to pile up for some time. For example, the Greenland ice sheet melted more in the summer of 2002 than at any time in the twenty-four years in which its status was tracked. Carbon levels in the atmosphere were about 275 parts per million before industrial times; today they are about 370 parts per million. Average global temperatures have been putting the earth in its warmest period in a millennium, and rising. September 2003 was the warmest September worldwide since records started being kept in 1880.

We can also expect simple-minded disbelief in global warming based on local conditions—the "How can they say there's global warming when it's snowing again?" response. This ignores the fact that global warming has to do with average global temperatures over sustained periods, not fleeting weather in one place or another. Indeed, one prediction of global warming is that the eastern seaboard may become colder in winter, not warmer. This is because thawing sea ice and heavier rainfall in the North Atlantic may contribute to the formation of cold fronts in this region. So easterners shouldn't expect global warming to deliver a windfall of balmy January weather any time soon.

Some scientists, who are presumably better informed than the average Joe or Jane, still insist that they don't know how much influence humans have on climate, and whether global warming is occurring at all. But these scientists are increasingly in the minority, even if their views are attractive to some industrial leaders and policymakers.

The one thing that might make global warming go away is if humankind cuts back on its burning of fossil fuels. Most industrial nations, including Japan and the countries of the European Union, agreed to do just this in the Kyoto Protocol, but in 2001 President Bush refused to accept that treaty. At issue was the Kyoto position in favor of mandatory greenhouse gas restrictions, versus Bush's refusal to accept anything but voluntary measures. In late 2002, Bush started to send signals that he might moderate that position, and there were some signs that Congress might move toward gradual mandatory restrictions.

Even if the developed world moves to implement mandatory greenhouse gas restrictions, the developing world may not be quick to sign on. With globalization encouraging even the poorest countries to compete as industrial nations, smokestacks and car exhausts are churning in many more places than before. In China, for example, coal use is rising faster than almost anywhere else in the world—a serious matter because coal, when burned to generate electricity, releases more greenhouse pollution than oil or natural gas. The International Energy Agency in Paris forecasts that the increase in greenhouse gas emissions in China from 2000 to 2030 will nearly equal the level of growth in the whole industrialized world. India, another country rising in industrialization, is also rising in its emissions of greenhouse gases, while deforestation of the Amazon in Brazil may also be contributing to global warming.

As the world tries to balance its hunger for energy with the need to curb greenhouse gas emissions, alternative sources of energy may begin to look appealing. Nuclear power may come back into vogue, after its long period in the wilderness because of public safety concerns. Solar and wind power, long dismissed as "sunshine and breezes," may begin to look more serious. Ideas that once sounded science-fictiony may be seriously developed, such as space-based solar power. This could come from orbiting satellites that would receive sunlight and transmit it to the earth in the form of microwaves.

If, despite everyone's best efforts, global warming does not slow down, Band-Aid measures may start to proliferate. In a *New York Times* op-ed piece, Oliver Morton recommended dropping a giant tarp on the summit of Africa's Mount Kilimanjaro to protect the mountain's retreating snowcap. Unless such a measure is taken, Morton argues, the snows of Kilimanjaro may become a thing of the past.

Band-Aid measures won't help solve the most dire predictions of global warming: hurricanes more ferocious than any before seen; the Dust Bowl returning to the Great Plains; New York City flooded as a result of melting polar caps. Before things reach that point, it is possible that humanity will notice with more soberness that the globe is getting warmer, and do something about it.

The Incredible Shrinking Science

81 You know a technology has arrived when Michael Crichton writes a thriller about it. His germ-warfare novel *The Andromeda Strain* appeared a few years before bacteria were genetically engineered for the first time; his cloned-dinosaurs novel *Jurassic Park* appeared a few years before the first mammal was cloned. In 2002 he published *Prey*, about a swarm of microscopic robots built through nanotechnology, the industrial application of science on a very small scale. As Crichton's clouds of murderous, shape-shifting nanoparticles wreaked havoc on their creators, real nanotechnologists could take comfort in knowing that their field was now as hot as the latest bestseller.

The idea of nanotechnology dates back to a 1959 speech by Richard Feynman, "There's Plenty of Room at the Bottom," but the term itself was coined more recently by K. Eric Drexler and popularized in his 1986 book *Engines of Creation*. It shares the prefix *nano-* (extremely small) with the nanometer, which is 1 billionth of a meter, or 100,000 times as thin as a human hair. Nanotechnology takes place on a scale of 100 nanometers or less—a scale that is home to viruses, individual molecules, and the tiniest features of microchips. For most of history, the nanoscale was off-limits to human tinkering. People could chop down trees and thread needles, but not until recent decades could they directly manipulate molecules, even atoms, to produce working machines on a nanoscale. The aim of nanotechnology is to arrange atoms in a specified order to do useful work, and to do so cost-effectively. Cost-effectiveness is easier to achieve if molecular machines themselves do the task: nanomachines that can self-replicate and mechanically position atoms to make useful products. If the right kinds of molecular machines can be built, a whole range of products may follow, incorporating sophisticated technology invisible to the naked eye: everything from new medical treatments to quantum computers to microprecise crime scene investigation to self-cleaning kitchens.

In recent years, science has been making progress toward this nanofuture. Carbon nanotubes were invented, cylindrical molecules of carbon that are stronger than steel and can conduct more current than silicon. Scientists developed nanowires, virtual strings of atoms only a few nanometers thick, and a nanothermometer that can measure temperature changes at the molecular level. IBM developed the Millipede, a data storage device that uses nanoprobes to store one terabit of data per square inch. New York University scientist Nadrian Seeman is conducting research into building complex, atomically precise structures using DNA. In 2003, MIT and Harvard Medical School scientists built a tiny system of blood vessels that is a step to building whole organs for use as transplants. The same year, Israeli scientists for the first time used biological self-assembly to create a functional electronic nanodevice. With a toolkit of DNA, carbon nanotubes, bacterial proteins, antibodies, silver, and gold, they produced a self-assembling nanotransistor.

As nanotechnology, backed by taxpayer dollars, gains momentum in the laboratory, the business world is signing on to reap the potential profits. Some nanotech materials are already on the market: nanoscale clay particles to strengthen car bodies; carbon nanotubes contributing greater stiffness to Babolat tennis rackets. In December 2003, President Bush signed a law authorizing $3.7 billion in federal subsidies for nanotechnology research and development over the next four years. The

National Science Foundation projects that sales of nanotech products will reach $1 trillion by 2015. With all the hoopla, venture capital has been flowing steadily into nanotech companies, and the few publicly traded startups, such as Nanogen, have been attracting investors. Investors are especially hungry to put money in companies such as IBM that have strong portfolios of intellectual property—valuable nanotechnology patents that other companies will need to license to get their work done.

Still, there are reasons to be wary of the nanotech bandwagon. One is the danger that the sector is being overhyped: all one has to say is "dot-com" to remind investors of how easily tech stocks can generate bubbles that burst. The fancy molecular machines that all the fuss is about are not yet here, and no one knows for sure which companies will be the winners and losers once they do arrive.

Another problem is that the health and environmental hazards of nanotechnology are as yet little explored. DuPont researchers discovered in 2002 that when they injected carbon nanotubes into the lungs of rats, 15 percent of the animals died—not an encouraging sign as nanotubes proliferate in industry. No doubt there will be increasing regulation and controversy as the nanotechnology field develops, just as there has been for biotechnology. But just as biotechnology has continued to develop with great speed in the last few decades, nanotechnology will probably do so as well in the years to come. The results are likely to be small in size but vast in impact.

Integrated Devices

82 As people multitask their way through life, their gadgets also have to provide multiple services. Years ago, the TV-VCR or phone-fax combo was enough. Then the personal computer integrated the DVD player. Now there are even more complicated items that combine more electronic consumer elements, such as organizers and phones, recorders, cameras, and players. Even the trusty PC will be an all-in-one information and entertainment powerhouse. It's all a far cry from the old *Honeymooners* Handy Housewife Helper that could slice, dice, and core an apple.

Some integrated items gain immediate popularity by combining desired but heretofore unavailable services. One is the palmtop that is also a global positioning system (GPS) receiver. In addition to linking recording and editing elements from one's Windows PC, the palmtop also employs the GPS receiver to tell you where you are now and give directions to where you want to go.

Other integrated devices have become popular by combining already commonplace elements in novel ways. One such device is predicted to be the all-in-one computer/media center. Known by Microsoft as the Media Center, the computer will integrate various capabilities. It will be a digital television, music player and music collector, digital photo archive, and game center. Thus far, however, there has been some commercial and consumer resistance to the computer-as-center. Filmmakers and music companies fear the center's link to the Internet will increase film and music piracy. Consumers reject its high price and lack of ability for customization. Still, industry executives say the integrated entertainment center is on its way. In the *New York Times*, Jen-Hsun Huang, executive at video card maker NVIDIA, said, "In five years it will absolutely reshape the consumer electronics industry."

Until it does become commonplace household equipment, it joins the other multitasking products that are taking a while to become part of the household. For example, many Americans have still not gotten used to making compilations for the MP3 players or even how to master the combination cell phone and personal organizer.

Integrated products have been adopted very quickly in some business arenas. For example, they demonstrated their usefulness and have been widely accepted in the 2004 presidential campaign. There, commonly used devices have included hand-held reorganizers that send text messages that coincide with video feed from a film crew. Reporters delivering text now also use various digital gadgets, such as wireless laptops, digital tape recorders with software that downloads speech as an audio file, digital video cameras, and a cell phone. The increased connections make it possible for reporters to hand in copy whenever and wherever they want, not just at the campaign filing center that had the necessary hookups.

In the 21st century, multitasking devices cover the human realms of work and leisure. But it has yet to learn to multitask love. For that, most people still prefer to conduct a single function—wooing one partner at a time.

Newgenics

83 The idea of "designer babies"—children bred or bioengineered for superiority—has been a staple of science fiction for years, from the scenery-chewing Khan of *Star Trek* fame to the 1997 Ethan Hawke movie *Gattaca*. This idea has usually been associated with eugenics, the discredited, state-administered 20th-century efforts (by Nazis and others) to weed out genetic undesirables. Yet, the customizing of embryos is no longer science fiction but fact, and a new, privately driven kind of eugenics is afoot. Call it newgenics: not a coordinated effort to build a master race, but a decentralized trend in which parents try to give their kids a genetic edge by any available means.

Even setting aside the wonders of genetic engineering, the kids'-competitive-edge business is a huge industry. It spans everything from Kaplan SAT prep courses to orthodontia to infant formulas that are supplemented with fatty acids supposed to bolster your baby's intellect. Short kids can get growth hormone to enhance their height; fidgety kids can get Ritalin to improve their concentration. Add present-day know-ledge of the human genome and gene manipulation, and the possibili-ties become even greater. For parents willing to plunk down big bucks to spruce up their already-born children, why not go the extra step and have the children born to order?

This brave new commercial world has been brewing since the 1970s, when production of human embryos in a test tube—in vitro fertilization, or IVF—came into being as a way of helping infertile couples conceive. This was the same decade when genetic engineering first began to be practiced, with genes snipped from one organism and implanted into another to create products such as bacteria that could crank out human insulin for use by diabetics. Both of these technologies—IVF and genetic engineering—spawned successful industries, the former providing embryos for implantation in the wombs of formerly barren mothers; the latter yielding a host of new medicines, crops, and genetically engineered lab animals. Together, they created an amazing possibility. If human genes could be spliced at will into bacteria, they could, in theory, be spliced into human embryos, such as those produced by IVF technology. In theory, genetic engineers could endow the human embryo with genes for this or that trait—blue eyes, genius intelligence, a great pitching arm. All that was needed was exact knowledge of which genes did what—knowledge that was mostly lacking back in the 1970s.

Today, knowledge of which genes do what is still very incomplete, but it has been advancing steadily, and it took a major step forward on April 14, 2003. That was the day that the Human Genome Project announced completion of its multiyear effort to sequence all 3 billion DNA letters in the human genetic inheritance, or genome. Even now, scientists are using that mammoth genetic roadmap to try to understand specifically how genes figure in diseases and contribute to our various traits. As their knowledge grows, it is increasingly likely that IVF labs will be able to offer parents designer babies or superbabies, with just the traits they've been looking for.

Indeed, through different technologies, parents have already been practicing newgenics (Edward Black's term in his book *War against the*

Weak). Back in the late 1970s, a millionaire inventor named Robert Graham founded a sperm bank for the production of "genius babies," with sperm donated by exceptionally bright or athletic individuals. More than 240 children were conceived through the bank; a sampling of 15, surveyed by Slate.com in 2001, turned out to be bright and healthy, though not yet Nobel Prize–winners. This may seem like a fringe case of newgenics, but another example is completely mainstream: genetic screening. This technology, in use since the 1980s, is the basis for amniocentesis, a common procedure in which amniotic fluid from an expectant mother is tested for various genetic markers. Through amnio-centesis, older pregnant women throughout the world are informed whether their fetus has an extra copy of chromosome 21, the cause of Down syndrome; if it does, many of these women opt to abort the fetus. Similar choices are being made every day to rule out the birth of children who have other genetic diseases, or are simply the wrong sex: in China and India, for example, parents regularly use prenatal testing to ensure that their child will be a boy.

The latest twist is to combine IVF and genetic screening so that parents can select the optimal embryo among several conceived for them in the lab. Through preimplantation genetic diagnosis, or PGD, couples who have a history of genetic diseases, such as cystic fibrosis or hemo-philia, can rule out any embryos with genes for those diseases, allowing only a healthy one to be implanted in the mother's womb. In one case, that of the Nash family in Colorado in 2000, it was used to ensure the birth of a child who had the same tissue type as his already-born sister, and could therefore provide her a stem cell transplant she needed. If you think PGD is only being used in extreme situations such as this, think again. In some U.S. fertility clinics, PGD is already being used to ensure that only an embryo of the right sex is implanted. According to *Washington Monthly*, fertility specialists are receiving requests to screen embryos for homosexuality and hyperactivity, whenever, and if ever, that becomes possible.

Intentional genetic engineering of human embryos—the deliberate splicing in of desired genes or removing of undesired ones—is still not being practiced. But it has happened as a side effect. Babies conceived in the 1990s through a process called cytoplasmic transfer have altered mitochondrial DNA, resulting from the injection of cytoplasm from the eggs of a fertile donor into the eggs of an infertile patient. That altered genetic material will be passed on to those children's descendants, if any—making this possibly the first example of germline (or inheritable) genetic engineering in humans.

With the market for newgenics as large as it is, and with genetic knowledge and rapidly advancing technology, it seems inevitable that parents will soon be customizing their babies to an even greater degree than they are already doing. Human cloning is fraught with both technical and legal obstacles, but should these be resolved, parents may even be able to clone little genetic replicas of themselves.

The only brake will probably come from legislators convinced that newgenics is a bad idea. The case against newgenics is already being made from many directions: conservative Christians arguing that it entails aborting or distorting of embryos; left-wing opponents seeing a divide coming between rich people who can afford superbabies and poor people who can't. One critic, Francis Fukuyama, argues in his book *Our Posthuman Future* that our basic ethical principles and political rights (such as equality) are based on judgments about human nature. Therefore, he says, alterations to human nature, such as those that might arise from the creation of a race of designer babies, threaten those principles and rights and should be avoided through state regulation.

To a greater or lesser degree, state regulation will be imposed, but it is unlikely to stop the forward rush of newgenics. Unlike the old state-sponsored eugenics, newgenics is fundamentally a matter of individual parents wanting the best for their children, and paying whatever they can afford to bring it about. That drive is rooted in old-fashioned human nature, and mere laws and regulations are unlikely to stop it. If the government cracks down too hard, irate voters (influenced by the fertility industry lobby) will probably vote out legislators who put too many legal curbs on their freedom to customize their children. Newgenics, in one form or another, is here to stay.

The Return of Freud

84 The story of Sigmund Freud's reputation is as dramatic a case history as that of any of his patients. During his lifetime (1856–1939), the founder of psychoanalysis was a household word and a font of controversy, attracting both admirers and detractors. After his death, his concepts—the Oedipus complex; repression, transference, and projection; the central role of the unconscious—became a kind of psychiatric orthodoxy, practiced on many psychoanalysts' couches and filtering through literary studies and popular culture. But by the 1970s, cracks had appeared in Freud's reputation, and by the 1990s he was under heavy attack when he wasn't being dismissed altogether. Unscientific and opportunistic were among the kinder things said about him; misogynistic, paranoid, and dishonest among the harsher. Yet, individual Freudian concepts are beginning to get a new life, and Freud's works are coming to be prized for their literary and humanistic value, if not their scientific accuracy.

The notion of the unconscious is particularly hot these days. In recent years, empirical studies have documented the existence of numerous important unconscious processes, including subliminal influence, self-deception, first impressions, and preconscious volition (the initiation of a decision before the mind has become aware of it). In his 2002 book *Hidden Minds*, Frank Tallis argues that Freud deserves credit for having uncovered the power of the unconscious that modern science is mapping out. This degree of credit may be more than Freud deserves: he didn't invent the idea of the unconscious, just one version of it, and the version that scientists are documenting today bears little resemblance to the version he did invent. Nevertheless, Freud certainly made the unconscious famous, and remains associated with it in the popular mind. So it is likely that, through vehicles like Tallis's book, Freud's reputation will benefit from the general resurgence of interest in the unconscious.

Freud is also benefiting from the discoveries of cognitive science, which tend to show that the mind operates through specific, in-built modules, such as the "habit system" and the "supervisory attention system," rather than as a unified entity dominated by a central, conscious command. In the new model, there is no single central command, and the different modules of the mind interact with, support, battle, and suppress each other in various combinations. For example, neuroscientists Michael Gazzaniga and Roger Sperry have studied patients whose left brain hemisphere is divided from the right hemisphere, and have found that the right hemisphere can choose actions on its own, without the knowledge of the left hemisphere. The left hemisphere's contribution is in generating an account (possibly an incorrect one) of why the person chose what he or she did.

There is nothing in the cognitive science model that corresponds specifically to Freud's tripartite division of id, ego, and superego, but there are defense mechanisms that suppress or explain away facts that would be inconvenient for one's self-image. These have been documented in studies like those of Randolph Nesse and Alan Lloyd. "Though modern psychologists and psychiatrists tend to reject orthodox Freudian theory," says Steven Pinker in *The Blank Slate*, "many acknowledge that Freud was right about the defense mechanisms of the ego."

Most therapists today don't practice strict Freudian analysis, and the pharmaceutical industry has heavily pushed the notion that drugs such as Prozac can make common mental disorders go away. But most research indicates that these drugs are of limited value and that talk therapy is needed as well. Recent studies show that common mental disorders such as depression are more widespread than previously thought, so talk therapy is probably going to be a growing field. Talk therapy of all schools is indebted to Freud and remains associated with him—and this too will aid in keeping his name alive.

Even as science breathes new life into Freud's reputation, the humanities is doing its own job of resurrection. Penguin is launching the New Penguin Freud, edited by Adam Phillips, in which each of Freud's works will be retranslated with a minimum of technical vocabulary and issued as a separate paperback for readers' literary pleasure. Even if some readers only buy Freud to criticize him, Freud will still be selling books—and nothing succeeds like success. For this and other reasons, Freud is likely to remain popular, and to enjoy qualified but growing esteem.

Rosie the Robot Redux

85 Where are all the robots we were supposed to have? Why don't any of us have a mechanical maid like the Jetsons' Rosie the Robot, or a rolling buddy like Will Robinson's friend Robot in *Lost in Space*, or even a killer cyborg like the Terminator? The fact is, the robots are already here, but not in the shape we expected them. Welcome to the age of robo-gadgets.

After decades of research in the fields of artificial intelligence (AI) and robotics, scientists no longer expect that they will manufacture a genuine "Rosie the Robot" anytime soon: an artificial person that seems virtually human as it bickers with human masters, irons their clothes, cooks their meals, and flirts with other robots. The complexity of such a virtual human is beyond present-day science. But by concentrating on smaller modules of human behavior, such as navigating around obstacles or smiling, AI and robotics researchers have been remarkably successful at creating machines that perform certain particular human tasks or mimic particular human traits. Some of these machines have been around for decades—industrial robots assembling cars; animatronic presidents at Disney World—but until recently, they required a technically trained service crew and were affordable only to corporate budgets. Now, with advances in basic science at places like the MIT Artificial Intelligence Laboratory (in operation in some form since at least 1959);

faster, cheaper micro-processors; and burgeoning commercial interest, robots with advanced AI are beginning to penetrate the consumer market. Though technologically sophisticated, these robo-gadgets are designed for ease of use and middle-class pocketbooks.

First there were toys, like My Real Baby, an animatronic infant doll from Hasbro that responded expressively to a child's handling (laughing when tickled; crying when not fed); and AIBO, Sony's doglike entertainment robot. These just-for-fun robo-gadgets began appearing early this century, and their sales have depended on the vagaries of children's tastes. They have been followed by utilitarian robo-gadgets, such as the Roomba, a robotic vacuum cleaner from iRobot, a company whose origins lie in the MIT AI Lab and that previously developed My Real Baby in collaboration with Hasbro. The debut of the Roomba in December 2002 received a big publicity blitz, with spots on *The Today Show* and *Live with Regis and Kelly*. Priced at $199.99 and adorned with a *Good Housekeeping* seal, the saucer-shaped device vacuums automatically, intelligently avoids stairs, and even cleans under beds while you watch television or do whatever else you like. *Esquire* magazine called the Roomba "a self-propelled, self-navigating sucker that dances around furniture and avoids terrified pets while you practice your speed eating."

Other utilitarian robo-gadgets are starting to appear, including Robomower, a robotic lawn-mower from Friendly Robotics, priced at about $750. The coming years will see a profusion of robo-gadgets, each automating some area of household drudgery. Which robo-gadgets succeed will depend on price and ease of use. Initial sales will be driven by the coolness factor (one Amazon.com customer called the Roomba "the coolest thing I ever bought"), but sales will peter out quickly unless the robo-snowblower, robo-garbage-carrier, or robo-dishwasher is affordable and does its job without much fuss.

Some robo-gadgets will be barely recognizable as robots. The Segway Human Transporter, currently available for about $4,500, looks like a two-wheeled scooter, but underlying its uncanny ability to maintain balance is some seriously high-tech computer wizardry. A company called Yobotics is using its expertise in walking robotics to develop the

RoboWalker, a powered device that disabled people can wear like mechanized braces to augment or replace their leg functioning. Robo-gadgets are increasingly being used for activities that require extreme delicacy, such as surgery, or that are dangerous for humans, such as searching rubble for survivors or venturing onto battlefields. Flying Predator drones—airborne robots operated by humans from afar—attacked Iraqi antiaircraft batteries in the Iraq war in 2003; fully automated, unmanned fighter jets are now under development. On the ground, the U.S. Army used an unmanned robot vehicle called PackBot, developed by iRobot, to conduct search and surveillance in Afghanistan in 2002.

Other devices might be called virtual robo-gadgets: software programs that make use of AI advances, such as fuzzy logic, which allows computers to deal with imprecise assessments, and neural networks, which learn through experience on the analogy of human brains. When you visit Amazon.com and are greeted with a list of personalized book or CD recommendations, you are meeting a virtual robo-gadget: a recommender system that analyzes patterns in your previous choices to predict what else you might like. (Ironically, e-retailers have found that these recommender systems work better when human editors regularly tweak them.) AI progams will increasingly be used in banking, police surveillance, stock-picking, medical diagnosis, mechanics' shops—even such humble activities as gambling. In December 2002, an Australian researcher unveiled MAIT, an automated sports tipster that reportedly outperformed the best human tipsters at predicting the results of Australian Rugby League matches.

A full-service robot maid is still a far-future dream, but robo-gadgets in the near future will be able to do multiple tasks—not just vacuum but also detect money on the floor, for example. That will fit with the current trend of hybrid devices, gadgets that offer more value to customers by doing more than one thing. Some robots will be designed as "base-bots," versatile platforms to which useful functions can be added as the technology develops, just as a home PC gains new functions as new software is added. Indeed, future robo-gadgets may be integrated with the home computer, accessing its processing power through a wireless connection. Off in the distance, the dream of the robotic servant will continue to drive innovation. *New Scientist* reported in 2001 that a company called Probotics was developing a robot named Cye who could fetch you a beer from the refrigerator. "That's something I know I can build," said Henry Thorne of Probotics. "In 15 years I want it to be able to fix your toilet."

The Science of Happiness

86 A generation ago, hardheaded scientists couldn't be bothered with a concept like "happiness." Liquid oxygen and protons—*that* was science. "Happiness" was a vague concept fit for wedding speeches and greeting cards. But increasingly scientists have become interested in the nature of happiness and whether they can use rigorous research to increase the total stock of it. As their discoveries proliferate, look for new drugs, techniques, and science-based advice on how to become more cheerful, content, and serene—in a word, happier.

One important discovery of recent years is that happiness has a genetic component. Through studies of identical twins reared apart, psychologist David Lykken has found evidence for a gene-based "Happiness Set Point": a basic level of contentment that an individual tends to have no matter what fortunes or misfortunes life throws at that person. According to *New York Times* columnist Richard A. Friedman, MD, some people appear to be born with a "joyous temperament," known as hyperthymia, which makes them cheerful and optimistic in both good times and bad. Their mirror opposites are people with dysthymia, a chronic, mild depression that makes them incorrigibly gloomy, something like the donkey Eeyore in the Winnie-the-Pooh stories.

Researchers are now hard at work trying to pinpoint the genes that have an impact on happiness. In 2003, scientists discovered one candidate: a gene involved in the brain's use of serotonin, a chemical messenger, or neurotransmitter, believed to influence mood. In a study of 800 adults, people with a certain form of this serotonin-transporter gene were at higher risk of depression than people with a different form. At the moment, such studies are in their infancy, but in time, they may lead to new treatments to remedy depression and boost happiness.

Genetic research is linked to studies of the biochemistry of happiness: that is, what happens in the brain as neurons swap neurotransmitters to communicate with one another, and how that affects mood. Beginning in the 1980s, biochemical research yielded an important new class of antidepressants, the selective serotonin reuptake inhibitors, or SSRIs. The most famous member of that class was Prozac (fluoxetine), but many others have arisen, including Luvox (fluvoxamine), Paxil (paroxetine), Zoloft (sertraline), and Celexa (citalopram). They are now commonly prescribed for depression, along with older treatments such as heterocyclics (tricyclics) and newer ones such as Wellbutrin (buproprion).

Many of the 19 million Americans estimated to be clinically depressed have benefited from one or more antidepressant pharmaceuticals, and new drugs are constantly in development, whether to minimize side effects or improve effectiveness. Current avenues for research include trying to boost the growth of new nerve cells in a region of the brain called the hippocampus, and attempting to block release of the stress hormone cortisol.

As pharmacological remedies improve and become more widespread, some people worry that the country will become a nation of happiness zombies, induced by drugs to feel blissful instead of going out and achieving satisfaction through hard work. "[A] fraudulent happiness is just what the pharmacological management of our mental lives threatens to confer upon us," wrote the President's Council on Bioethics in a recent report. This concern seems to be based on a misunderstanding of what antidepressants do. Unlike cocaine or heroin, SSRIs are not addictive and do not produce a euphoric high. They don't tend to reduce the desire to do hard work, but enable it in people who might otherwise be too depressed to work. A study at the University of California at San Francisco showed that nondepressed volunteers were not made any happier by taking the SSRI Paxil.

Happiness is a complex phenomenon, and no reputable scientist thinks that a single gene or chemical makes or breaks happiness. As Antonio Damasio argues in *Looking for Spinoza: Joy, Sorrow, and the Feeling Brain* (2003), there is increasing evidence that body states as well as brain states contribute to feelings of joy or sorrow. Lykken, in his book *Happiness: The Nature and Nurture of Joy and Contentment* (2000), proposes that there are many actions we can take to make the most of our Happiness Set Point, such as focusing on the things that give us pleasure and counteracting negative emotions. Cognitive-behavioral therapy, which focuses on teaching people to change negative patterns of thought, has shown some effectiveness in treating depression. In *Destructive Emotions: A Scientific Dialogue with the Dalai Lama* (2003), Daniel Goleman offers scientific evidence that compassion, as stimulated by Buddhist meditation techniques, can induce a state of joy—and, conversely, that emotions such as hatred and craving can make for misery. Goleman's evidence comes from a conference attended by psychologists, neuroscientists, philosophers, and Buddhist monks. Its eclectic roster is itself a sign of how far scientists today are willing to go in their quest to understand happiness.

The Searchers

87 The United States has become a search engine nation. According to News.com, searching is the second biggest activity on the

Internet, next to e-mail. Every day on the World Wide Web, some 200 million searches are made, for information serious to silly. This trend will continue and will expand over the next several years; what will change are the varieties of search engines used. Search users will demand and will get more refined search engines that will mine text in more varied, personalized ways to lead users to their answers more quickly and easily.

Currently, most users turn first to the Google search engine. The *New York Times* reports that as of 2003, Google conducts 55 percent of all searches on the World Wide Web. For an average word, it finds hundreds of pages of citations, then ranks the listings by use of algorithms. The algorithms rank higher the sites that have the largest number of links. Google says that this process represents "the uniquely democratic nature of the Web." Yet, the algorithms as they are constituted also favor the major brand-name sites that are commonly known and the minor sites that have a big cult following (such as those focusing on conspiracies, for example).

In the future, other search engines may take different approaches. Yahoo! which uses Google's algorithmic searches, is seeking to develop its own algorithmic search. Yahoo! acquired two related companies, Inktomi and Overture, and forecasters predict a new Yahoo! search engine by early 2005.

It and other new search engines will probably try in various ways to figure out what kind of answer the user seeks before the engine begins searching. To accomplish that, the next generation of search engines will take in as much data as it can about the user's searching habits. For example, future engines want to build what SearchEngineWorkshops.com calls "little robots that 'come to know you' over a period of time, based on past searching habits." This is meant to help the engine refine the search and deliver a desired answer.

In addition, other companies are using different ways to view information. For example, Groxis and Kartoo organize their data visually, while Vivisimo sorts its information into groups of categories.

For more delicate categorization of text, people will increasingly consult text-mining tools that go far beyond what search engines can do. According to the Web site of the Text Mining Research Group at the University of Waikato, text mining is "about looking for patterns in natural language text, and may be defined as the process of analyzing text to extract information from it for particular purposes." It "uses recall and precision . . . to measure the effectiveness of different information extraction techniques, allowing quantitative comparisons to be made." While search engines gather documents with shared keywords, a text-mining program sifts through, categorizes, and makes connections within huge amounts of texts in minuscule amounts of time. It uses algorithms to determine the context behind words, set up categories, and draw connections among those categories. Now used largely for academic study and commercial research, text-mining programs could become popular with the information-laden consumer.

As for now, Google dominates the search engine market, with annual revenues estimated at $750 million and gross profit margins of 30 percent. But users may be so hungry for variety and complexity in their searches that search rivals like Yahoo! and text-mining programs may have a secure place. Google's more than 50,000 servers may not be enough.

Yet, as *Search Engine Guide*'s Andy Beal says, users have to decide between how personally tailored they want their search findings and how much privacy they are willing to give up to get it. He predicts that "the search results we receive in just a couple of years from now could make current search engine technology look as archaic and cumbersome as picking up a Yellow Pages book is today. However," he continues, "in order to achieve this new search nirvana" we will have to learn to cooperate with the search engine providers and "quell our fears and trepidations surrounding the protection of our privacy."

Spider Goats: The Age of Biobased Products

88 What do you get when you cross a spider with a goat? Answer: the beginning of an age of high-tech biobased products. Biobased products, which rely on plant and animal materials as their main ingredients, are nothing new. Wooden furniture and organic fertilizer are ancient and still-used examples of this category. But biotechnology, a set of tools for manipulating genes, has transformed the once homely field of biobased manufacturing into one that is exotic and poised for tremendous growth.

There is no better example than Montreal-based Nexia Biotechnologies, Inc. In concert with the U.S. Army, Nexia announced in 2002 that it had spun the first synthetic spider silk with properties similar to natural spider silk. As fans of *Spiderman* know, spider silk has long been admired for its amazing toughness and lightness: ounce for ounce, a strand of webbing that is only one-tenth the width of a human hair is five times stronger than steel. But until now, no one has been able to produce spider silk in sufficient quantities to make it commercially viable. Nexia, however, used genetic engineering to raise goats that carry spider genes, so that the females produce milk liberally laced with spider silk proteins. When these dragline proteins are harvested and spun into fibers, the result is a material tradenamed BioSteel. Nexia hopes to turn BioSteel into gold by using it to make everything from sutures and bulletproof vests to lightweight components for spaceships and minivans.

Some biobased products are attractive to industry because of properties that cannot otherwise be procured, such as the light superstrength of spider silk. Another example comes from extremophiles, microbes that live in superhot geysers, the ocean depths, and other punishing environments. These microbes produce enzymes that function even under extreme conditions of temperature, pressure, and pH, and those enzymes are attractive to industry as catalysts in production processes.

Diversa Corporation specializes in discovering and cloning just such enzymes. DNA itself is attractive for its potentially enormous computing power. Experiments have shown that DNA can be used as a "molecular computer," processing information on a tinier scale and with potentially far greater speed than silicon-based models.

Other biobased products are attractive not for their special properties, but for their environmental cleanliness. Until now, industrial manufacturing has relied heavily on plastics and other products made from petroleum, a resource that is nonrenewable and polluting. By contrast, plant and animal materials never run out and, in most cases, are biodegradable, so that they leave the environment in a more pristine condition than petroleum would. Biobased materials are now appearing in everything from fuels and fabrics to solvents and lubricants, and an increasing number of them make use of advanced biotechnology. In 2002, Cargill Dow launched a corn-based, bioengineered, environmentally friendly substance, NatureWorks, that can be used in place of plastic and polyester in clothing, bedding, and packaging. For some time, biotech companies have been engineering microorganisms that can eat up oil spills and other toxic messes (a field called bioremediation) or churn out mass quantities of vitamins and industrial enzymes.

As demand grows for these kinds of products, industrial biotech (biotechnology with industrial applications) may soon become as big a business as medical biotech. Consulting Resources Corporation foresees growth in this field of 17 percent a year over the next decade. In *The Shape of Things to Come*, Richard W. Oliver predicts, "The new economic engine that will soon power the new world of business is biomaterials. . . . Our entry into the age of Bio-Materials—biotechnology and the exciting world of new materials—holds the promise of gaining control over matter." Says Tom Mitchell, president and CEO of Genencor International, Inc., a pioneer in industrial biotech, "Fifteen years from now, we may look back and see that industrial biotech benefits are as great as biotech's impact on human health."

The War on Germs

89 In the old days, it seemed that germs were on the run. Vaccines and antibiotics effectively protected people from ancient microbial scourges such as polio, diphtheria, and pneumonia. Smallpox, in 1980, became the first disease to be completely eradicated by vaccination. Germs were spoken of lightly in advertising campaigns: Americans counted on their Listerine to kill millions of germs on contact.

Then AIDS emerged, killing more than 100,000 Americans by 1990. Tuberculosis, a disease believed to be a thing of the past, began recurring in epidemic form. Antibiotics, once surefire treatments for bacterial respiratory infections, frequently failed to do the trick because bacteria were developing antibiotic resistance. In 2003, scientists scrambled worldwide to do battle with yet another new disease, SARS (severe acute respiratory syndrome). Today, no one assumes germs are on the run.

Complicating the war on germs is the danger of deliberate infection by terrorists. In fall 2001, anthrax attacks on the eastern seaboard killed five people and sickened fourteen. Experts say that the country is still unprepared for another bioterrorist attack. Asked about this issue by *National Geographic News* in April 2003, Laurie Garrett, author of *The Coming Plague* (1994), said "[A]nybody . . . who is on the ground in public health in this country will tell you we are a far cry from being ready for such a thing."

Even without terrorism, public health officials have their hands full dealing with the germs nature delivers. The outbreak in Asia of a virulent new strain of avian influenza, or bird flu, has been challenging infectious disease experts around the world. So far, the disease has mostly been restricted to birds, but there have been a few human cases, the majority of those fatal.

One consolation in this case is that, for the most part, avian influenza has so far not been transmitted person to person, which would make containment harder than bird-to-person transmission. Another consolation is that contemporary science affords weapons for dealing with such a new strain. For example, scientists in the World Health Organization's influenza network used a new method called reverse genetics to develop a vaccine and diagnostic test for the virus, which is known as A(H5N1). The technique involves replacing the genes that make the virus harmful to birds with genes that are harmless. On the other hand, international health officials clearly felt overwhelmed by the rapid spread of the disease across half of Asia—so much so that they urged countries in Asia to consider the herculean task of vaccinating billions of birds against the disease.

Avian influenza demonstrates one of the ways that new diseases emerge: by incubation in an animal reservoir, then transmission from animals to humans, sometimes as a result of a new mutation.

Another risk factor for the spread of disease is government incompetence. The Chinese government initially denied the seriousness of the SARS outbreak, which contributed to its spread. Another risk factor is the same modern transportation that permits medicines and epidemiological teams to be transported rapidly around the world. Speaking about the devastating 1918–1919 Spanish influenza pandemic, Jeffrey Taubenberger of the Armed Forces Institute of Pathology in Washington told ABCNews.com: "In 1918, the flu spread at the speed of ships and trains. Now we have jumbo jets crossing the oceans on a routine basis. In many ways a virus might be more dangerous now than back then."

Whatever happens with this or that disease, complacency is a bad idea. For the foreseeable future, the struggle of humans against germs is likely to resemble not so much a victory lap as persistent urban warfare.

What a Tangled Web: Network Theory

90 In the 1980s chaos theory (or complexity theory) was the emerging science that spawned journal articles, attracted research dollars,

generated popular books, and had everyone excited. In the 2000s the emerging science du jour is network theory.

To a network theorist or network scientist, a network is any set of individual nodes connected by links—your high school graduating class; the Internet; Al Qaeda; the stock market; airports; power grids; epidemics; brain cells; the entire human population. Since the mid-1990s, network scientists have been analyzing such real-world networks, looking for the principles that govern them. They draw on a tradition of network (or graph) mathematics that reaches back to the 18th-century Swiss mathematician Leonhard Euler, but they have dramatically advanced the field by using sophisticated computers to do the heavy number-crunching. Like the earlier chaos theory, which centered on chaotic or complex systems, including networks, network theory has begun to attract big research dollars, stir academic debate, and penetrate popular consciousness.

One way to understand network theory is through the John Guare play *Six Degrees of Separation*, which drew on a 1967 experiment by psychologist Stanley Milgram that tried to show that anyone in the United States could reach anyone else through a chain of fewer than six people. Another way is through the game Six Degrees of Kevin Bacon, which draws on the same source. The "six degrees" phenomenon points to the existence of what are called "small-world" networks: networks in which the path of links between any two nodes tends to be short. The phenomenon also provided the title for a 2003 book on network theory by Duncan J. Watts, *Six Degrees: The Science of a Connected Age.*

The findings of network theory are now being applied in many fields, including sociology, computer science, economics, disease, and war. For example, network theorists have shown that many small-world networks are characterized by hubs; a hub is a node with many links, in contrast to ordinary nodes, which have relatively few links. In network theory jargon, hub-laden networks are called "scale-free." The destruction of hubs can devastate a scale-free network, even though the destruction of several randomly selected nodes might not. As network theorist Albert-László Barabási explains in his book *Linked: The New Science of Networks* (2002), this principle has vast implications: for example, security personnel should realize that the apparently indestructible Internet could be crippled by destroying some of its hubs; and epidemiologists might try to stop disease outbreaks by identifying and treating hubs (e.g., Typhoid Mary) in the transmission network.

The U.S. military is working with network theorists to fight terrorism, and with good reason: 9/11 and its aftermath showed the resilience of two prominent networks, Wall Street and Al Qaeda. The destruction of the World Trade Center failed to shut down Wall Street for more than a few days, because the U.S. business world is not a simple hierarchy in which all functions depend on one center; it can't be shut down simply by destroying one of its prominent edifices. The same holds true for Al Qaeda, which despite the invasion of Afghanistan and the removal of some of its top leaders was not destroyed. To understand how to defeat Al Qaeda and protect the United States from future attacks, network theory is needed.

Network theory is now rippling through the publishing world, underpinning books from Malcolm Gladwell's *The Tipping Point* (2000) to Ed Keller and Jon Berry's *The Influentials* (2003), which profiles local leaders "who come from every city and town and who shape the opinions and trends in our country." Other books set out to explain network theory to the uninitiated, including those mentioned previously by Watts and Barabási, and Mark Buchanan's *Nexus: Small Worlds and the Groundbreaking Science of Networks* (2002).

Network theory intersects with a variety of other fruitful notions, including networked business, a business model based on linkages with partners; smart mobs, leaderless groups of people using technology; and emergence, the spontaneous self-organization and adaptive behavior that emerges from networks of simpler entities, such as cells, ants, and Web users. Books such as *Emergence: The Connected Lives of Ants, Brains, Cities, and Software* (2001) by Steven Johnson and *Sync: The Emerging Science of Spontaneous Order* (2003) by Steven Strogatz not only talk about a great many emergent phenomena, but are themselves examples of such a phenomenon: the network of books that are now talking about networks, and will probably be doing so for some time.

10

The Sexes

Blondes Forever

91 In September 2002, major international news outlets reported that in 200 years natural blondes would become extinct. More precisely, news reports said that research by the World Health Organization found that there would be too few people with recessive blonde genes in the grandparents' generation to continue the blonde trait beyond 2202. The last natural blondes, they said, would be in Finland, the country with the highest concentration of natural blondes.

Within days, the report was found to be untrue. CNN, ABC, and the BBC Web site retracted their statements. The World Health Organization (WHO) said in a statement that it "has no knowledge of how these news reports originated but would like to stress that we have no opinion on the future existence of blonds." Ultimately, according to the *Washington Post*, the erroneous information was traced to an article in a German magazine that cited a WHO source that could not be verified. So the blonde will go on.

While natural blondes are not an endangered species, their numbers may decrease in the future, says Jonathan Rees, professor of Dermatology at the University of Edinburgh. According to Rees, "The frequency of blondes may drop but they won't disappear." In remarks for BBC Online, he says, "Genes don't die out unless there is a disadvantage of having that gene or by chance. They don't disappear." He adds, "The only reason blondes would disappear is if having the gene was a disadvantage and I do not think that is the case."

Truth be told, only 0.001 percent of adults are naturally blonde, but thanks to effective, inexpensive hair dyes and increased popularity of light hair across the continents, the number of blondes will increase. They'll just be bottle blondes. Since the early 20th century, people have been able to buy chemically activated blonde hair dye, and now, reports *USA Today*, 40 percent of all hair color sold is blonde. In the United States alone, one in three American women dye their hair blonde (while one in twenty American women are natural blondes), reports Joanna Pitman's book *On Blondes*. Of them, many, such as singer Beyonce Knowles and athlete Serena Williams, are African-American. Others, like singer Eminem, are male (and men account for over $200 million of the hair care market). Reasons for becoming blonde range from the desire to look younger, feel sexier, be cool. Since the 1970s, when L'Oreal enticed people to try blonde hair color with the words, "Because I'm worth it!" being blonde has also become a statement of self-affirmation.

In fashion-conscious Japan, sales of blonde hair coloring have increased dramatically; for one major hair color company, blonde coloring accounts for one-fourth of its sales in Japan. There, a head of rich black hair that was traditionally called a "woman's life" is now just as likely to be a lighter shade, sometimes blonde. Sales of blonde coloring continue to be strong throughout Europe, where women have been lightening their hair for generations. Most famous of recent vintage is the late Princess Diana, who went from plain brunette to blonde celebrity.

The fact that a minor report predicting the demise of blondes would raise international interest (while the demise of an obscure language may primarily interest scholars) points to the ongoing fascination with blondes. For over 2,000 years, people have been drawn to the blonde as a symbol of youth, power, and sexuality. So it continues. As a hairstyling mogul said in *USA Today*, "Blond hair is a global fashion." The $1.4 billion hair care market backs him up, as does research indicating that bottle-blonde women are more attractive to men than natural blondes.

Father Goose

92 If you could get in a time machine to visit a playground thirty years ago and compare it to a playground today, the children cavorting on the swings and slides would look about the same. But if you took a good look at the adults kissing scraped knees and breaking out snacks, you would notice a difference: thirty years ago practically all the adults would have been women, whereas today at least a few of them are likely to be men. Move over, Mother Goose; Father Goose has arrived.

The feminist movement scored big inroads in getting women into the workplace and teaching them they did not have to be stay-at-home moms. As a windfall for fathers, it made it possible for men to get out of the workplace and be stay-at-home dads. At first, the standard model for a stay-at-home dad, as in the 1983 movie *Mr. Mom*, was one who lost his job and was forced into the humiliating and awkward position of changing diapers all day while his wife brought home the bacon.

But increasingly, fathers are choosing to stay home with their children because they like their children and enjoy spending time with them. In some cases, an additional factor is that the mother cares more about her career than the father cares about his. In other cases, financial sense is the deciding factor: if the mother earns more at her job than the father earns at his, that might be reason enough to make the father the stay-at-home parent. Usually, couples where the father stays home with the kids have a strong commitment to handling child care personally, rather than leaving it to a nanny or day care program. The only question on the table is which parent will do the job.

Fathers will probably never be 50 percent of the nation's stay-at-home parents. Mothers will likely predominate in this business for the foreseeable future. Even so, the number of stay-at-home dads has been growing and will probably continue to grow. According to research estimates, the number of stay-at-home dads in the United States quadrupled from 1986 to 2000, reaching 2 million and making this model the fastest-growing type of family.

As this trend continues, a variation on the full-time dad is likely to gain prominence: the family in which both parents work half-time jobs and watch the kids half-time. Sometimes economic considerations drive this model, but often it is a simple matter of sharing the wealth: both parents want to work and both want to enjoy their children. Blue-collar men have led this trend, splitting shifts with their wives so both can work and raise the kids. A policeman or fireman, for example, may work the overnight shift, sleep during the day while the kids are at school, then take care of the kids when they come home from school. After dinner, his wife, who has worked during the day, takes charge of the kids and the cycle begins again.

This model is ideal for freelancers, telecommuters, and other people who work from home. The authors of this book, for example, have collaborated on writing it while splitting shifts of caring for their daughter. The shift-system of child care is more unusual for couples with a full-time, white-collar job outside the home, but even here where there's a will, there's a way. In November 2003, *New York Times* columnist Lisa Belkin reported on several couples who each share a single high-level position—neonatologist, astrophysicist, pastor—with each parent in the couple doing the job half-time and taking care of the children the rest of the time.

Another unusual but growing model is that of two fathers—members of a gay couple—in which one father stays home with the children while the other works. There are 60,000 male couple households with children in the United States, and 26 percent of them include a stay-at-home parent. According to a report in the *New York Times*, that figure is one percentage point more than for married couples with children. That should not be surprising: gay couples have usually gone through considerable obstacles to obtain children to raise, and they are unusually committed to raising those children themselves rather than entrusting them to nannies or day care centers.

Becoming a stay-at-home dad has its drawbacks. Some are the same ones faced by stay-at-home moms: boredom with making peanut-butter sandwiches and engaging in playground chitchat about children's snow gear; the feeling that one's career aspirations are dying on the vine; the sense that one's contribution to society is not really valued. Fathers may face an additional sense of isolation and anxiety that comes from being surrounded by mommies and suspected of not being fully a man. A 1996 study by Robert A. Frank, Ph.D., showed that 63 percent of at-home fathers felt somewhat isolated, compared to 37 percent of at-home mothers.

The benefits? Several studies indicate that children benefit from having a full-time, stay-at-home parent, and that they receive particular advantages if that parent is the father. According to a Fall 2000 article in *Christianity Today*, a study from the Center for Successful Fathering in Austin, Texas, says that when a father is actively involved in parenting, children benefit with higher grades, fewer anxiety disorders, greater ambition, and lower risk of delinquency or teen pregnancy. Another study found that such children scored higher on verbal skills and academic achievement. Not measured in such studies are the benefits to the father—relearning how to play; living at a slower, saner pace for a few years; and not missing a moment of that most fleeting of joys, the growing up of one's children.

Grrrl Power

93 What do wearing string bikinis, shooting flamethrowers, calling oneself a slut, and attending college have in common? To varying degrees, they're representations of grrrl power. The term refers to the increasing ways girls and women can define themselves and exist in society, largely without approbation. They can be girls who reject the sexualization in clothes and attitudes that usually accompany the physical changes of young adulthood. Or they can be sexual aggressors, and not be concerned with being a "nice girl." They can engage and excel in formerly exclusively masculine actions, like lethal martial arts, saber wielding, and murder, which are the stock-and-trade of the female avengers in movies like *Charlie's Angels* and *Kill Bill*. They can even like and excel in sports. Or they can simply exaggerate the markers of female sexuality—clothing, makeup, artistic expression—to laugh at female stereotypes and also find a place in them.

A recent example of grrrl power in the marketplace is the bikini, 21st-century version. It's not your mother's bikini. It's not just for ogling or tanning. It's a female statement of sex and power. Craig Brommers, vice president for marketing at Speedo, told the *New York Times*, "People are wanting skimpier cuts than they ever have before. At the same time, more girls are active in sports than they ever have been before, and for them wearing a bikini is an issue of empowerment in the sense of 'here is my body—it is strong and fit.' There is so much more at issue here than merely 'sexiness.'"

Women with grrrl power also have a less serious sense of solidarity than their feminist predecessors. In movies like the two *Charlie's Angels*, the women are giddy cohorts who solve crimes, not the marchers of decades ago who found solidarity in seriousness. Equally light are the many books that celebrate female unity, like the *Girlfriends* series and the *Ya-Ya Sisterhood* books of a few years ago. The many celebrations of goddesses and witches can also be displays of grrrl power, as they use previously downplayed images to generate strength.

While the 1960s might have been the Age of Aquarius and the 1980s the Al Franken Decade, the early 21st century may be the era of grrrl power. Females coming of age during this period will be part of generations of women that achieve more in greater numbers than ever before. More self-confidence, more financial independence, more education. In fact, they will be facing a glut of educational success—and, as with all cultural tidal waves, some unintended consequences.

While for hundreds of years, males have outnumbered females as college students, the trend in every state, income bracket, and racial and ethnic group in the United States is reversing. As of 2003, 133 females get BA degrees for every 100 males. By 2010, it is projected that the numbers will be 142 women to 100 men, and by 2020, it will be 156 to 100. Once women are entrenched as the main sex on college campuses, how will they define themselves? What will the fighting spirit of grrrl power become when women are the dominant force in society?

Less Sex

94 For many reasons, Americans young and old are either having or promoting the idea of having less sex. Part of it is in reaction to the possibility of getting AIDS (acquired immune deficiency syndrome). Part is the centuries-old argument from Christian and other religions to preserve virginity until marriage. Another part, especially prevalent among married or cohabitating couples, is practical: lack of time. Among unmarried young people, there have been fewer pregnancies and a small number who promise to avoid sexual relations until marriage. Given the increasing speed of everyday life and the ongoing presence of AIDS and other sexually transmitted diseases, this trend may continue.

The consequences of sexual activity in the United States point to the need for caution. According to the 2001 report from U.S. surgeon general David Satcher, on American sexuality, about 12 million persons are infected with sexually transmitted diseases (STDs) each year. The most commonly reported STD is chlamydia. The incidence of cases is highest among teenagers fifteen to nineteen years old. Teenagers and African-Americans are most often infected with gonorrhea. In all, there are about 750,000 AIDS cases reported across the country, and about 900,000 persons who live with HIV. Forty-five million Americans are infected with genital herpes. As for pregnancies, about half occurring each year are unintended. In part, this has resulted in over 1.3 million abortions per year. These numbers mean that about 50 percent of pregnancies end in abortion.

In an effort to lessen the early experience of sex, some schools teach classes that inform about contraception but also abstinence. According to reports, these programs have no effect on the date of sexual initiation. Classes that teach about contraception do not increase sexual activity.

Public calls for sexual caution come from various sources. Since the early 1990s, various Protestant and Catholic Church youth groups have established chastity clubs. Using names such as "Best Friends," "Choose," and "Next Generation," its members vow to abstain from sexual intercourse until marriage. Popular celebrities such as Enrique Iglesias have publicly chosen chastity before marriage.

Church teaching on sex still carries sway in the secular society. Perhaps the most well-known in the United States, the Catholic Church, calls for adherents to abstain from sexual relations before marriage. On abstinence, there is some agreement between church and state. Over the past several years, the U.S. government has committed support and funds to sex education that promotes abstinence until marriage. In 2001, the federal government spent $115 million on conveying the "abstinence-only" message to young people through public school health curricula. Additional funds have been earmarked for the program in the future. A 2003 Global HIV/AIDS Prevention Amendment included the earmark that 33 percent of all prevention funds must be used exclusively for abstinence before marriage programs.

Also existing are nongovernment organizations that promote abstinence before marriage. One of them, Chastemates.org, notes at its Chastemates Learning Center Web site, "Abstinence from sexual activities before marriage has a very positive HEALTH message unrelated to any specific religious message."

With or without school, parental, or medical influence, fewer young people are having sex. In the Archdiocese of Detroit Natural Family Planning Newsletter, a national survey revealed that in the 1990s, sexual activity among some young people decreased. For example, in 1988,

60.4 percent of fifteen- to nineteen-year-old males had engaged in sexual activity; by 1995, the number had dropped to 55.5 percent. Similarly, sexual activity among fifteen- to nineteen-year-old females was 55 percent in 1990; by 1995, it was 50 percent. Depending on one's outlook, it seems the younger generation is either less concerned or more concerned about sexual relations.

Life after Feminism

95 Four decades after Betty Friedan published *The Feminine Mystique* in 1963 and the postwar wave of feminism began, American women seem to live with more power and comfort than they once did. Some of the battles have already been fought or at least launched. Women make up at least half of college undergraduates and nearly half the work force. There is also more social freedom. They can cohabit, live alone, or marry. Again, statistics bear this out. They show that cohabitation and living alone are on the rise for women. Marriage rates remain fairly constant, though those who want to marry do so earlier than they did a generation ago.

In these ways, one of the main points of feminism has come to pass—feminism of the post–World War II era is a part of everyday life. But in the 21st century, feminism has also taken on new forms. There is no longer (if there ever was) a unified goal, like "Sisterhood is Powerful." From postfeminism to libertarian feminism, various causes take the feminist mantle, and each serves a different goal. Some versions of feminism are broadly social in outlook, some targeted and political. Some are championed by women, some by men. All involve how women can and should live.

The new millennium began with talk of a third wave of feminism. One book about it, *Manifesta: Young Women, Feminism, and the Future* by Jennifer Baumgardner and Amy Richards, posits this feminism as a mix of personal liberation and commitment to social justice for all women. They still believe, however, that motherhood and domestic life unavoidably cause entrapment and patriarchal control. Motherhood is "the opposite of liberation," they say.

This limited view of life with the opposite sex and the need to equate independence with solitude is part of what Katie Roiphe criticizes in her book *The Morning After: Sex, Fear, and Feminism*. While supposedly promoting free speech and openness about sexuality, the feminism that she observed during the late 20th century among the highly educated is narrow and unbending.

Others see that postfeminism can mean nothing more than returning to the past. Columnist Maureen Dowd observes a postfeminist return to the supposedly pampered wife of the mid-20th century. She writes that "[m]any women I know, who once disdained their mothers' lifestyles, no longer see those lives as boring and indulgent. Now, they look back with a tad of longing." As statistical backup, she cites a survey by *Cosmopolitan* magazine in which two-thirds of 800 females agreed that, given the chance, they "would rather kick back than climb the corporate ladder." To social critic Susan J. Douglas, this retrograde form of postfeminism is more than a social phenomenon. It is a right-leaning government and industry-fueled "engineering process" whose aims are to keep from instituting profamily social welfare programs and to make money for major corporations. To the author, it is "Postfeminism Inc."

The "individualist feminists" of ifeminism.com see their version of modern feminism as an embrace of personal freedom, choice, and personal responsibility. In short, it is a form of libertarianism. In their online introduction, ifeminism.com states that "ifeminism turns the old stereotype of feminism on its head." Rather than looking to reform government laws on equality, individualist feminists promote libertarian ideals to remove government involvement in people's lives. In particular they wish to remove government interference with women's sexual activities. "You cannot create equality with men by embedding gender privilege for women into the law," they say. Individualist feminist heroes include novelist Ayn Rand, founder of the *Catholic Worker* Dorothy Day, and cultural critic Camille Paglia.

Many young women simply seek a way to live with feminism in their everyday life. As former-graduate-student-turned-Web-columnist Melissa Gelula wrote for the online journal *Sexing the Political*, "I sense that many women, who, like me, found the feminism at some point in their lives, and never thought they'd let it go, might secretly wonder about its continued applicability in their personal, parenting, or professional lives, and may struggle to keep it alive in a culture that's still very counter all-things liberatory."

To feminist and social critic Katha Pollitt, living with modern feminism may require revitalizing it and making it a forceful ideology. To do that, she suggests, it may be necessary to once again make it what it was in the 1970s: "a do-it-yourself, direct-action social movement." Can it really mean going back to "Free to Be You and Me"?

Looking for Love Online

96 Forget church socials. The world's new matchmaker is the computer. The trend of finding a mate through Internet power was established during the late 20th century, and will continue and become more refined through the 21st. In a chronicle of current online dating practices, Jennifer Egan in the *New York Times* noted that according to ComScore Networks, millions of Americans are devoting much time and money to finding love online. In the month of August 2003 alone, 40 million Americans visited an online dating site. During the first six months of 2003, they spent $214.3 million on personals and dating sites. And there are so many choices for how and where they want to look that they can tailor their search. The market for love search mechanisms has proven so popular and so profitable that they have become increasingly specialized. Already there are compatibility-based matchmaking sites like eHarmony.com, schoolmate reunion sites like Classmates.com, faith-based dating sites, as well as Internet personal ads and new takes on the mail-order bride route. There are also less savory, more transitory hookups that have no national ad campaigns. One way or another, online dating sites will lead more lovers down the wedding aisle or into the rent-by-the-hour hotel room during the 21st century.

Most of the basic matchmaking sites aim to offer choices based on compatible interests and personalities. Sites like eHarmony.com and others have prematch personality analyses that are more likely to reveal suitable candidates. PerfectMatch.com also relies on personality tests to match candidates. But these are designed by relationship expert Dr. Pepper Schwartz, and once potential mates are presented, candidates can correspond with them by PerfectMate instant messaging. Another approach is to promise the most advanced techniques to offer an international pool of applicants, as does FriendFinder.com. Rather than relying on outdated "Dating Science," FriendFinder lets people, as its press release reads, find the "optimal balance between technology and natural human behavior."

Virtual reunion sites will continue to build on an even stronger force than that of the standard dating sites. Instead of hoping to get a new ideal mate, the virtual reunion sites draw on long-harbored memories of what might have been. As one female veteran of a virtual reunion site said in the *New York Times*, "You grew up with these people. You share their lives, and they are the ones you feel you can trust. There is something comforting about going back home." Major sites specializing in finding long-remembered high school students are Classmaters.com, Reunions.com, and GradFinder. Classmates.com is one of the most established sites, in operation since 1995. It has 32 million registered members and about 1.8 million paid subscribers. A similar search site for remembered people who were or were not classmates is Switchboard.com. It, like other matchmaking sites, generates money from enrolling customers in a database of potential mates and providing e-mail addresses of possible mates.

Other online dating sites are targeted to niche desires. Jdate.com is designed to bring together people of Jewish heritage. The Vanity Date site is aimed at building a database of good-looking if vapid potential partners. It is aimed at matching beautiful-looking people with others who are the same.

Some sites work to enhance the meeting of mates by offering socializing activities as well as video and voice services. For example, Match.com offers monthly parties, some of them based on special interests like cooking. Generally, at these and other online activities, prospective partners flirt, but keep their distance. As author Egan says in the New York Times Magazine, "[T]here's a general sense that it shouldn't go on for too long."

Also popular are Internet personal ad sites, such as the *New York Observer* Web site and the Nerve dating site. For various reasons, however, the ads are more iffy than virtual reunion or established dating sites. One reason is that they, like their print predecessors, promote lying. Research has found that men sell themselves as taller and unmarried, while women say they are younger and shapelier.

For those put off by the earnestness of dating sites, there are also antidating online sites. These sites disavow the possibility of finding a mate by already established means and turn to less emotion-based techniques. For example, on Solvedating.com, a site in development, supporters will be introduced to a mix of mathematic equations, population statistics, and "love economics" to find a soul mate.

As to the future, there seems no reason to end online dating. It is easy to do, serves a need, and fits an increasingly online society. Columnist David Brooks observes that it also restores the necessary leisure of courtship. Online dating sets up a structure to dating by requiring that the couple spend time online becoming acquainted before meeting in person, much less entering into intimate relations. Brooks calls the phenomenon of online dating "a revolution in the way people meet and court one another," and the process itself "ruthlessly transactional and strangely tender."

Macho Women

97 What do women want? In the postfeminist 21st century, they'll let you know. Judging from the psychological studies on aggression and the many ways that women can define themselves as aggressive, it seems that assertive women are entering a mature, established phase of existence. There may be no more aggressive women than there ever were, but the ones who exist will make themselves more public. Whether they will be successful at their goals is another matter.

Aggressiveness has become such an accepted term of empowerment that it has become the unifying component for many specialized women's organizations. Far from the consciousness-raising groups that formed generations ago, these groups celebrate the physicality and force they have taken to their desires. For example, aggressive athletes can find community through organizations such as the Women's Aggressive Skating Network (WASN), which is for women who have "challenged themselves in this very exciting fun sport of aggressive inline skating." For the woman who wishes to increase her assertiveness, there are many classes sponsored by colleges and professional organizations, such as "Assertiveness Training for Women in Business" workshops held by the American Management Association. Supposedly it trains women to use assertiveness to "get things done and get what you want."

Gender differences and how they are demonstrated through aggression has been the focus of scientific studies. Among researchers is British social scientist Anne Campbell, who studies sex differences in aggression from infancy to adulthood, and University of Rochester anthropologist Signithia Fordham, who studies the nature of female aggression. In her studies, Fordham examines why much female aggression is indirect, downplaying its power.

Still, in everyday society there remains much ambivalence toward aggressive women. It shows up in the many ways women and men portray female aggression. For some, it is humorous violence, as in the online "Fairy Tale for Assertive Women" that tells the story of how a "self-assured" princess rebuffs the marriage proposal of an oafish prince-turned-into-toad by turning him into a "repast of lightly sauteed frogs' legs seasoned in a white wine and onion cream sauce." Yet, others poke fun at both female and male aggression, as in the role-playing online game called "Macho Women With Guns." According to its creators, it is "the game of an alternative world twisted beyond the bounds of chauvinism and reason" where women packing phallic heat seek to gain respect by restoring a civilization that has collapsed under the weight of men displaying their weapons.

Meanwhile, macho men have their own set of problems. At least they do if they are the *drosophila serrata*. According to a genetics study at the University of Queensland, the Australian fly that has the greatest amount of pheromones may be the most likely to attract a mate but does not generate high numbers of offspring that survive. Reports one of the study's evolutionary geneticists on its findings, "[T]he attractive males put so much effort into buying the red Ferrari to attract females, they have no money to put into the education of their kids." For males, too, beauty is a curse.

Manly Men

98 While metrosexuals win approving gazes from big-city singles and from their own reflection in the mirror, the 21st century has another masculine type. He is the overtly masculine male who acts rather than ponders himself. He is the Manly Man, and rather than setting style trends, he is running the nation.

The manly man first came to attention after the attacks of New York and Washington, D.C., on September 11, 2001. Not only were firefighters and policemen acknowledged for their bravery and sacrifice, they were, as weeks passed, seen as objects of appreciation. According to a woman interviewed for Fox News, the attraction goes deeper than the helmets and uniforms. It's "[n]ot just because they are the picture of strength and masculinity, but also because they've done the hardest, most noble job of all, which is to put their own lives second to others," said Liz Quilty, a Boston layout artist. But, adds a New Yorker involved with a fireman, there is the lure of the uniform. "I tell you, when he's got that outfit on, it's like (sigh)," Felice Recupero told *USA Today*.

The 9/11 tragedy also solidified the macho mien and political outlook of President George W. Bush and his administration. For months, Secretary of State Donald Rumsfeld was its representative, an ideological heartthrob to many men and a regular sex symbol to some women. Since 2003, a new manly leader has emerged, the governor of California, Arnold Schwarzenegger. Exuding sexuality, he has an appeal similar to that of Rumsfeld and the male members of the Bush administration, who also appear to be able to control whatever situation they face.

While the manly man seems firmly entrenched in society for the foreseeable future, the reasons behind his rise are varied. Unlike metrosexuals, who may be a natural outgrowth of the cultural change that occurred during the last decades of the 20th century, the manly man is a reaction to it. Norman Mailer and others have called it a backlash against feminism. Former President Bill Clinton points to a national uncertainty that leads people to prefer "somebody who's strong and wrong than somebody who's weak and right." In the *Nation*, writer Richard Goldstein says, the "neo-macho man" unites both misogyny and anger at 9/11 to create an accepted form of the dominant male or "male avenger." He cites this newly accepted macho stance as a reaction to deep-seated "sexual terror" among men. As Goldstein says, "The intimate nature of this anxiety [sexual terror] prevents it from being addressed, and as a result, it operates in powerful, unapparent ways."

For ultimate good or ill, the manly man has permeated everyday American thinking. There is surefire proof: in his new form, he has entered pop culture iconography. A famous trademark has been regenerated with testosterone. In what Georgia-Pacific executive vice president Michael Burandt calls "the single most important step forward in the nearly three-decade history of the brand," the Brawny Paper Towel man has been redesigned. Gone is his blond hair, big mustache, and denim shirt. Instead there is a flannel shirt, dark hair, and chisel-cut face, all based on an actual firefighter. When it gets to the level of national packaging, it means the manly man is here to stay.

Metrosexuals

99 In 1994, British social critic Mark Simpson introduced a name for the modern urban feminized but straight male—the metrosexual. In his article for the *Independent*, "Here Come the Mirror Men," he describes them as fashionable, self-loving men who may be gay, straight, or bisexual but are united in their interest in pursuing their narcissistic way of life and attracting other young men to "study them with a mixture of envy and desire." Continental examples included British singer Robbie Williams and soccer star David Beckham. In 2002, Simpson elaborated on the type for U.S. audiences in his Salon.com article "Meet the Metrosexual" and soon, metrosexuality became a buzzword in popular American slang.

But the meaning of the term has changed in translation to American. Rather than standing primarily for quasi-erotic and pansexual narcissism (Simpson says the metrosexual "has clearly taken himself as his own love object"), metrosexuality has instead been transformed into a nearly healthy concern for grooming and hygiene. Already a book, *The Metrosexual Guide to Style: A Handbook for the Modern Man* (2003) by one-time daytime TV actor Michael Flocker is at least in part a guide for attracting women. Not surprisingly, American celebrities pegged as metrosexuals do display style but are linked to female companions— including Sean "Puffy" Combs and Brad Pitt (both cited on *Good Morning America*), and movie star Ben Affleck. But the definitive met- rosexual media exhibit is the television show *Queer Eye for the Straight Guy*, about adding the gay aesthetic touch to a heterosexual's home and self.

Over the coming years, it appears that metrosexuality will have its strongest voice as a marketing tool. In the 2003 report by the communi- cations agency Euro RSCG Worldwide called *The Future of Men USA*, a study charted men from twenty-one to forty-eight years of age on their thinking about what constitutes masculinity. The report posits that adult men now are "secure" in their sexuality and in their personal choices to "do what they want, buy what they want, enjoy what they want— regardless of . . . [whether] . . . some people might consider these things unmanly."

For manufacturers of personal care products, this translates into a new market to be tapped. In Mark Simpson's words, a metrosexual is "an advertiser's walking wet dream." The men's clothing and beauty care market is projected to reach tens of billions of dollars by the mid- decade, and at least until they age into *Death in Venice* pensioners or just grumpy old men, metrosexuals are a desired market. The group provides a handy term for the intended target of the growing field of male self-care products, such as Unilever's body spray Axe, which offers deodorant protection and a masculine fragrance that increases a man's confidence. Reports the L'Oreal spokesperson who championed Ben Affleck as their latest "ambassador," "Ben embodies a new gen- eration of men who show their strength in their personality, but are not afraid to care for their appearance." A shopping magazine for men based on the women's shopping periodical *Lucky* was also launched in 2004.

How future generations will judge metrosexuals is unknown. They may be considered weak and effete, but well dressed, like yesterday's dandies and fops. They may be the 21st century's representatives of timeless style. Or they may be latter-day Napoleons, awash in their own power. It is more likely that metrosexuals will be cited as one of the ongoing examples of what historian Ann Douglas called the feminization of American culture. The well-coiffed, well-dressed Afflecks are modern-day exemplars of this centuries-old trend. Moisturizer is for everybody!

More Free Milk: Cohabitation Abounding

100 Two generations ago, parents cautioned daughters not to move in with a boyfriend because he would never marry them: "Why buy the cow when they can get the milk for free?" they said. According to the 2000 Census, few people are listening. The census reported that the number of unmarried persons living together as partners increased by 72 percent over the past decade. Further, those cohabiting span the demographic and economic spectrum, and include all ethnic groups. Marshall Miller of the Alternatives to Marriage Project, a national nonprofit organization for unmarrieds, notes in his organization's statement that society has "seen unmarried cohabitation transformed from something scandalous to something most people do before they marry or instead of marrying." Cohabitation has moved in for good.

In 1970, only one of ten couples lived together without being married. But between 1960 and 2000, the number of cohabiting opposite-sex couples has increased ten times, from 439,000 to 4.7 million couples. As of 2003, unmarried people account for about 5.5 million households. With about 55 million married couples, married people predominate in the United States, but overall their number is diminishing. In 1990, married couples accounted for 55.1 percent of U.S. households; as of 2000, they account for 52 percent. Both numbers pale at the 1950 numbers: 78 percent of U.S. households had married people.

Other census information points to the variety of types and reasons for cohabitating. To begin with, there is no typical age for cohabitating. One-third of all cohabitants are between twenty-five and thirty-four, 23 percent are over forty-five, and 4 percent are senior citizens. The average period of cohabitation is two years. Living together as preparation for marriage is now commonplace: about half of women who have married and have reached age thirty have lived with their mates first. Almost half of cohabiting couples have children. In all, there are 3.3 million children living with an unmarried parent who is cohabiting with a person he or she is not married to. Senior citizens who cohabitate but do not marry usually do so to retain their pension, Social Security, and Medicare benefits. Homosexual couples unable to formalize their relationship in marriage also add to the number of cohabitating couples. Economics also enters into the decision to cohabitate. People below the poverty level are more likely than other economic groups to live together; according to some estimates, up to one-third of cohabiting couples with children live below the poverty line.

Even as cohabitation increases, conflict continues over its long-term effects on relationships and the family. Studies in the mid-1990s have suggested that cohabiting couples are generally not as committed to their partner or the relationship as married people. Studies in the *Journal of Family Issues* in 1995 and in *Journal of Marriage and the Family* in 1996 report that cohabiting couples are less likely to be satisfied with their relationship and are less likely to be monogamous.

A 2003 study by Penn State University researchers in the *Journal of Marriage and the Family* found that living together before marriage is still linked to higher rates of troubled unions, divorce, and separation. The study compared the marital happiness of couples from 1964 through 1980, when cohabitation was not commonly practiced, to couples during the years 1981 to 1997, when it was. In both cases, cohabitating couples in both groups had a higher incidence of marital unhappiness and a higher than average divorce rate. One reason was increased incidence of infidelity. Married women were five times less likely to have an additional sex partner than do cohabiting women. In part, say researchers, the negative outcomes are linked to the choice of riskier partners that living together encourages.

Characteristics of cohabiting partners were the focus of another study done at Johns Hopkins University. There researchers found that cohabiting couples tended to look for characteristics "such as education which can reflect a short-term ability to contribute to the relationship," as opposed to people seeking spouses, who look for "ascribed characteristics (such as age and religion) that reflect long-term considerations."

Yet, studies also find that while the cohabitation rate has gone up over the last twenty years, the divorce rate has not. Since 1980, it has remained at about 50 percent, and in the early 21st century, it has leveled at 43 percent.

Cohabitation is also being legitimized by the various forms of legal recognition it is receiving from governments and businesses. By 2005, over 3,500 private companies, colleges, universities, and state and local governments will be offering benefits for domestic partners such as health insurance and family leave. Already as of 2003, over one-third of the Fortune 500 companies offer employee benefits to workers' domestic partners

Commenting on these changes in the way people live together, Dorian Solot, executive director of the Alternatives to Marriage Project, proclaims, "Getting married isn't the only way to live happily ever after." Millions of unmarried cohabiting Americans are testing that statement now, and millions more are going to try in the next decades. In various forms, they will contribute to the even larger trend of the 21st century, the redefined family. Unmarried couples, stepfamilies, and gay families will join married parents with children as accepted types of the American family, which will live on. Says Robert Schoen, demographer at Johns Hopkins University, "Yes, family forms are changing, but the family does not show any signs of fading away."

Index

marketing (continued)
  to children, 130–32
  diversity, 134–37
  by gender, 140–42
  mass customization of, 138–39
  to metrosexuals, 245
masculinity, 242–44
media centers, 206
media consolidation, 6–8
meditation, 82
meetups, 101
melanomas, 89
men
  as fathers, 230–32
  macho, 242–44
  marketing to, 141–42
  metrosexuals, 244–26
menopause, 83–85
metrosexuals, 244–46
middle class, shrinking, 29–30
mini-nukes, 164–66
multicultural people, 31–34
multitasking, 98–99
music industry, piracy and, 48–49
Muslims, 183–84
mutual fund scandals, 19–20

N, O

nanotechnology, 203–5
neoagnosticism, 187–90
neoimperialism, 172–75
network theory, 224–26
networked businesses, 16–18
New Economy, 12

newgenics, 207–10
Nigeria, 168
nuclear weapons, 164–66
obesity, 26–29, 85–86, 143
online dating, 238–40
online literature, 54–57
online shopping. *See* e-commerce
orthodoxy, 179–80
ozone layer, 89

P

Pakistan, 164
parenting styles, 122–24, 230–32
Patriot Act, 125, 150
personal advertising, 138–39
pharmaceutical industry, 17–18, 78–80
pharmacogenomics, 75–77
population growth, 36–38
postfeminism, 236–38
privacy, patient, 87–88
progressive relaxation, 81–82

R

racial divisions, 31–34
radio, 45, 115
religion. *See also* agnosticism
  Christianity, 178–80
  Islam, 183–84
  link between health and, 190–92
  open-mindedness about, 193–95
replacement surgeries, 70–73
Republican Party, 156, 157–58
retail trends, 2–3
robots, 110, 213–16